RAND McNALLY

D1547157

World Atlas
Know Geography™

Grades 4-9

Vice President
Publishing & Education
Joan Sharp

Product Management Director
Jenny Thornton

Design Director
Joerg Metzner

Cover Design
Dawne Lundahl

Interior Design
Michelle LeBlanc -Smith

Writing
Elizabeth Leppman, PhD
Joella M. Morris

Author
Celeste Jones Fraser

Editors
Brett R. Gover
Joella M. Morris

Production
Carey Seren

Cartographic Project Managers
Marzee Eckhoff
Rob Ferry
Nina Lusterman

Cartography
Gregory P. Babiak
Justin Griffin
Marc Kugel

Research
Susan Hudson
Elizabeth Leppman, PhD
Felix Lopez
Raymond Tobiaski

Manufactured by Rand McNally
Skokie, Illinois 60077

Printed in U.S.A.
January 2018
PO# 57439
ISBN 0-528-01895-7

If you have any questions, concerns or even a compliment,
please visit us at randmcnally.com/contact, e-mail us at:
consumeraffairs@randmcnally.com, or write to:

Rand McNally
Consumer Affairs
P.O. Box 7600
Chicago, Illinois 60680-9915

randmcnally.com

SUSTAINABLE FORESTRY INITIATIVE
Certified Chain of Custody
Promoting Sustainable Forestry
www.sfiprogram.org
SFI-01681

TABLE OF CONTENTS

THE DISCOVERER'S TOOLS

Introduction

In this atlas, you will find maps, photographs, graphs, tables, and diagrams. Together, all these tools will give you a clear picture of the geography of regions, countries, and the world. The first section in this atlas, The Discoverer's Tools, will help you master the tools for unlocking a world of information. Each tool provides you a different perspective and different information. As you use this atlas, study all the tools—it will be a journey of discovery.

DID YOU KNOW?

Maps and globes show you pictures of the earth standing still. In real life, however, the earth is always moving. It spins on an imaginary line called an axis at about 1,000 miles per hour. It takes 24 hours to make one complete spin, or rotation.

WORLD

NORTH POLAR VIEW

SOUTH POLAR VIEW

LEGEND

WORLD VEGETATION

Globes vs. Maps

A **globe** is a model of the whole Earth. Because it is round like the Earth, a globe is an accurate representation of our planet. Shapes, sizes, distances, and directions are all shown correctly on a globe. A **map** is a flat picture of the whole world or just a part of it, such as a country, state, or city. Maps are drawn from an overhead perspective—from the view you would get looking down from above.

Different maps show different information. For example, a map might show the streets of a city, the shape of the land, weather patterns, or places where mining takes place. The size of the area shown on a map is determined by what the mapmaker wants to show. The top map on this page is a map of the whole world. The map below it is a map of the United States, without Alaska and Hawaii. Can you see how the map of the United States is just one small part of the map of the world?

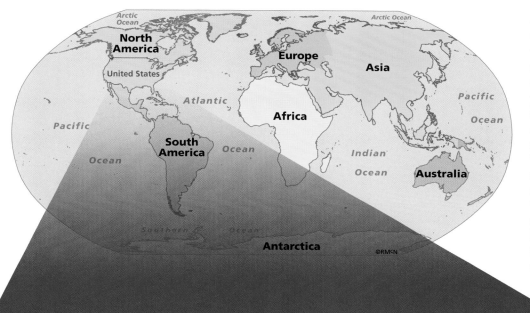

DID YOU KNOW?

An atlas is a collection of maps. This atlas is a collection of more than 100 physical, political, and thematic maps.

Thematic Maps

Have you ever seen a weather map on television that uses different colors to show places with different temperatures? That map is a **thematic map**. It shows information about a **specific topic** and where a particular condition is found. The thematic maps in this atlas give you information about specific topics or themes.

This atlas has ten world thematic maps. These maps let you compare the same kinds of information for areas around the world. For example, you could use the World Climate Map to see what places in the world have a climate similar to the climate where you live.

This atlas also has thematic maps in the sections about each of the continents. Several different thematic maps often appear on facing pages. This allows you to compare different topics for the same area. For example, if you compare a climate map and a population density map for South America, what do you think you might discover?

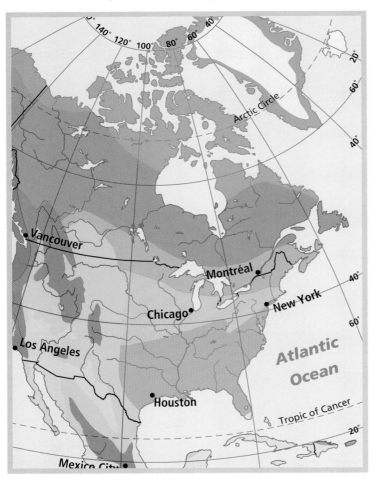

Physical Maps

On the physical maps, different **land elevations** and **ocean depths** are shown by different colors. Major **physical features**, such as the Rocky Mountains in North America, and major rivers, such as the Colorado River, are named. Countries and some cities are also named.

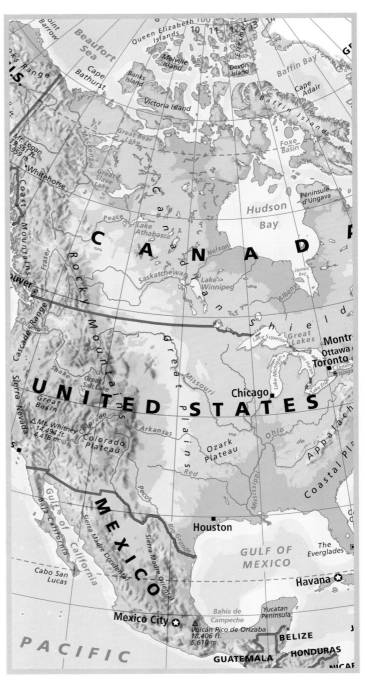

Political Maps

It would be impossible to show all the Earth's features on a single map. So, mapmakers create maps that show only a few things. For example, political maps show **political units**—areas under one government, such as countries, states, provinces, territories, and cities. Countries, states, and provinces are shown in different colors so that you can recognize type and have different symbols to show their populations.

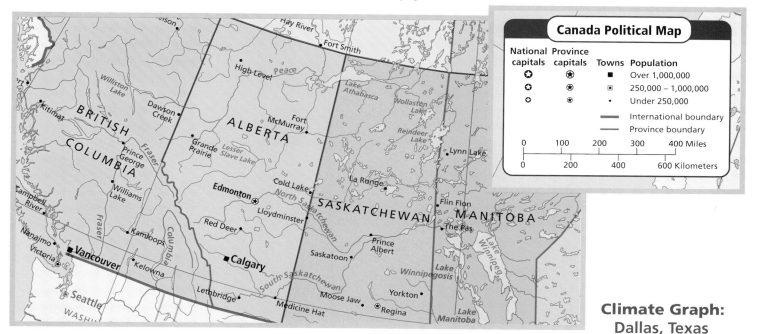

Climate Maps

Climate is the kind of weather a place has over long periods of time. Climates are measured by average temperature and precipitation. The term *precipitation* refers to moisture that falls to the earth in the form of rain, mist, hail, snow, or sleet.

On the climate maps in this atlas, each color represents a different climate region. Climate graphs accompany each climate map. Each graph shows the average monthly temperatures and precipitations for a specific city.

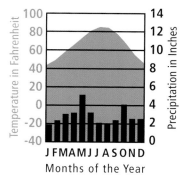

Climate Graph: Dallas, Texas

Climate Map

- Dry - very little rain
- Moderate - warm summer and mild rainy winter
- Continental - mild summer and snowy winter
- Highlands - varies with altitude

Environments Maps

Environments maps show what type of land is found in different areas. Each color represents a different type of **environment**, such as desert, forest, cropland, or **urban**. *Urban* refers to areas covered by cities and their suburbs.

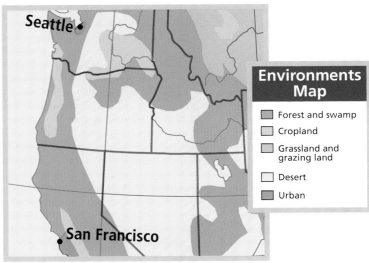

Environments Map

- ▨ Forest and swamp
- ▢ Cropland
- ▨ Grassland and grazing land
- ▢ Desert
- ▨ Urban

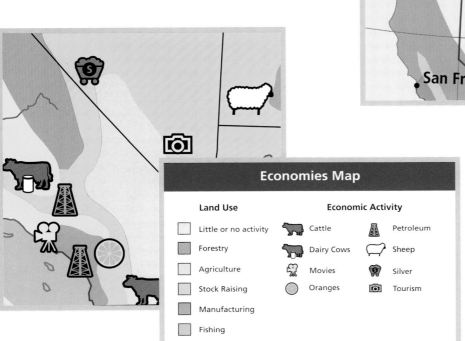

Economies Map

Land Use

- ▢ Little or no activity
- ▨ Forestry
- ▢ Agriculture
- ▢ Stock Raising
- ▨ Manufacturing
- ▨ Fishing

Economic Activity

- 🐂 Cattle
- 🐄 Dairy Cows
- 🎬 Movies
- 🟠 Oranges
- ⛏ Petroleum
- 🐑 Sheep
- Ⓢ Silver
- 📷 Tourism

Economies Maps

The purpose of economies maps is to show how people make a living in different areas. The colors show how the land is used. In the sample map shown, yellow stands for agriculture. The economies maps in this atlas also include symbols representing products and economic activities that are especially important in certain areas. In the sample map shown on the left, these products and activities include oranges, petroleum, and tourism.

Population Density Maps

Because people are not spread out evenly on the earth's surface, mapmakers have created **population density** maps. These maps show which areas have lots of people, which have a moderate number of people, and which have few people. The colors stand for the numbers of people per square mile. As you can see in the sample map, the darker the color, the more people there are per square mile. Population is densest in the regions with the darkest color.

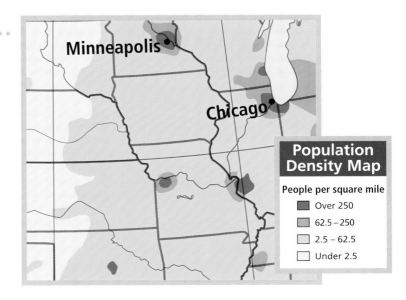

Population Density Map

People per square mile

- ▨ Over 250
- ▨ 62.5 – 250
- ▢ 2.5 – 62.5
- ▢ Under 2.5

Map Projections

The only way to make a flat map of the round Earth is by changing its shape. Mapmakers must stretch some areas and shrink other areas. For this reason, maps cannot show the world as it really looks.

Only a globe can do that. Mapmakers have developed many different methods of representing the round earth on a flat surface. These different methods are called **map projections**.

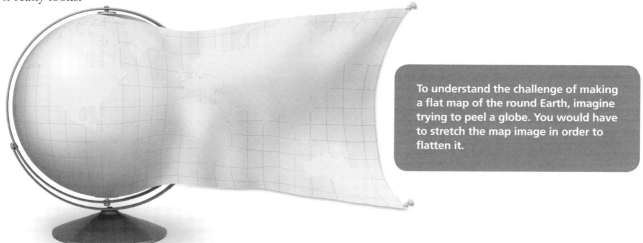

To understand the challenge of making a flat map of the round Earth, imagine trying to peel a globe. You would have to stretch the map image in order to flatten it.

Mollweide Projection

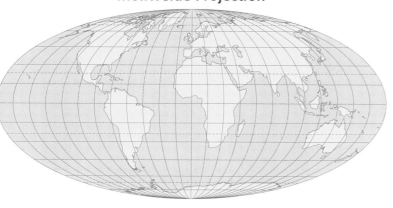

Robinson Projection

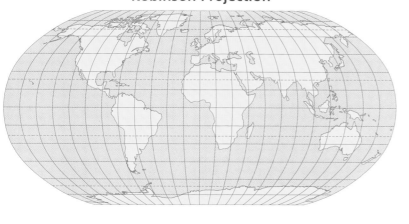

Types of Map Projections

Mapmakers choose different projections, depending on how the map will be used. Each map projection is different in the way it shrinks and stretches areas of the world. The maps on this page show three different kinds of map projections.

Mercator Projection

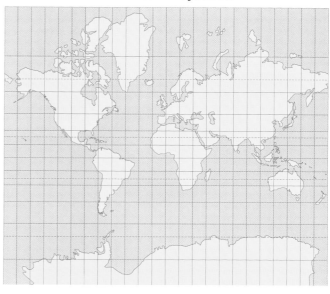

Orienting Yourself on the Earth

All directions on the Earth are based on the location of the **North and South Poles**. These are fixed points on the globe that never change. When you go north anywhere on the Earth, you are heading toward the North Pole. The same is true for going south and the South Pole.

This means that on the Earth and on maps, north and south are always opposite one another. West and east are always opposite one another, too. However, unlike the north and south directions, there is no east or west pole.

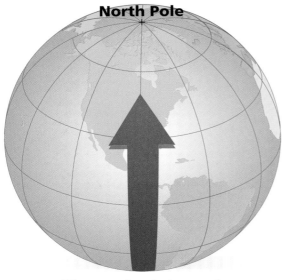

The arrow is pointing **north** towards the North Pole.

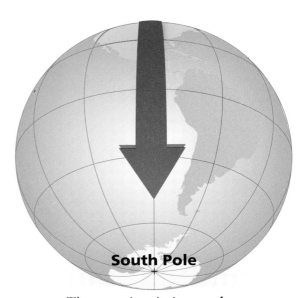

The arrow is pointing **south** towards the South Pole.

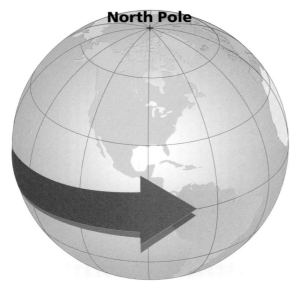

The arrow is pointing **east**.

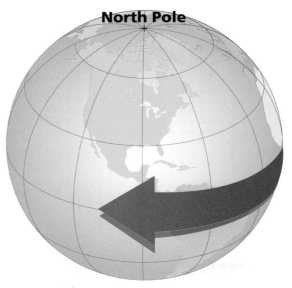

The arrow is pointing **west**.

Cardinal and Intermediate Directions

North, south, east, and west are called **cardinal directions**. The directions in between them, such as northwest, are called **intermediate directions**. Most maps include a **compass rose**, or direction symbol.

North Arrows

Some maps show only a **north arrow**. A north arrow indicates the direction toward the North Pole. What about the other directions? Once you know at least one direction, you can always figure out all the others. They never change in relation to each other.

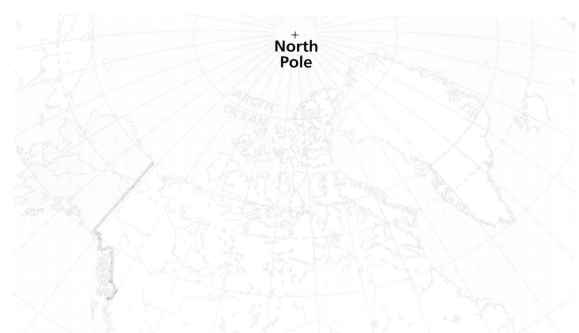

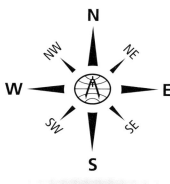

Compass rose

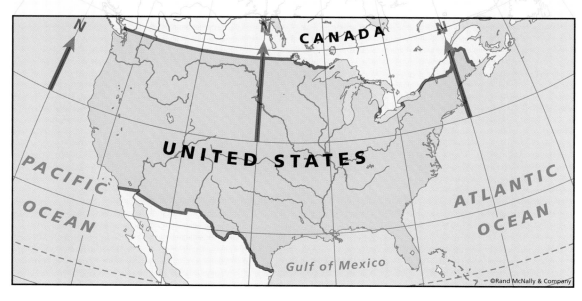

It is important to remember that north is not always straight up toward the top of the map. The United States map above has three north arrows. The map has been extended to show that each arrow points to the North Pole. The arrows are curved because this projection shows the roundness of the Earth.

Lines of latitude, also called **parallels**, run east and west across globes and maps.

Lines of longitude, also called **meridians**, run north and south on globes and maps.

Latitude and Longitude

In order to identify any location on the Earth, people have invented a **grid system** of crisscrossing lines that circle the Earth.

Lines of **latitude** circle the Earth east and west. Latitude is the distance measured north or south of the Equator. The **Equator**, 0 degrees latitude, is halfway between the North Pole and the South Pole.

The North Pole is 90 degrees north latitude, and the South Pole is 90 degrees south latitude. Distance from the Equator can be expressed as any number between 0 and 90 degrees, north or south latitude.

Lines of **longitude** run north and south between the two poles. The line representing 0 degrees longitude is called the **Prime Meridian**. Longitude is the distance measured east or west of the Prime Meridian. Distance from the Prime Meridian can be expressed as any number between 0 and 180 degrees, east or west longitude.

Every location on the Earth has a **global address** made up of its latitude and longitude numbers. For example, the city of New Orleans, Louisiana, is located at 30 degrees north latitude, 90 degrees west longitude, so its address is 30° N, 90° W.

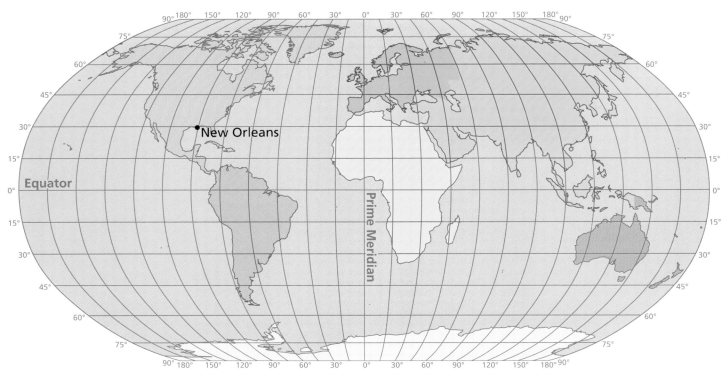

Legend for Physical and Political Maps

Water Features

ATLANTIC OCEAN — Ocean or sea

Lake (physical map)

Lake (political map)

Salt lake (physical map)

Salt lake (political map)

Seasonal lake

Nile — River

Niagara Falls — Waterfall

Land Features

A S I A — Continent

Mt. Mitchell 6,684 ft. △ 2,037 m. — Mountain peak

Kilimanjaro 19,340 ft. ▲ 5,895 m. — Highest mountain peak

A l p s — Physical feature (mountain range, desert, plateau, etc.)

Borneo — Island

Cultural Features

——— International boundary

——— State, province, or territory boundary

EGYPT — Country

KANSAS — State, province, or territory

PUERTO RICO (U.S.) — Dependency

Population Centers

National capital	State, province, or territory capital	Town	Population
✪	✪	■	Over 1,000,000
✪	✪	▫	250,000 — 1,000,000
✪	✪	·	Under 250,000

Land Elevations and Ocean Depths

Land elevation

3,000 meters	9,840 feet
2,000 meters	6,560 feet
1,000 meters	3,280 feet
500 meters	1,640 feet
200 meters	656 feet
0 Sea level	0 Sea level

Water depth

0 Sea level	0 Sea level
200 meters	656 feet
2,000 meters	6,560 feet

Map A

Vallejo
San Pablo Bay
San Rafael
Concord
Berkeley
Golden Ga
San Francisco
Oakland
San Francisco Bay
Hayward
Fremont
Palo Alto
PACIFIC OCEAN
San Jose

0   10   20   30 Miles

Different Scales for Different Maps

Maps can be drawn to different **scales**. The three maps on this page all focus on San Francisco, California. The maps are the same size, but have different scales. On Map A, one inch represents about 30 miles. On Map B, one inch represents about 4 miles. On Map C, one inch represents about one-half mile.

Because of their different scales, the three maps represent different sizes of areas on the Earth.

DID YOU KNOW?

Map C shows the most detail of San Francisco as a city, such as its streets and parks.

Map B

ALCATRAZ ISLAND
GOLDEN GATE BRIDGE
Golden Gate
GOLDEN GATE NATIONAL RECREATION AREA
Lincoln Blvd
PRESIDIO OF SAN FRANCISCO
The Embarcadero
Van Ness Av
Market St
Geary Blvd
Golden Gate Pk.
Fulton St
JAMES LICK
San Francisco
Great Hwy
Lincoln Way
19th Av
Sunset Blvd
Portola Dr
280
Ocean Av
Monterey Blvd
35
Lake Merced
SOUTHERN
FRWY
Mission St
101
John McLaren Pk.

0   1   2   3   4 Miles

San Francisco

Map C

Buchanan St
Laguna St
Octavia St
Vallejo St
Broadway St
Pacific Av
Jackson St
Washington St
Lafayette Park
Clay St
101
Sacramento St
California St
Gough St
Franklin St
Van Ness Av
Pine St
Bush St
Sutter St
Post St
Geary Blvd
Polk St
Larkin St
Cleary

0   1/4   1/2 Mile

Index

The **index** is a list in alphabetical order of most of the places that appear on the maps. Each place entry in the index is followed by its map key, or alpha-numeric grid location, and the number of the page on which it appears.

Did You Know?

Each "Did You Know?" presents an interesting fact about the world.

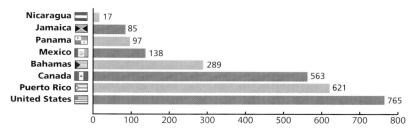

DID YOU KNOW? Lake Michigan gets its name from an Algonquin Indian word, *michigami*, which means "big lake."

What If?

Each "What If?" asks you to use information from the atlas and other sources to answer a critical thinking question. There are no right or wrong answers, but be sure you can present facts to support your opinions.

WHAT IF? If all of Australia received plenty of rain, how might the population distribution be different?

Graphs, Charts, and Photographs

The graphs, charts, and photographs in the atlas help illustrate information from the maps. They may help you see the same information in a different way. They may also provide additional information about the themes of the maps. The photographs show you how the features shown on the map look in the real world.

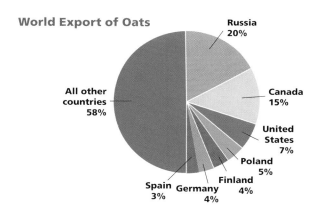

World Export of Oats
Russia 20%, Canada 15%, United States 7%, Poland 5%, Finland 4%, Germany 4%, Spain 3%, All other countries 58%

Automobiles per 1,000 people
Nicaragua 17, Jamaica 85, Panama 97, Mexico 138, Bahamas 289, Canada 563, Puerto Rico 621, United States 765

Geographical Terms

The large illustration to the right is a view of an imaginary place. It shows many of Earth's different types of landforms, bodies of water, and human-made features. The following vocabulary list defines many of the features on the map.

See if you can find an example of each feature on the maps in the atlas.

Archipelago
A group of islands

Canyon
A deep, narrow valley with high, steep sides

Coast
Land along a large lake, a sea, or an ocean

Desert
A large land area that receives very little rainfall

Forest
A large area covered with trees

Gulf
A large part of an ocean or a sea that lies within a curved coastline; a gulf is larger than a bay

Harbor
A sheltered body of water where ships can safely anchor

Hill
A small area of land that is higher than the land around it

Island
A piece of land that is surrounded by water

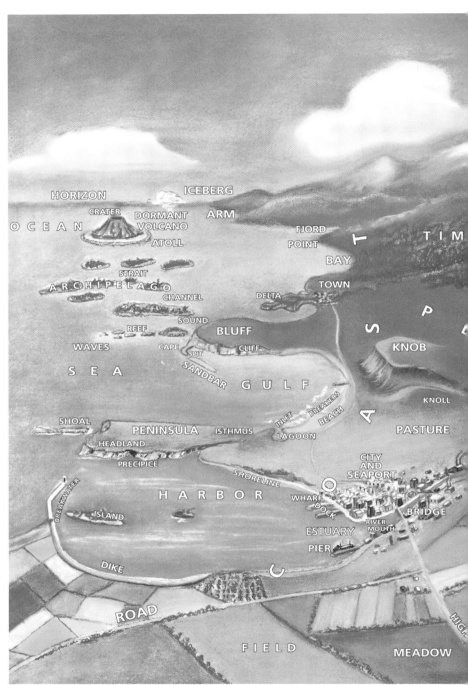

Isthmus
A narrow piece of land that joins two larger areas of land

Lake
A body of water completely surrounded by land

Mountain
Land that rises much higher than the land around it

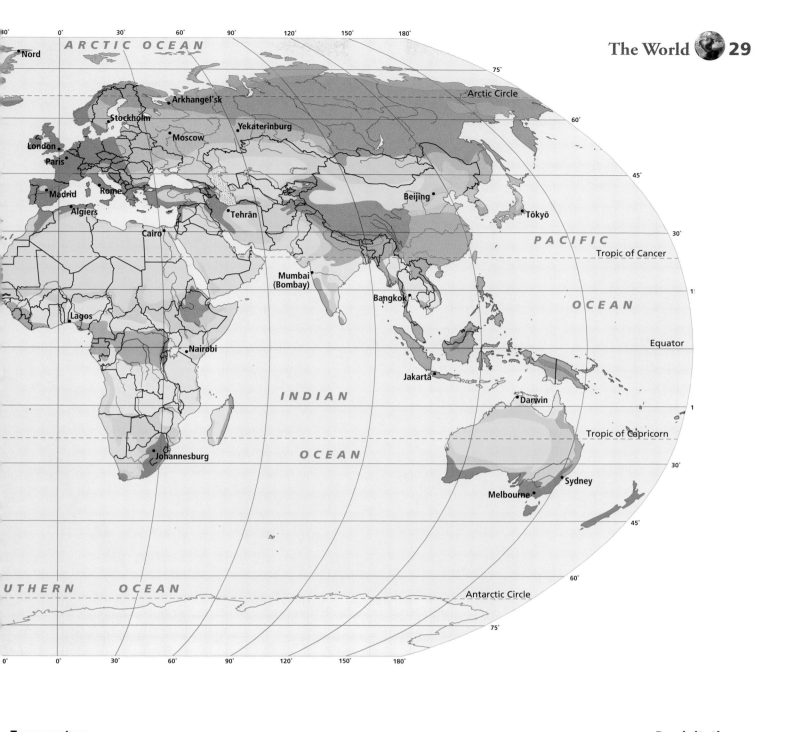

ARCTIC OCEAN

• Nord

Arctic Circle

• Arkhangel'sk

• Stockholm

• Yekaterinburg

• Moscow

London •

Paris •

• Beijing

• Madrid   • Rome

• Algiers

• Tōkyō

• Tehrān

• Cairo

PACIFIC

Tropic of Cancer

Mumbai
(Bombay)

OCEAN

• Bangkok

• Lagos

• Nairobi

INDIAN

• Jakarta

• Darwin

Equator

Tropic of Capricorn

OCEAN

• Johannesburg

• Sydney

• Melbourne

SOUTHERN   OCEAN

Antarctic Circle

Temperature

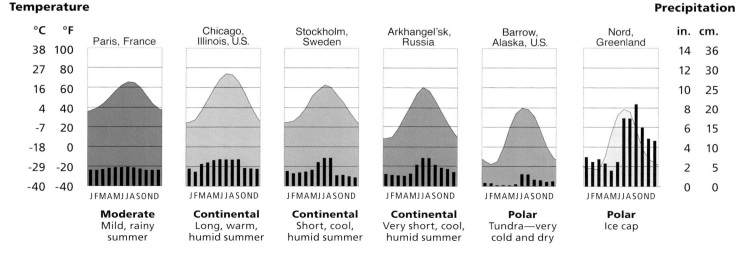

°C	°F	Paris, France	Chicago, Illinois, U.S.	Stockholm, Sweden	Arkhangel'sk, Russia	Barrow, Alaska, U.S.	Nord, Greenland	in.	cm.
38	100							14	36
27	80							12	30
16	60							10	25
4	40							8	20
-7	20							6	15
-18	0							4	10
-29	-20							2	5
-40	-40							0	0
		JFMAMJJASOND	JFMAMJJASOND	JFMAMJJASOND	JFMAMJJASOND	JFMAMJJASOND	JFMAMJJASOND		
		Moderate Mild, rainy summer	**Continental** Long, warm, humid summer	**Continental** Short, cool, humid summer	**Continental** Very short, cool, humid summer	**Polar** Tundra—very cold and dry	**Polar** Ice cap		

Precipitation

World Environments Map

This map shows different environments throughout the world. The environment of a place is its physical setting and conditions. Some environments, such as forest and tundra, are natural. Other environments, such as cropland and urban areas, have been created by humans. This map shows many of the world's largest urban areas.

The theme of this map is land environments, but approximately 75% of Earth's surface is covered by water. This causes Earth to look blue from space. For this reason, Earth is sometimes called the "blue marble."

Only 3% of the water on Earth is fresh water. The other 97% of Earth's water is salt water.

Environments Map

- Forest
- Swamp
- Crop & woodland
- Cropland
- Crop & grazing land
- Grassland
- Desert
- Tundra
- Barren
- Urban

© Rand McNally
Made in U.S.A.
M-102169-3

Earth as seen from space

Forest

This tropical rain forest in South America is green all year because the climate is hot and rainy. By contrast, forests in the middle latitudes lose their leaves when the weather turns cold.

Swamp

Low-lying, uncultivated land where water collects and certain types of trees and other vegetation may grow

Crop and woodland

Land made up of low-density forests; It is suitable for the cultivation of crops, such as grain, vegetables, or fruit.

Cropland

Flatter land where the climate is mild tends to be where most of the world's crops are grown. This farm is in Pennsylvania.

Crop and grazing land

Fields covered with grass or herbage, it is suitable for grazing livestock and cultivating crops.

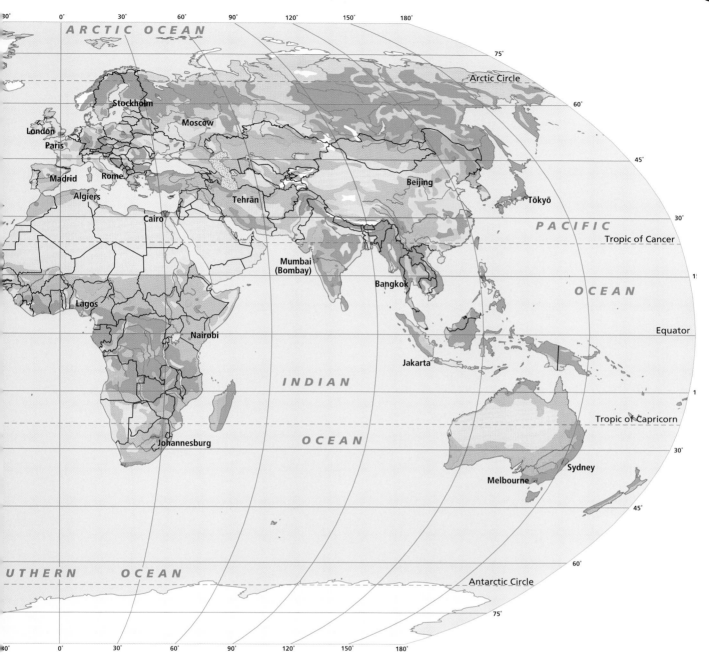

ARCTIC OCEAN

75°

Arctic Circle

60°

Stockholm

Moscow

45°

London

Paris

Beijing

Madrid   Rome

Tehrān

Tōkyō

Algiers

PACIFIC

30°

Cairo

Tropic of Cancer

Mumbai
(Bombay)

OCEAN

Bangkok

Lagos

Equator

Nairobi

INDIAN

Jakarta

Tropic of Capricorn

OCEAN

Johannesburg

30°

Sydney

Melbourne

45°

SOUTHERN   OCEAN

60°

Antarctic Circle

75°

Grassland

Natural grasslands, like this one in Oklahoma, are found where the climate is somewhat dry. These regions are not wet enough for growing crops, but perfect for grazing animals.

Desert

The Sahara is the largest desert in the world. With less than five inches of rain per year, it is a place with very few plants.

Tundra

In tundra regions, like this one in Russia, the ground stays nearly frozen even in summer. The only plants that can grow there are low grasses and mosses.

Barren

Level land that is unable to support the growth of crops, trees, or vegetation

Urban

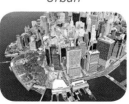

New York City is one of the world's great cities. Many of the urban areas on the map above have over one million people.

World Population Density Map

This map shows which parts of the world have many people and which have few people. Areas with many people living there have **dense** populations. The largest areas of dense populations are in East Asia, South Asia, and Europe. Vast areas of the world are too cold, too dry, or too mountainous for dense population.

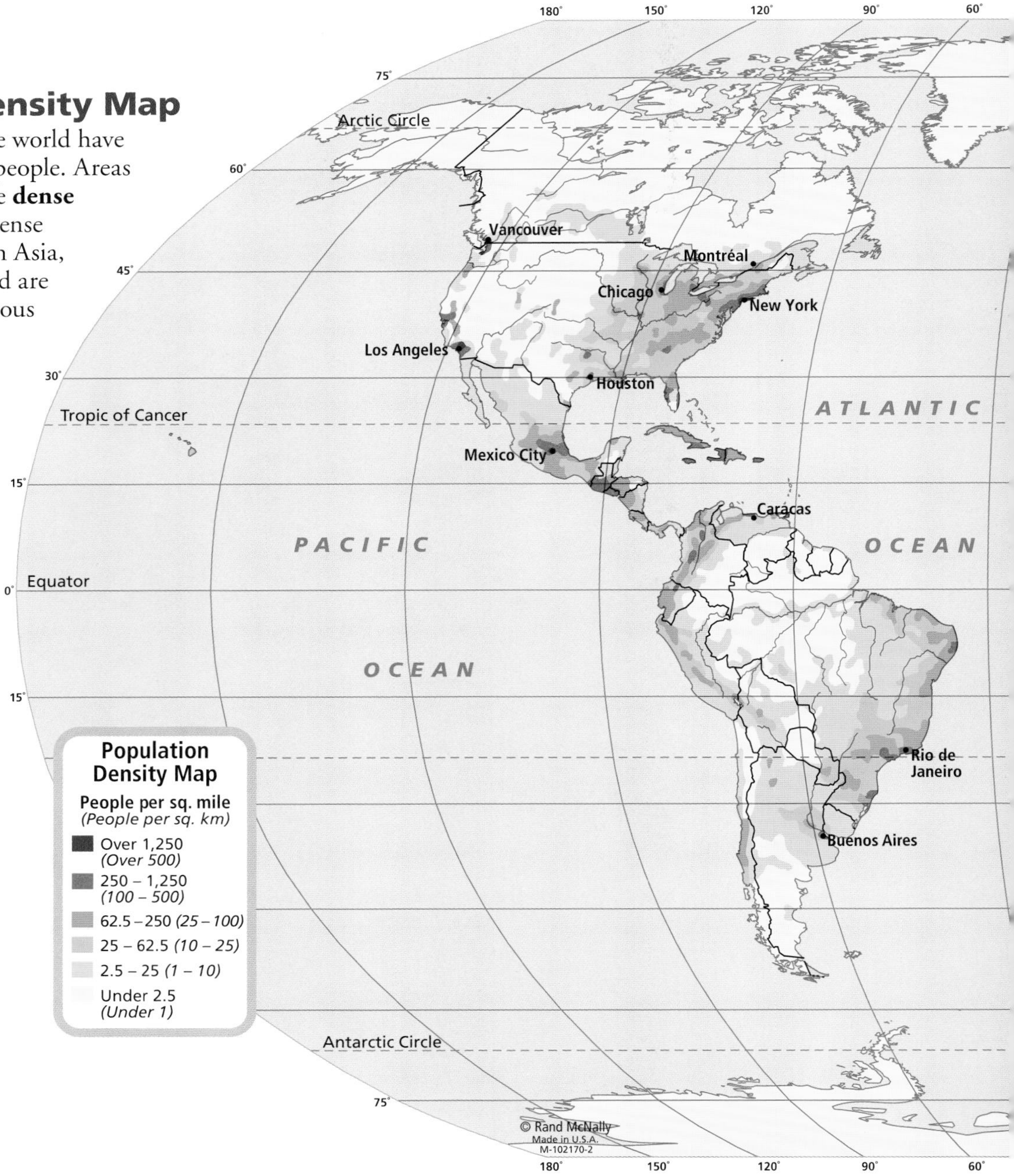
180°
150°
120°
90°
60°
75°
Arctic Circle
60°
Vancouver
Montréal
45°
Chicago
New York
Los Angeles
30°
Houston
Tropic of Cancer
ATLANTIC
Mexico City
15°
Caracas
PACIFIC
OCEAN
0° Equator
OCEAN
15°
Rio de Janeiro
Buenos Aires
Population Density Map
People per sq. mile
(People per sq. km)
Over 1,250 (Over 500)
250 – 1,250 (100 – 500)
62.5 – 250 (25 – 100)
25 – 62.5 (10 – 25)
2.5 – 25 (1 – 10)
Under 2.5 (Under 1)
Antarctic Circle
75°
© Rand McNally
Made in U.S.A.
M-102170-2

World Population Growth

For most of human history, the world's population grew very slowly. About 250 years ago, it began to grow faster as people learned to control illnesses. However, today people in many parts of the world are having smaller families, and the rate of growth may be slowing down.

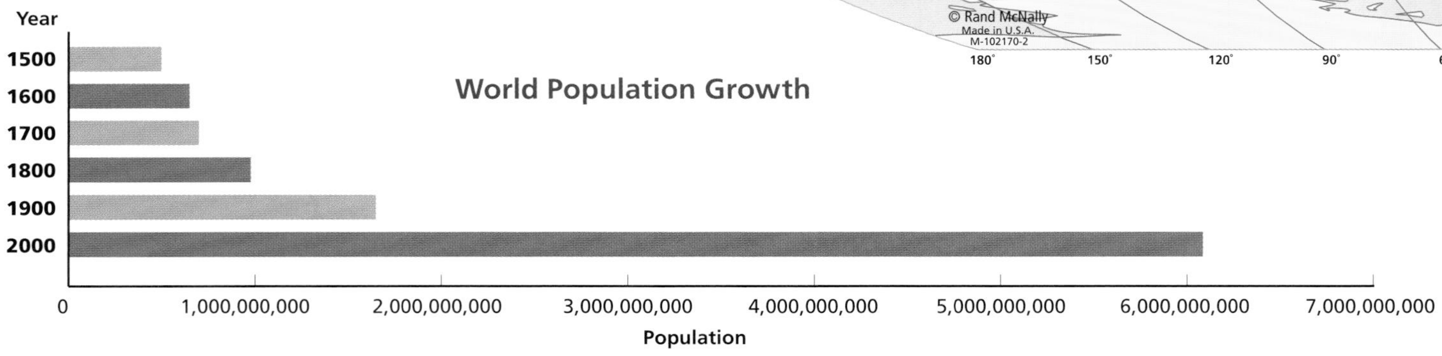
Year
1500
1600
1700
1800
1900
2000
World Population Growth
0
1,000,000,000
2,000,000,000
3,000,000,000
4,000,000,000
5,000,000,000
6,000,000,000
7,000,000,000
Population

Children Around the World

North America

North America

Middle America

South America

Europe

ARCTIC OCEAN

Arctic Circle

Stockholm
Moscow
Yekaterinburg
London
Paris
Madrid
Rome
Algiers
Tehrān
Cairo
Beijing
Tōkyō

PACIFIC

Tropic of Cancer

OCEAN

Mumbai (Bombay)
Bangkok
Lagos
Nairobi

INDIAN

Jakarta

Equator

OCEAN

Tropic of Capricorn

Johannesburg

Sydney
Melbourne

THERN OCEAN

Antarctic Circle

Hong Kong, China, is a city with a very high population density.

Africa

This street market is in India. India's population is one of the densest in the world.

Middle East

La Paz, the capital of Bolivia, is a medium-size city. It has a density of 62.5 to 250 people per square mile.

Asia

The surrounding area of a village in Africa has an average density of 2.5 to 62.5 people per square mile.

Asia

In the Australian Outback, settlements such as this cattle ranch are separated by miles of open land.

Australia

Some regions of the world have very few people. One such region is the Sahara, a vast desert in northern Africa.

World Patterns of Economic Activity

This map shows the kinds of jobs people have around the world. Each color on the map shows the most important economic activity for that area.

Look at the bright yellow area of Canada and the United States. According to the map legend, agriculture is the most important economic activity there. If you went to this area, you would see farm fields, orchards, and farm animals such as dairy cows and pigs. You would probably see grain elevators, feed stores, and other businesses that support farming. Of course, you would see banks, office buildings, stores, and factories, but not as many as you would see in the areas colored red.

According to the map legend, the most important economic activities in the red areas are manufacturing and commerce. Manufacturing is making goods. Automobiles, computers, clothing, and skateboards are examples of goods.

Commerce is the buying and selling of goods. Commerce also includes the buying and selling of services. Medical care, banking, education, and cable television are examples of service industries. In Canada, the United States, Europe, and Japan, more people work in service industries than in manufacturing or agriculture. If you went to the areas shown in red, you would see a concentration of banks, office buildings, factories, and stores. Many of the world's largest manufacturing and commerce areas are shown on this map.

According to the map legend, hunting, forestry, and subsistence farming are the most important economic activities in the brown areas. In these areas you would find people working on small farms, growing food for themselves and their families. You would find people hunting and fishing to get food for themselves and their families.

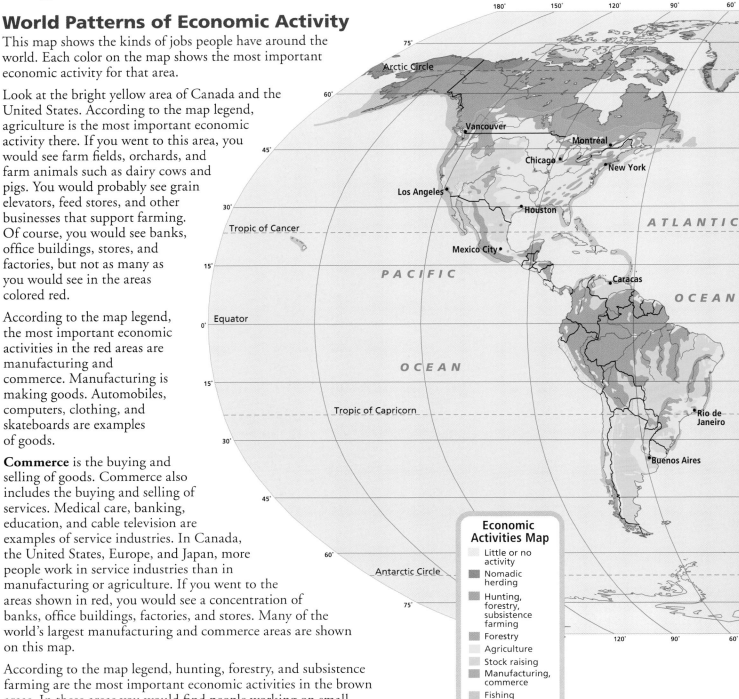

Economic Activities Map

- Little or no activity
- Nomadic herding
- Hunting, forestry, subsistence farming
- Forestry
- Agriculture
- Stock raising
- Manufacturing, commerce
- Fishing

Nomadic herding

Hunting

Subsistence farming

Forestry

ARCTIC OCEAN

Arctic Circle

75°

Stockholm

60°

London
Moscow

Paris

45°

Beijing

Madrid
Rome

Tōkyō

Algiers

30°

Cairo

PACIFIC

Tropic of Cancer

Tehrān

15°

OCEAN

Mumbai
(Bombay)

Bangkok

Lagos

Equator 0°

Nairobi

INDIAN

Jakarta

15°

OCEAN

Tropic of Capricorn

30°

Johannesburg

Sydney

Melbourne

45°

60°

THERN OCEAN

Antarctic Circle

75°

© Rand McNally
Made in U.S.A.
M-102171-2

Agriculture

Stock raising

Manufacturing

Commerce

Fishing

World Mineral Fuel Deposits

Deposits of coal, petroleum, and natural gas are found in very limited parts of the world. What types of deposits does the United States have? Which continents have many coal deposits?

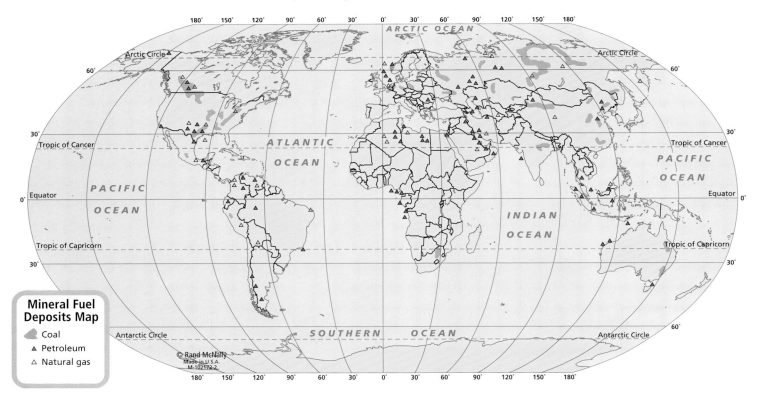

Mineral Fuel Deposits Map
- Coal
- ▲ Petroleum
- △ Natural gas

© Rand McNally
Made in U.S.A.
M-102172-2

World Coal Production

China and the United States, which have extensive deposits of coal, lead the world in coal production.

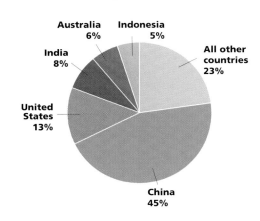

Australia 6%
Indonesia 5%
India 8%
All other countries 23%
United States 13%
China 45%

World Petroleum Production

Saudi Arabia, Russia, and the United States produce more than one-third of the world's oil.

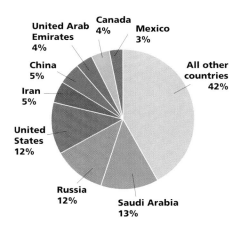

United Arab Emirates 4%
Canada 4%
Mexico 3%
China 5%
Iran 5%
All other countries 42%
United States 12%
Russia 12%
Saudi Arabia 13%

World Uranium Production

Australia and Kazakhstan lead the world in production of uranium, which is used as a fuel in nuclear energy plants.

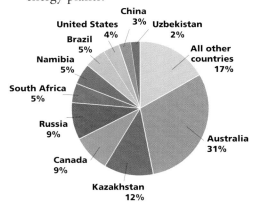

China 3%
United States 4%
Uzbekistan 2%
Brazil 5%
All other countries 17%
Namibia 5%
South Africa 5%
Russia 9%
Australia 31%
Canada 9%
Kazakhstan 12%

World Energy Consumption

Manufacturing, heating, and transportation are the three main ways that people use energy. This explains why the largest users of energy are industrialized countries that have large populations and relatively cold climates.

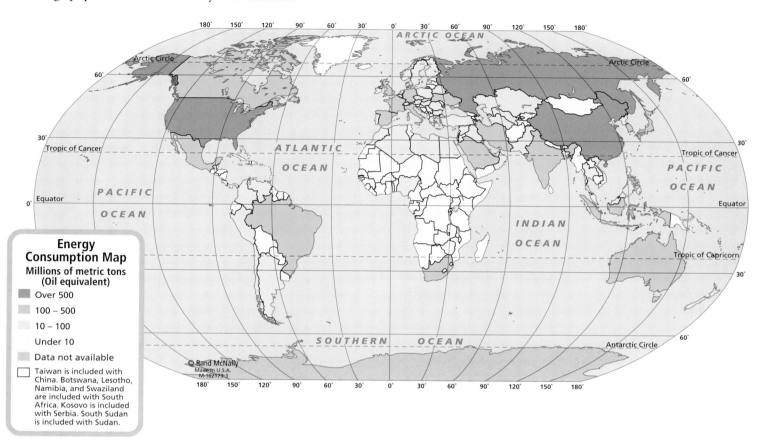

Energy Consumption Map
Millions of metric tons (Oil equivalent)

- Over 500
- 100 – 500
- 10 – 100
- Under 10
- Data not available
- Taiwan is included with China. Botswana, Lesotho, Namibia, and Swaziland are included with South Africa. Kosovo is included with Serbia. South Sudan is included with Sudan.

© Rand McNally
Made in U.S.A.
M-102173-3

Energy Terms

Coal

A rock created from ancient plant life under enormous pressure; It is burned to produce heat and create steam for running machines or making electricity. Most coal, when burned, emits sulfur, a major component of acid rain.

Geothermal power

Uses water heated naturally beneath the earth's surface; The steam that results powers engines that create electricity. Geothermal power is a clean source of energy, but it is available only in very limited areas.

Fossil fuels

Formed from remains of plants and animals over millions of years; Fossil fuels are not renewable sources of energy, because it takes vast amounts of time to create them. Coal, oil, and natural gas are fossil fuels.

Hydroelectricity

Generated by fast-moving water that is used to power generators; Dams on rivers provide sources of rapidly moving water. Hydroelectricity is a clean source of power, but the dams can have negative effects on their surroundings.

Natural gas

A form of petroleum; This flammable gas is used mainly as fuel for stoves, furnaces, and hot-water heaters. Natural gas is a clean-burning fuel.

Nuclear energy

Created by splitting atoms; The energy is used to heat water that makes steam to drive electricity generators. The safety of nuclear plants and the hazardous wastes they create are of great concern.

Petroleum

A liquid, also called oil; Petroleum is the most widely used source of energy in the world. It is used to produce gasoline, kerosene, and fuel oil. It is also used to manufacture plastics and other products.

Wind power and solar energy

Two sources of renewable energy; They are not in wide use today, but in some places the use of wind to make electricity is increasing.

Plate Tectonics

According to the theory of plate tectonics, Earth's surface is divided into more than a dozen plates. These plates move very slowly—just a few inches a year. As they move, they collide or grind past each other. Most of the world's volcanoes and earthquakes occur at the places where plates meet.

Many plates collide with or grind past the Pacific Plate. Find the Pacific Plate on the Plate Tectonics map. The Ring of Fire is the name given to the band of earthquakes and volcanic activity around the Pacific Ocean.

225 million years ago: *Most of the world's land was together in a single "supercontinent." Scientists call this giant continent Pangaea.*

180 million years ago: *Pangaea split up into separate landmasses.*

65 million years ago: *The oceans as we know them today began to take shape. South America and India moved away from Africa.*

The present day: *India has joined with Asia, Australia has moved away from Antarctica, and North America has separated from Europe.*

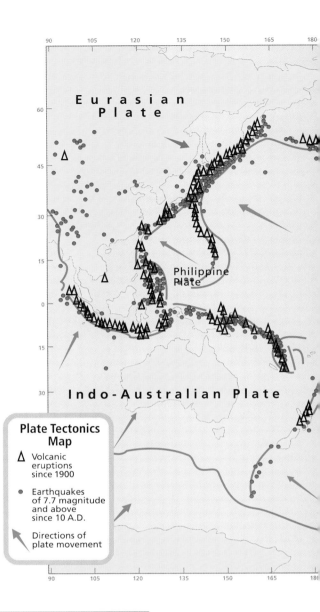

Plate Tectonics Map

△ Volcanic eruptions since 1900

● Earthquakes of 7.7 magnitude and above since 10 A.D.

↖ Directions of plate movement

Some Notable Earthquakes

Year	Magnitude (Richter Scale)	Place	Estimated Deaths
2011	9.0	Near Honshū, Japan	20,352
2010	7.0	Near Port-au-Prince, Haiti	316,000
2004	9.1	Sumatra, Indonesia	227,000 killed by earthquake and tsunami
1990	7.4	Iran	50,000 killed by earthquake and landslides
1976	7.5	Tangshan, China	255,000
1970	7.9	Peru	66,000
1964	9.2	Prince William Sound, AK	128 killed by earthquake and tsunami
1948	7.3	Turkmenistan	110,000
1927	7.9	Qinghai, China	200,000
1923	7.9	Japan	143,000 killed by earthquake and fire
1908	7.2	Italy	70,000 killed by earthquake and tsunami
1906	7.8	San Francisco, CA	3,000 killed by earthquake and fire

Damage from the 1906 San Francisco earthquake

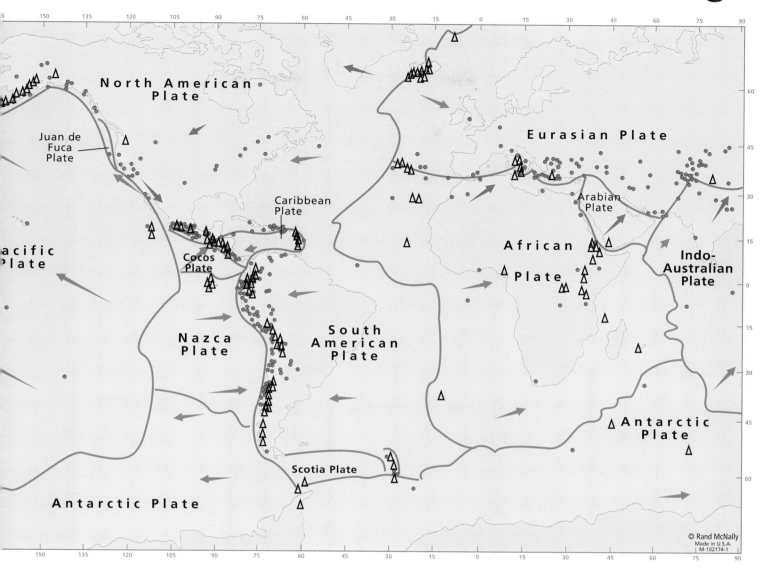

Some Notable Volcanic Eruptions

Year	Volcanic Explosivity Index (VEI)	Name (location)	Estimated Deaths
2010	4	Eyjafjallajökull (Iceland)	Disrupted air travel for 20 countries
1991	6	Mt. Pinatubo (Philippines)	900
1985	3	Nevado del Ruiz (Colombia)	25,000
1980	5	Mt. St. Helens (Washington, U.S.)	57
1963	3	Surtsey (Iceland)	Volcano creates new island
1902	4	Mt. Pelée (Martinique)	30,000
1883	6	Krakatoa (Indonesia)	36,000 killed, most by tsunami
1815	7	Gunung Tambora (Indonesia)	92,000
79	5	Vesuvius (Italy)	16,000 killed in Pompeii and Herculaneum

Eruption of Mt. St. Helens in 1980

World Time Zones

The world is divided into 24 standard time zones. As Earth turns on its axis each day, the sun is overhead at different places at different times. Each time zone is based on the place where the sun is overhead at noon. The boundaries are adjusted so that people whose activities are connected live in the same time zone.

You can figure out the standard time for any time zone in the world. Add one hour for each time you count as you go east. Subtract one hour for each time zone you count as you go west.

Prime Meridian

The Prime Meridian is also called the Greenwich Meridian, because it is centered on the Royal Greenwich Observatory near London in the United Kingdom. It represents 0° longitude. Time around the world is counted from the Prime Meridian.

International Date Line

The International Date Line is halfway around the world from the Prime Meridian, at 180° longitude. Like time zone boundaries, the International Date Line is adjusted from 180° so that people in the same country have the same day. The time is the same on both sides of the International Date Line, but the day is different. West of the International Date Line it is one day later than it is east of the International Date Line.

New Zealand, which lies just west of the International Date Line, is one of the first places in the world to greet each new day.

The precise location of the Prime Meridian is marked at the Royal Greenwich Observatory near London.

Examples of Time Changes

Auckland, New Zealand

12 midnight
June 26

Los Angeles, California, United States

4 a.m.
June 25

Montréal, Québec, Canada

7 a.m.
June 25

Rio de Janeiro, Brazil

9 a.m.
June 25

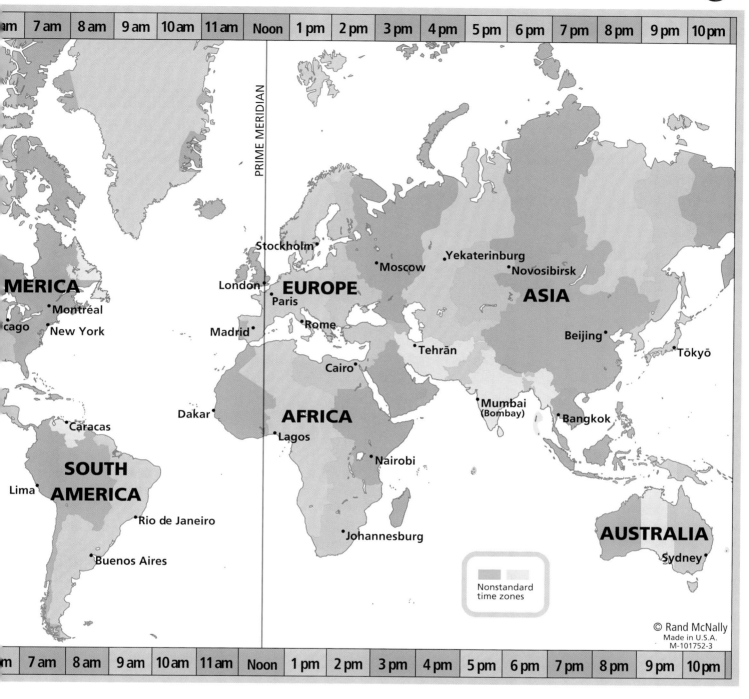

| | 7 am | 8 am | 9 am | 10 am | 11 am | Noon | 1 pm | 2 pm | 3 pm | 4 pm | 5 pm | 6 pm | 7 pm | 8 pm | 9 pm | 10 pm |

PRIME MERIDIAN

MERICA
Montréal
cago
New York

Stockholm
London
EUROPE
Paris
Madrid
Rome

Moscow
Yekaterinburg
Novosibirsk
ASIA

Beijing
Tōkyō

Cairo
Tehrān

Caracas

Dakar
AFRICA
Lagos

Mumbai
(Bombay)
Bangkok

SOUTH
AMERICA
Lima

Nairobi

Rio de Janeiro

Johannesburg

AUSTRALIA
Sydney

Buenos Aires

Nonstandard
time zones

© Rand McNally
Made in U.S.A.
M-101752-3

| | 7 am | 8 am | 9 am | 10 am | 11 am | Noon | 1 pm | 2 pm | 3 pm | 4 pm | 5 pm | 6 pm | 7 pm | 8 pm | 9 pm | 10 pm |

Paris, France   Moscow, Russia   Novosibirsk, Russia   Tōkyō, Japan

1 p.m.
June 25

3 p.m.
June 25

6 p.m.
June 25

9 p.m.
June 25

NORTH AMERICA

Denali, Alaska, United States

North America is the third-largest continent. About 506,000,000 people live there.

It stretches more than 5,400 miles (8,700 kilometers) from northern Canada to the Panama-Colombia border.

Three countries—Canada, the United States, and Mexico—make up most of North America. The Caribbean island countries, the countries of Central America, and the island of Greenland make up the rest of the continent.

Central America is a region within North America. It is made up of the countries of Belize, Guatemala, Honduras, El Salvador, Nicaragua, Costa Rica, and Panama.

Central America is part of a larger region of North America called Middle America. This region consists of Central America, Mexico, and the Caribbean countries.

Generally, the people of North America have used its rich natural resources to great advantage. But not everyone has benefited. There are people throughout the continent who struggle with poverty, particularly in Central America and some Caribbean countries.

Toronto, the largest city in Canada

San Francisco, California, United States

Pyramid of the Sun, Mexico

Caribbean starfish

A Historical Look At North America

About 20,000 years ago
First inhabitants of North America may have arrived from Asia across a land bridge that has since disappeared.

About 5000 B.C.E
Corn (maize) is first cultivated in Middle America.

About 1200-1500 C.E.
Aztec civilization is dominant in Mexico.

About 1500
Europeans explore North America.

Urbanization in North America

In the late nineteenth century and early twentieth century, many new factories were built in the United States and Canada. People moved from farms to cities to take jobs in factories and offices. They were joined by immigrants from many countries. After World War II, many people in cities moved to suburbs, and urbanized areas began to grow, especially along the East Coast between Boston and Washington, D.C. Today, people in Mexico are moving to cities and to suburbs. Some of them cannot find steady jobs, and the cities have trouble providing water, sewers, and schools for the rapidly growing populations.

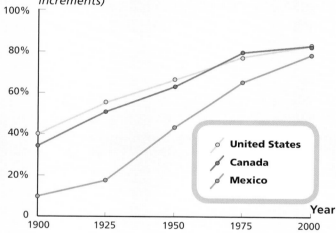

Rising Urban Population
Urban population as a percentage of total population, 1900-2000 (shown in 25-year increments)

Legend:
- United States
- Canada
- Mexico

Year

Pacific Ocean

Atlantic Ocean

Yellow represents densely populated areas.

© Rand McNally

New York City, the largest city in the United States

An abandoned farm on the Great Plains

Zachatecas, a city in Mexico

Suburban sprawl in Colorado

1776
The United States declares independence.

1867
Canada forms a confederation of four provinces.

1994
Canada, the United States, and Mexico sign the North American Free Trade Agreement, creating the largest free trade area.

1821
Mexico becomes independent.

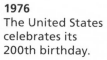

1976
The United States celebrates its 200th birthday.

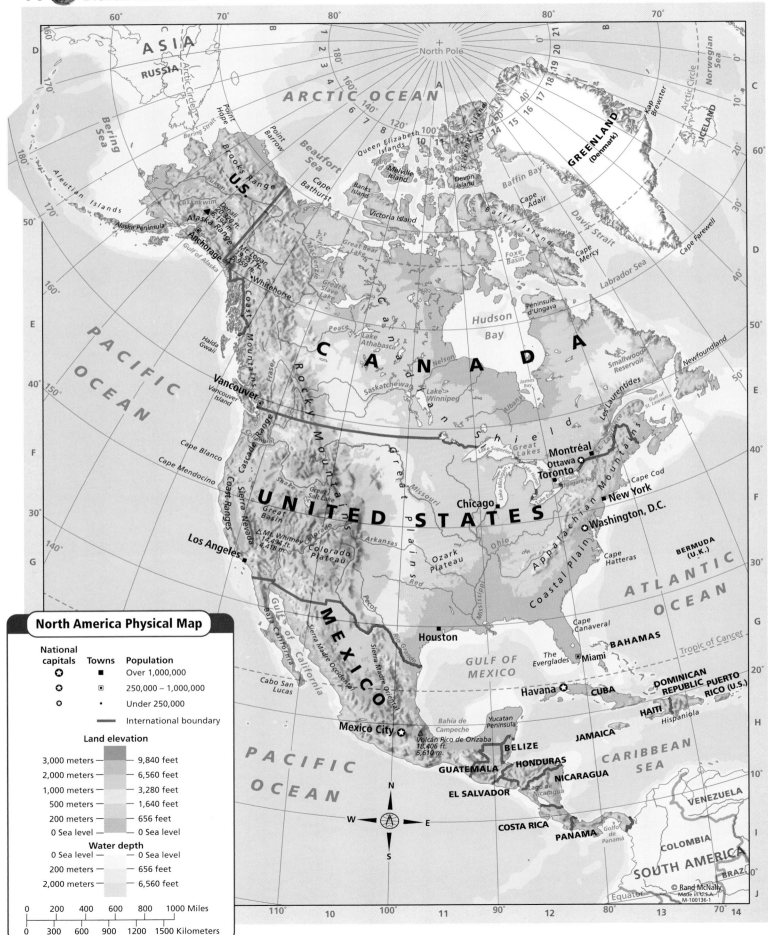

North America Physical Map

National capitals
- ⊛ Over 1,000,000
- ⊙ 250,000 – 1,000,000
- ⊕ Under 250,000

Towns Population
- ■ Over 1,000,000
- ▣ 250,000 – 1,000,000
- • Under 250,000
- —— International boundary

Land elevation

3,000 meters	9,840 feet
2,000 meters	6,560 feet
1,000 meters	3,280 feet
500 meters	1,640 feet
200 meters	656 feet
0 Sea level	0 Sea level

Water depth

0 Sea level	0 Sea level
200 meters	656 feet
2,000 meters	6,560 feet

0 200 400 600 800 1000 Miles
0 300 600 900 1200 1500 Kilometers

© Rand McNally
Made in U.S.A.
M-100136-1

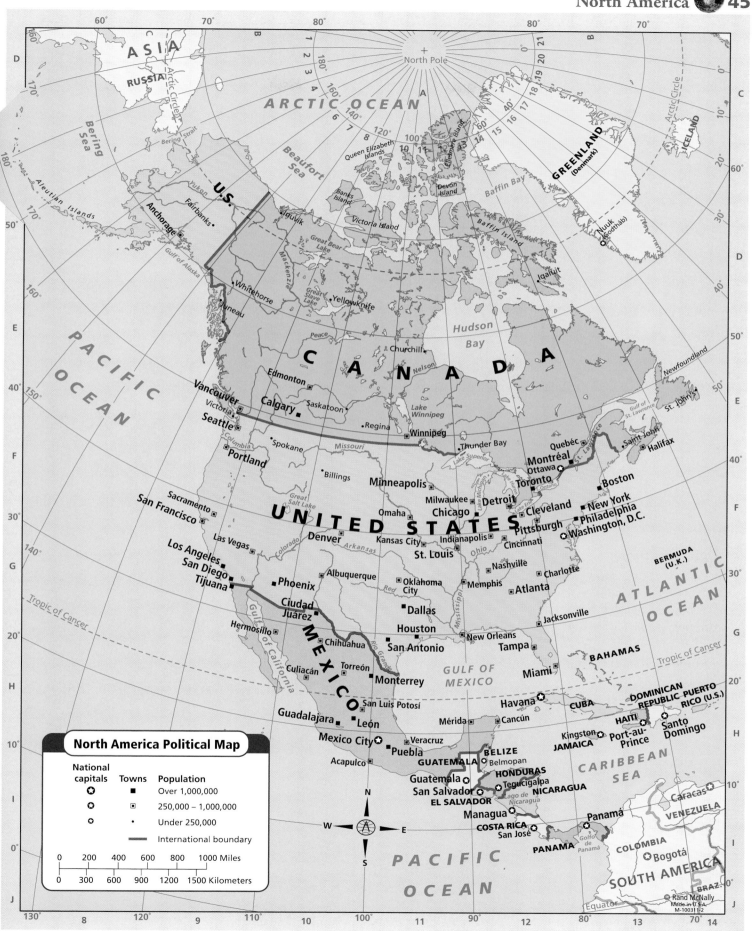

ASIA

RUSSIA

Arctic Circle

ARCTIC OCEAN

Bering Sea

Bering Strait

Aleutian Islands

North Pole

Queen Elizabeth Islands

Ellesmere Island

GREENLAND (Denmark)

ICELAND

Baffin Bay

Yukon

U.S.

Anchorage

Fairbanks

Inuvik

Banks Island

Victoria Island

Devon Island

Baffin Island

Nuuk (Godthåb)

Arctic Circle

Beaufort Sea

Mackenzie

Great Bear Lake

Whitehorse

Juneau

Gulf of Alaska

Great Slave Lake

Yellowknife

Peace

C A N A D A

Churchill

Hudson Bay

Iqaluit

PACIFIC OCEAN

Edmonton

Vancouver

Victoria

Calgary

Seattle

Saskatoon

Regina

Nelson

Lake Winnipeg

Winnipeg

Newfoundland

St. John's

Gulf of St. Lawrence

Columbia

Spokane

Missouri

Thunder Bay

Lake Superior

Québec

St. Lawrence

Saint John

Halifax

Portland

Billings

Minneapolis

Milwaukee

Lake Michigan

Detroit

Lake Ontario

Lake Erie

Montréal

Ottawa

Toronto

Cleveland

Boston

New York

Philadelphia

Washington, D.C.

ATLANTIC OCEAN

BERMUDA (U.K.)

UNITED STATES

Sacramento

San Francisco

Great Salt Lake

Omaha

Chicago

Pittsburgh

Denver

Las Vegas

Kansas City

St. Louis

Indianapolis

Cincinnati

Colorado

Arkansas

Ohio

Nashville

Memphis

Charlotte

Los Angeles

San Diego

Tijuana

Albuquerque

Phoenix

Oklahoma City

Dallas

Red

Atlanta

Jacksonville

Tropic of Cancer

Ciudad Juárez

Hermosillo

MEXICO

Gulf of California

Chihuahua

Rio Grande

Mississippi

San Antonio

Houston

New Orleans

Tampa

Miami

BAHAMAS

Tropic of Cancer

Culiacán

Torreón

Monterrey

San Luis Potosí

GULF OF MEXICO

Havana

CUBA

DOMINICAN REPUBLIC

PUERTO RICO (U.S.)

HAITI

Santo Domingo

Guadalajara

León

Mérida

Cancún

Kingston

Port-au-Prince

JAMAICA

CARIBBEAN SEA

Mexico City

Veracruz

Puebla

Acapulco

BELIZE

Belmopan

GUATEMALA

Guatemala

HONDURAS

Tegucigalpa

San Salvador

EL SALVADOR

NICARAGUA

Lago de Nicaragua

Managua

COSTA RICA

San José

PANAMA

Panamá

Golfo de Panamá

Caracas

VENEZUELA

COLOMBIA

Bogotá

SOUTH AMERICA

BRAZ.

PACIFIC OCEAN

Equator

North America Political Map

National capitals	Towns	Population
⊛	■	Over 1,000,000
⊛	▣	250,000 – 1,000,000
⊛	•	Under 250,000
		International boundary

0   200   400   600   800   1000 Miles

0   300   600   900   1200   1500 Kilometers

N
W (A) E
S

© Rand McNally
Made in U.S.A.
M-100311-2

Climate

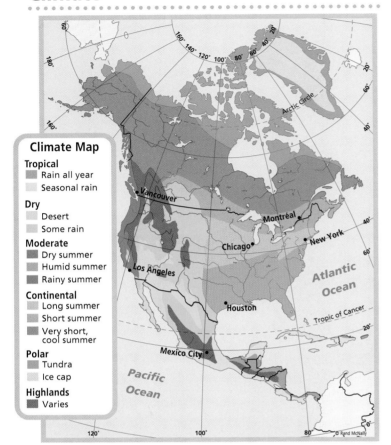

Climate Map

Tropical
- Rain all year
- Seasonal rain

Dry
- Desert
- Some rain

Moderate
- Dry summer
- Humid summer
- Rainy summer

Continental
- Long summer
- Short summer
- Very short, cool summer

Polar
- Tundra
- Ice cap

Highlands
- Varies

Environments

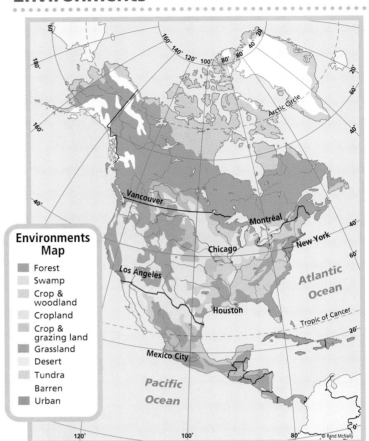

Environments Map
- Forest
- Swamp
- Crop & woodland
- Cropland
- Crop & grazing land
- Grassland
- Desert
- Tundra
- Barren
- Urban

Population

More than one-half of North Americans live in the United States. Canada is the continent's largest country in area, but it is home to only six percent of the continent's population.

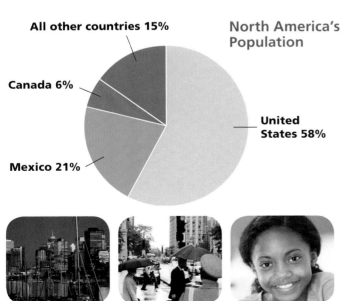

North America's Population

- All other countries 15%
- Canada 6%
- Mexico 21%
- United States 58%

Vancouver, British Columbia, Canada

Street scene in Chicago, Illinois

Girl in Haiti

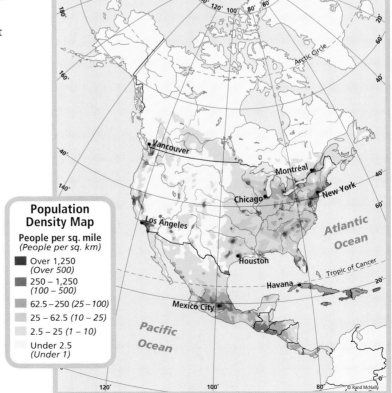

Population Density Map

People per sq. mile
(People per sq. km)
- Over 1,250 *(Over 500)*
- 250 – 1,250 *(100 – 500)*
- 62.5 – 250 *(25 – 100)*
- 25 – 62.5 *(10 – 25)*
- 2.5 – 25 *(1 – 10)*
- Under 2.5 *(Under 1)*

The Great Lakes

The Great Lakes lie along the border between the United States and Canada. Canals and rivers allow ocean-going ships to travel to the lakes and between them. Together, the lakes, canals, and rivers form a huge waterway that connects cities far inland with the ocean.

Size rank	Lake	Area sq. miles / sq. kilometers	Greatest depth feet / meters
1	Superior	31,700 / 82,100	1,332 / 406
2	Huron	23,000 / 59,570	750 / 229
3	Michigan	22,300 / 57,757	925 / 282
4	Erie	9,910 / 25,667	210 / 64
5	Ontario	7,320 / 18,960	802 / 244

Lake Superior is the largest of the Great Lakes.

The Welland Canal in Ontario, Canada, connects Lake Erie and Lake Ontario.

DID YOU KNOW?

Lake Michigan gets its name from an Algonquin Indian word, *michigami*, which means "big lake."

Relative Depths of the Great Lakes

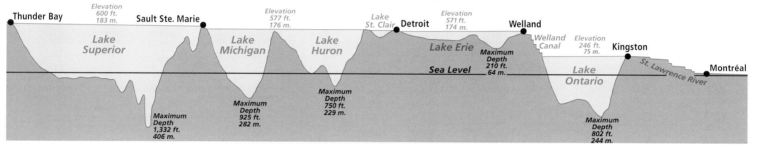

Thunder Bay
Elevation 600 ft. 183 m.
Sault Ste. Marie
Lake Superior
Maximum Depth 1,332 ft. 406 m.
Elevation 577 ft. 176 m.
Lake Michigan
Maximum Depth 925 ft. 282 m.
Lake Huron
Maximum Depth 750 ft. 229 m.
Lake St. Clair
Detroit
Elevation 571 ft. 174 m.
Lake Erie
Sea Level
Maximum Depth 210 ft. 64 m.
Welland
Welland Canal
Elevation 246 ft. 75 m.
Kingston
Lake Ontario
Maximum Depth 802 ft. 244 m.
St. Lawrence River
Montréal

Economic Activities

The map at right shows that agriculture is the most important economic activity for a large part of North America. Much of the continent's manufacturing and commerce is concentrated in a wide band between Chicago and New York.

In 1994, Canada, the United States, and Mexico enacted the North American Free Trade Agreement (NAFTA) to remove all trade restrictions between the three countries.

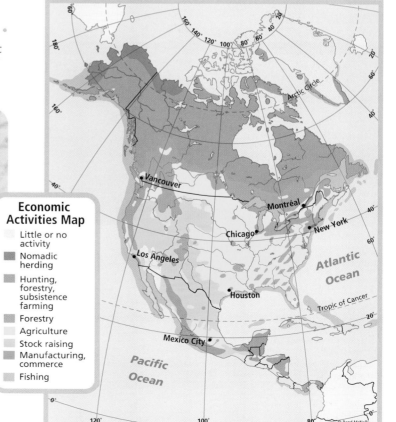

Economic Activities Map

- Little or no activity
- Nomadic herding
- Hunting, forestry, subsistence farming
- Forestry
- Agriculture
- Stock raising
- Manufacturing, commerce
- Fishing

Vancouver
Montréal
Chicago
New York
Los Angeles
Houston
Mexico City
Atlantic Ocean
Pacific Ocean
Tropic of Cancer
Arctic Circle

© Rand McNally

Fishing trawlers in California

Grain elevators in Alberta, Canada

Factory in Mexico

Natural Hazards

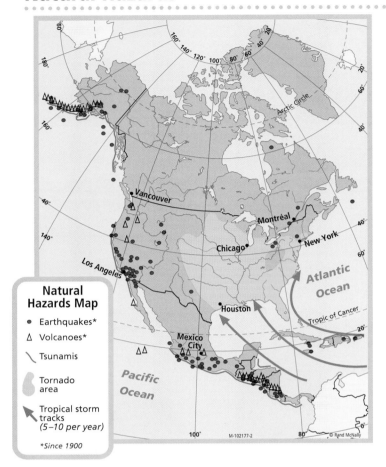

Natural Hazards Map

- • Earthquakes*
- △ Volcanoes*
- \ Tsunamis
- Tornado area
- ◤ Tropical storm tracks (5–10 per year)

*Since 1900

This satellite image shows a hurricane approaching the Atlantic coast of Florida.

Twister!

Tornadoes are rapidly rotating columns of air. They are usually funnel-shaped, and their winds may reach 200–500 miles per hour (320–800 kilometers per hour). They are usually less than one-quarter mile (400 meters) wide, but they can be extremely destructive. Texas has more tornadoes than any other state. Oklahoma ranks second in number of tornadoes, and Kansas ranks third.

Transportation

Automobiles in Mexico City add to the severe pollution problem there.

Automobiles per 1,000 people
More people in wealthy countries—especially those countries that do not offer much public transportation—own cars.

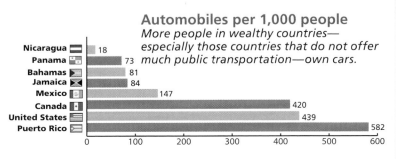

Nicaragua	18
Panama	73
Bahamas	81
Jamaica	84
Mexico	147
Canada	420
United States	439
Puerto Rico	582

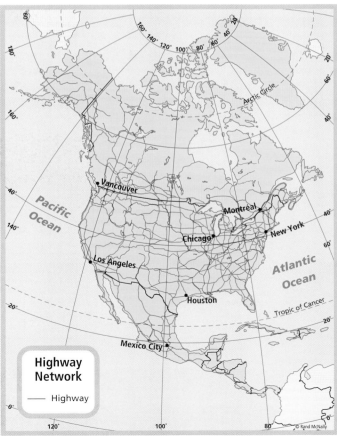

Highway Network

— Highway

Energy

Most nuclear power plants in North America are in the eastern and central United States.

The Hoover Dam in Nevada provides hydroelectric power to three states.

Wind power is a promising alternative energy source.

Electricity Production by Type

More than two-thirds of North America's electricity is produced by power plants that burn coal, oil, and natural gas. This is called thermal energy. Most of the remaining electricity comes from nuclear plants and hydroelectric, or waterpower, plants. Less than one percent of the continent's electricity is produced by geothermal plants, which tap into the heat of Earth's molten interior.

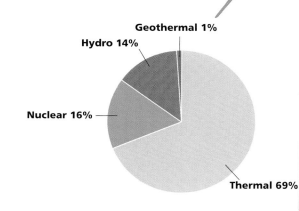

Geothermal 1%
Hydro 14%
Nuclear 16%
Thermal 69%

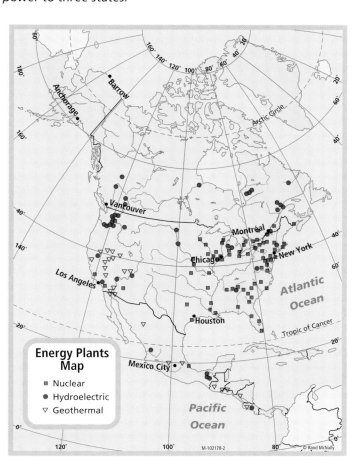

Energy Plants Map
- ■ Nuclear
- ● Hydroelectric
- ▽ Geothermal

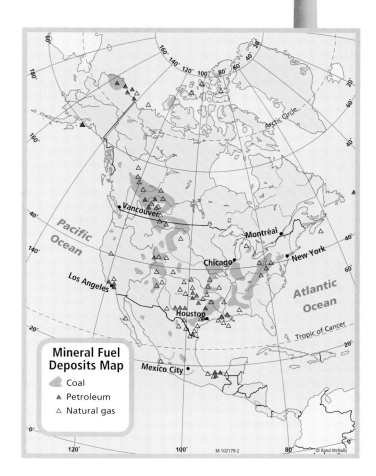

Mineral Fuel Deposits Map
- Coal
- ▲ Petroleum
- △ Natural gas

Looking at the United States

The United States stretches over great distances. The map to the right shows the points of land that lie farthest to the north, south, east, and west. The map also shows some of the country's extremes—places that rank at the top of their category.

Most maps of the United States show 48 of the states accurately, with Alaska and Hawaii dropped in as inset maps—usually off the coast of Mexico.

The other maps in this section will give you a new view of our country. They show all 50 states in their true locations and sizes.

Crater Lake, Oregon.

Mount Waialeale, Hawaii.

Westernmost Point
Cape Wrangell, Attu Island, Alaska
Longitude: 172° East

Coldest Place
Prospect Creek, Alaska
Lowest recorded temperature: -80°F

Highest Point
Denali, Alaska
Height: 20,320 feet above sea level

Deepest Lake
Crater Lake, Oregon
Greatest depth: 1,932 feet

Snowiest Place
Blue Canyon, California
Average yearly snowfall: 241 inches

Wettest Place
Mount Waialeale, Hawaii
Average yearly rainfall: 460 inches

Southernmost Point
Kalae, Hawaii
Latitude: 18° North

© Rand McNally
M-101368-1

THE SOUTHERNMOST POINT:

The southernmost point in the United States is found in Hawaii. Using latitude and longitude, explain its location in relation to southern Florida.

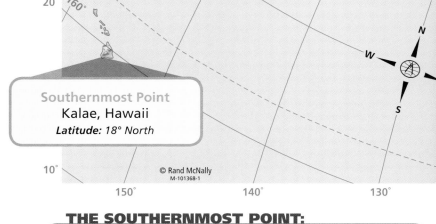

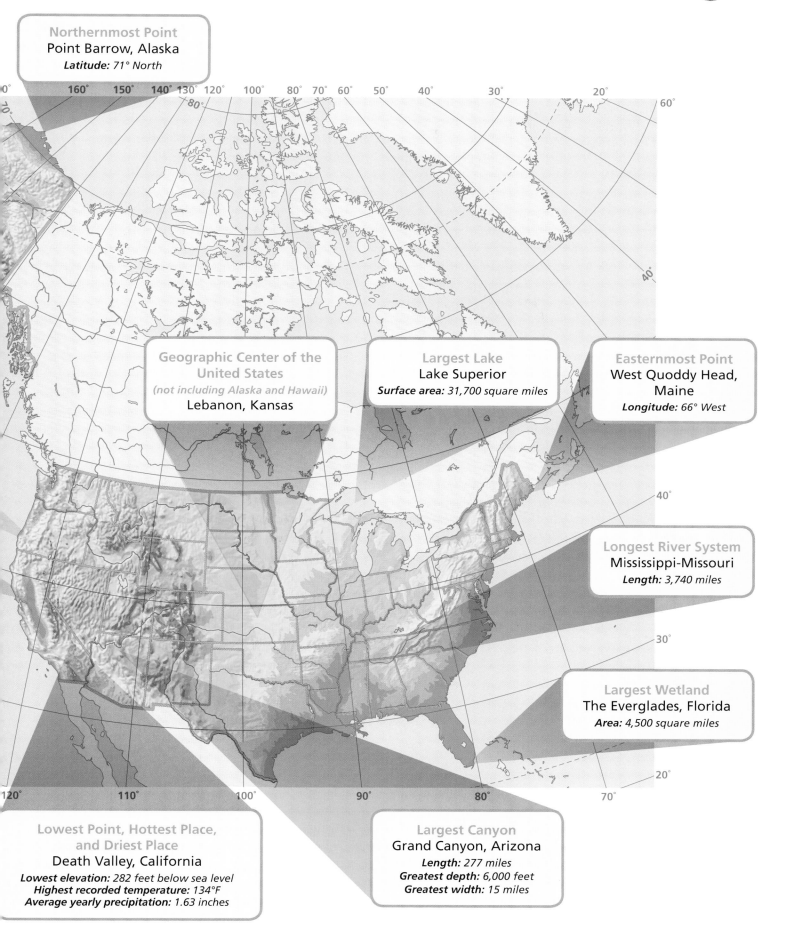

Northernmost Point
Point Barrow, Alaska
Latitude: 71° North

160° 150° 140° 130° 120° 100° 80° 70° 60° 50° 40° 30° 20° 60°

80°

40°

Geographic Center of the United States
(not including Alaska and Hawaii)
Lebanon, Kansas

Largest Lake
Lake Superior
Surface area: 31,700 square miles

Easternmost Point
West Quoddy Head, Maine
Longitude: 66° West

40°

Longest River System
Mississippi-Missouri
Length: 3,740 miles

30°

Largest Wetland
The Everglades, Florida
Area: 4,500 square miles

120° 110° 100° 90° 80° 70°

20°

Lowest Point, Hottest Place, and Driest Place
Death Valley, California
Lowest elevation: 282 feet below sea level
Highest recorded temperature: 134°F
Average yearly precipitation: 1.63 inches

Largest Canyon
Grand Canyon, Arizona
Length: 277 miles
Greatest depth: 6,000 feet
Greatest width: 15 miles

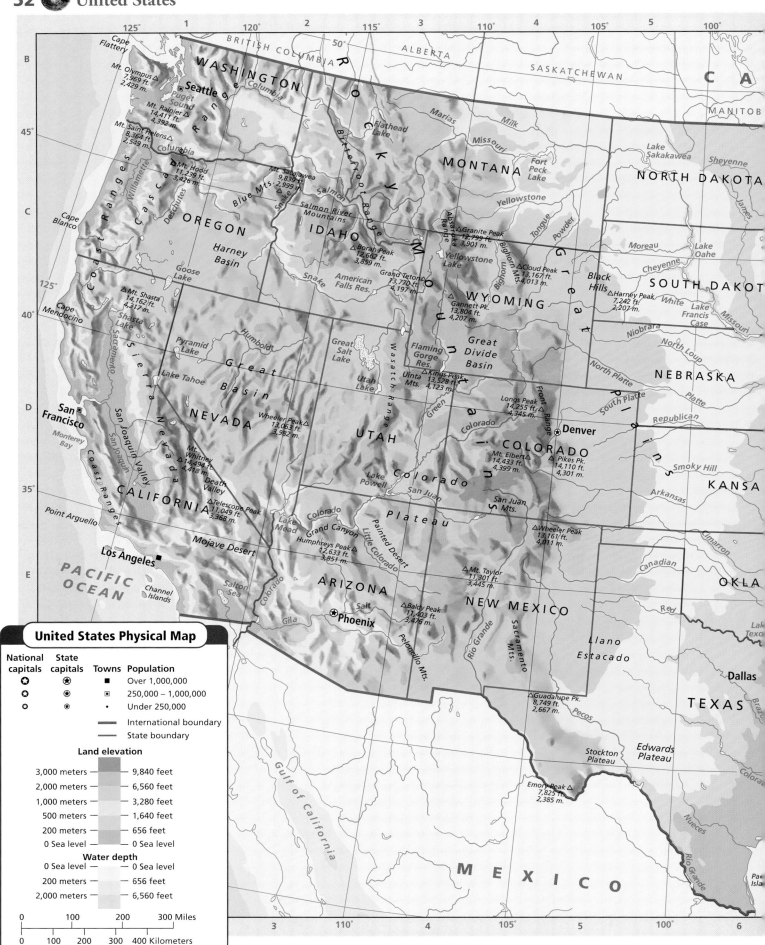

United States Physical Map

National capitals	State capitals	Towns	Population
✪	✪	■	Over 1,000,000
✪	✪	▣	250,000 – 1,000,000
✪	✪	•	Under 250,000
		▬▬	International boundary
		▬	State boundary

Land elevation

3,000 meters —	— 9,840 feet
2,000 meters —	— 6,560 feet
1,000 meters —	— 3,280 feet
500 meters —	— 1,640 feet
200 meters —	— 656 feet
0 Sea level —	— 0 Sea level

Water depth

0 Sea level —	— 0 Sea level
200 meters —	— 656 feet
2,000 meters —	— 6,560 feet

0   100   200   300 Miles

0 100 200 300 400 Kilometers

GULF OF MEXICO

ATLANTIC OCEAN

BAHAMAS

© Rand McNally
Made in U.S.A.
M-101115-2

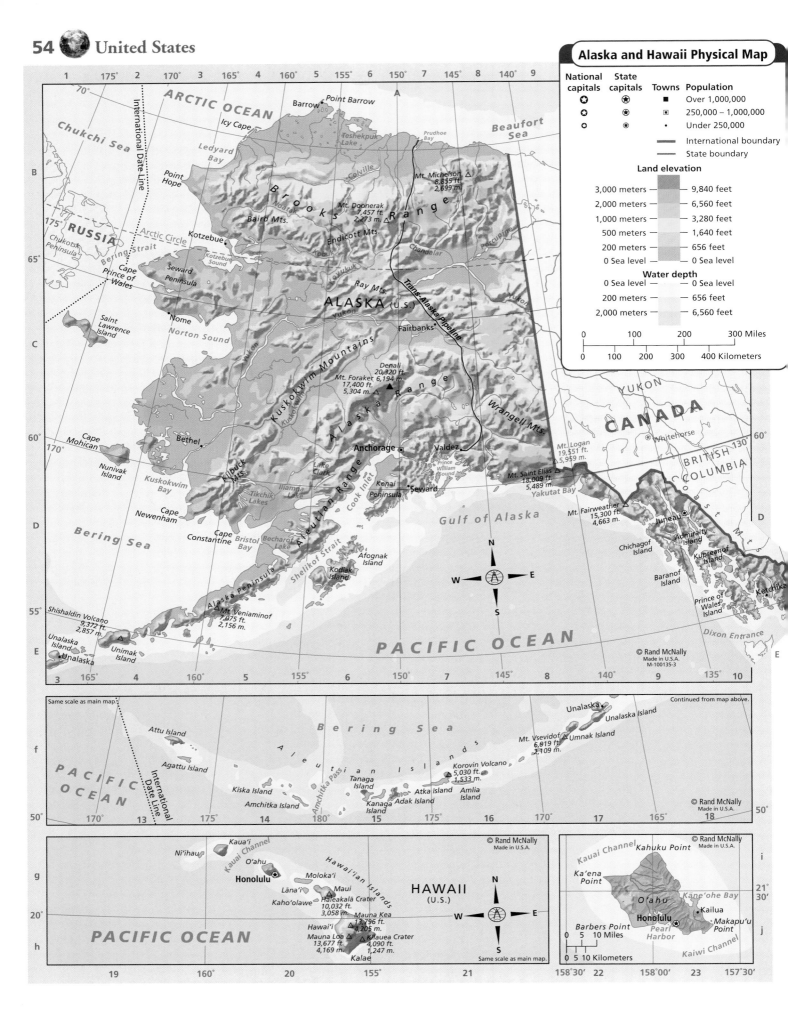

Alaska and Hawaii Physical Map

National capitals ⊛ **State capitals** ⊛

Towns Population
- ■ Over 1,000,000
- ▣ 250,000 – 1,000,000
- • Under 250,000

━━ International boundary
─── State boundary

Land elevation
3,000 meters	9,840 feet
2,000 meters	6,560 feet
1,000 meters	3,280 feet
500 meters	1,640 feet
200 meters	656 feet
0 Sea level	0 Sea level

Water depth
0 Sea level	0 Sea level
200 meters	656 feet
2,000 meters	6,560 feet

0 100 200 300 Miles
0 100 200 300 400 Kilometers

Main Map (Alaska)

ARCTIC OCEAN

Chukchi Sea

International Date Line

Point Barrow
Barrow
Icy Cape
Teshekpuk Lake
Prudhoe Bay
Beaufort Sea
Ledyard Bay
Colville
Point Hope
Brooks Range
Mt. Michelson △ 8,855 ft. 2,699 m.
Noatak
Baird Mts.
Mt. Doonerak 7,457 ft. 2,273 m.
Kobuk
Endicott Mts.
Chandalar
Porcupine

Chukotsk Peninsula
RUSSIA
Arctic Circle
175°
Kotzebue
Kotzebue Sound
Bering Strait
Cape Prince of Wales
Seward Peninsula
Selawik
Yukon
Ray Mts.
Koyukuk
ALASKA (U.S.)
Trans-Alaska Pipeline
Fairbanks
Yukon

Saint Lawrence Island
Nome
Norton Sound
Kuskokwim Mountains
Kuskokwim
Denali 20,320 ft. 6,194 m.
Mt. Foraker 17,400 ft. 5,304 m. △
Alaska Range
Wrangell Mts.
Mt. Logan 19,551 ft. 5,959 m. △
YUKON
Whitehorse
CANADA

Cape Mohican
170°
Bethel
Kilbuck Mts.
Lake Clark
Iliamna Lake
Anchorage
Prince William Sound
Valdez
Mt. Saint Elias △ 18,009 ft. 5,489 m.
Yakutat Bay
BRITISH 130° COLUMBIA

Nunivak Island
Kuskokwim Bay
Tikchik Lakes
Cook Inlet
Kenai
Seward
Kenai Peninsula
Mt. Fairweather 15,300 ft. 4,663 m. △
Chichagof Island
Admiralty Island
Juneau ⊛
Kupreanof Island

Cape Newenham
Bering Sea
Cape Constantine
Bristol Bay
Becharof Lake
Aleutian Range
Shelikof Strait
Afognak Island
Kodiak Island
Gulf of Alaska
Baranof Island
Prince of Wales Island
Ketchikan

Shishaldin Volcano 9,372 ft. 2,857 m.
Alaska Peninsula
Mt. Veniaminof 7,075 ft. 2,156 m. △
Dixon Entrance
© Rand McNally Made in U.S.A. M-100135-3

Unalaska Island
Unimak Island
Unalaska
PACIFIC OCEAN

N / W E / S

Aleutian Islands inset

Same scale as main map.
Continued from map above.

Attu Island
Bering Sea
Unalaska Island
Unalaska
Mt. Vsevidof 6,919 ft. 2,109 m. △
Umnak Island

PACIFIC OCEAN
International Date Line
Agattu Island
Aleutian Islands
Korovin Volcano 5,030 ft. 1,533 m. △
Amchitka Pass
Kiska Island
Tanaga Island
Atka Island
Amlia Island
Amchitka Island
Kanaga Island
Adak Island
© Rand McNally Made in U.S.A.

Hawaii inset

Kaua'i
Ni'ihau
Kauai Channel
O'ahu
Honolulu ✪
Moloka'i
Lāna'i
Maui
Kaho'olawe
Haleakalā Crater 10,032 ft. 3,058 m.
Hawaiian Islands
HAWAII (U.S.)
Mauna Kea 13,796 ft. 4,205 m.
Hawai'i
Mauna Loa 13,677 ft. 4,169 m.
Kīlauea Crater 4,090 ft. 1,247 m.
Kalae
PACIFIC OCEAN
© Rand McNally Made in U.S.A.
N / W E / S
Same scale as main map.

O'ahu inset

Kauai Channel
Kahuku Point
Ka'ena Point
O'ahu
Kāne'ohe Bay
Kailua
Barbers Point
Honolulu ✪
Pearl Harbor
Makapu'u Point
Kaiwi Channel
© Rand McNally Made in U.S.A.
0 5 10 Miles
0 5 10 Kilometers
21° 30'

Location of Alaska and Hawaii

The states of Alaska and Hawaii are separated from the 48 conterminous states. Canada lies between Alaska and the other states. Hawaii is a chain of islands in the middle of the Pacific Ocean.

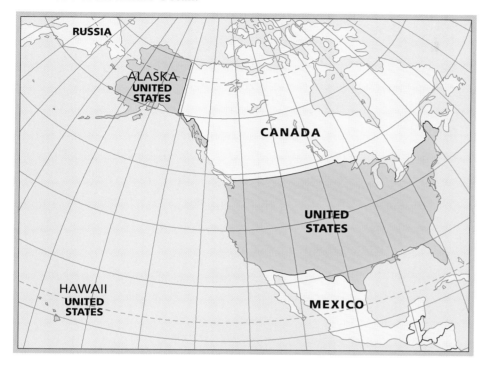

The coast of Maui is the second largest of the Hawai'ian islands.

The United States purchased the vast territory of Alaska from Russia in 1867. When Alaska became the 49th U.S. state in 1959, it increased the size of the country by nearly one-fifth.

Indian Reservations of the Conterminous United States

About 3 million Native Americans, or American Indians, live in the United States. About 22% live on or near reservations.

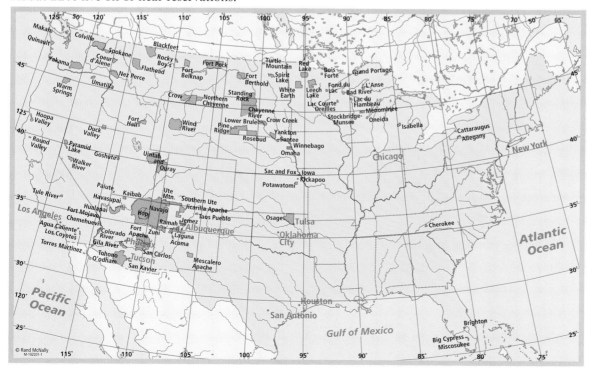

Pueblo Indian ruins in New Mexico reflect an ancient culture.

Navajo Reservation in Gallup, New Mexico.

Ceremonial clothing at a powwow in North Dakota.

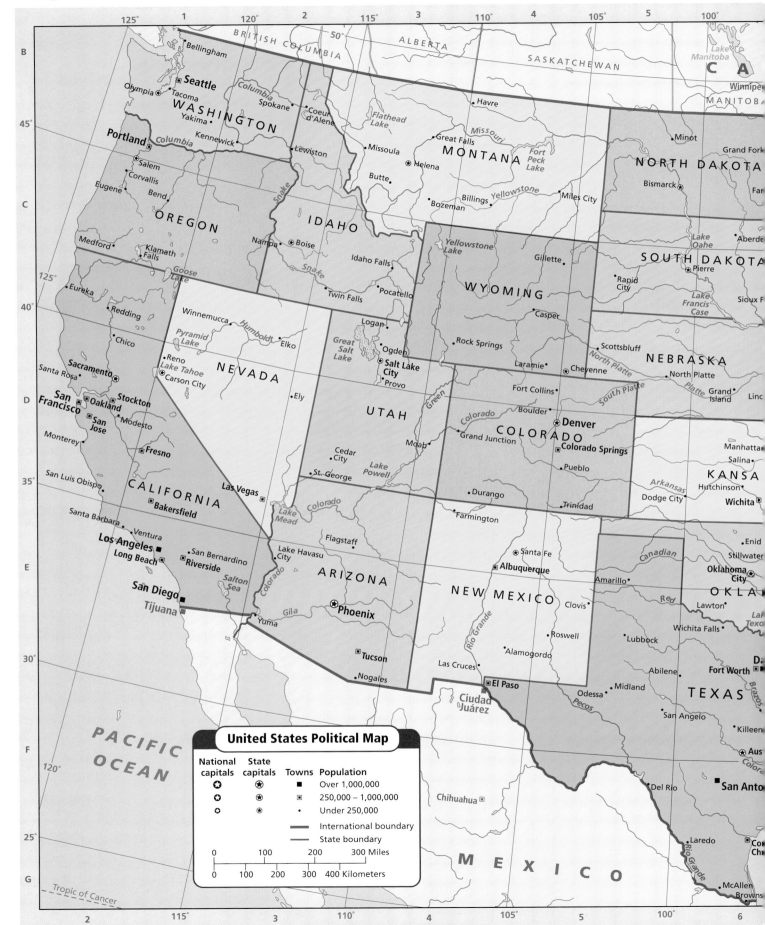

United States Political Map

National capitals
- ✪ Over
- ✪
- ✪

State capitals
- ✪
- ✪
- ✪

Towns Population
- ■ Over 1,000,000
- ▣ 250,000 – 1,000,000
- • Under 250,000

━━━ International boundary
─── State boundary

0   100   200   300 Miles
0 100 200 300 400 Kilometers

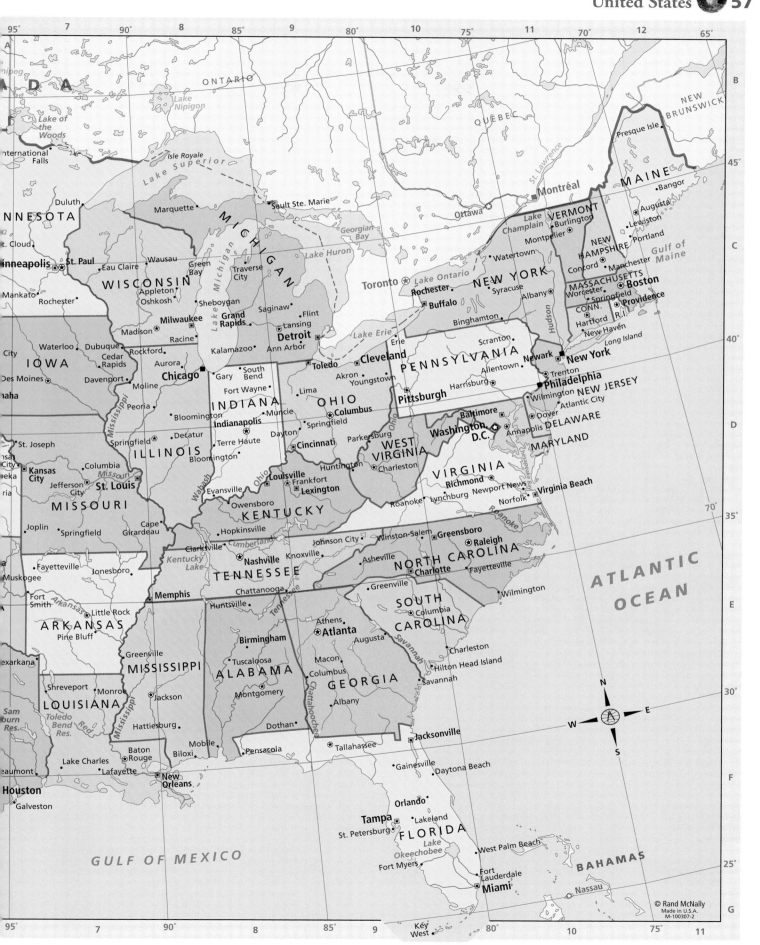

ATLANTIC OCEAN

GULF OF MEXICO

BAHAMAS

CANADA

ONTARIO

QUÉBEC

NEW BRUNSWICK

Lake of the Woods

International Falls

Duluth

Marquette

Sault Ste. Marie

Lake Superior

Isle Royale

MICHIGAN

MINNESOTA

St. Cloud

Minneapolis   St. Paul

Mankato

Rochester

WISCONSIN

Eau Claire

Wausau

Green Bay

Appleton

Oshkosh

Sheboygan

Traverse City

Georgian Bay

Lake Huron

Montréal

MAINE

Presque Isle

Bangor

Augusta

Lewiston

Portland

VERMONT

Lake Champlain

Burlington

Montpelier

NEW HAMPSHIRE

Concord   Manchester

Ottawa

Watertown

Gulf of Maine

MASSACHUSETTS

Worcester   Boston

Springfield   Providence

CONN.

R.I.

Hartford

New Haven

Toronto

Lake Ontario

NEW YORK

Rochester

Buffalo

Syracuse

Albany

Binghamton

Madison

Milwaukee

Grand Rapids

Saginaw

Flint

Lansing

Racine

Kalamazoo

Ann Arbor

Detroit

Lake Michigan

IOWA

Waterloo

Dubuque

Cedar Rapids

Rockford

Aurora

Chicago

Gary

South Bend

Fort Wayne

INDIANA

Lima

Akron

Youngstown

Cleveland

Toledo

Lake Erie

Erie

PENNSYLVANIA

Scranton

Allentown

Harrisburg

Pittsburgh

Newark   New York

Trenton

Philadelphia

NEW JERSEY

Wilmington

Atlantic City

Long Island

Hudson

Des Moines

Omaha

Davenport

Moline

Peoria

Bloomington

ILLINOIS

Springfield

Decatur

Terre Haute

Indianapolis

Bloomington

Muncie

OHIO

Columbus

Springfield

Dayton

Cincinnati

Parkersburg

Huntington

WEST VIRGINIA

Charleston

Baltimore

Annapolis

Washington, D.C.

Dover

DELAWARE

MARYLAND

Chesapeake Bay

VIRGINIA

Richmond

Newport News

Norfolk

Virginia Beach

St. Joseph

Kansas City

Topeka

Jefferson City

St. Louis

Columbia

MISSOURI

Missouri

Mississippi

Wabash

Ohio

Louisville

Frankfort

Lexington

Evansville

Owensboro

KENTUCKY

Hopkinsville

Kentucky Lake

Cumberland

Clarksville

Nashville

Knoxville

Johnson City

Winston-Salem

Greensboro

Raleigh

Roanoke

Lynchburg

NORTH CAROLINA

Asheville

Charlotte

Fayetteville

Joplin

Springfield

Cape Girardeau

Fayetteville

Jonesboro

Memphis

TENNESSEE

Chattanooga

Huntsville

Greenville

SOUTH CAROLINA

Columbia

Wilmington

Fort Smith

Muskogee

ARKANSAS

Little Rock

Pine Bluff

Arkansas

Greenville

MISSISSIPPI

ALABAMA

Tuscaloosa

Birmingham

Athens

Macon

Columbus

Atlanta

GEORGIA

Augusta

Savannah

Charleston

Hilton Head Island

Savannah

Texarkana

Shreveport

Monroe

Jackson

LOUISIANA

Toledo Bend Res.

Sam Rayburn Res.

Red

Mississippi

Hattiesburg

Montgomery

Dothan

Mobile

Biloxi

Pensacola

Chattahoochee

Tallahassee

Albany

Jacksonville

Gainesville

Daytona Beach

Baton Rouge

Beaumont

Houston

Galveston

New Orleans

Lake Charles

Lafayette

Orlando

Lakeland

Tampa

St. Petersburg

FLORIDA

Lake Okeechobee

West Palm Beach

Fort Myers

Fort Lauderdale

Miami

Nassau

Key West

N
E
S
W

Population

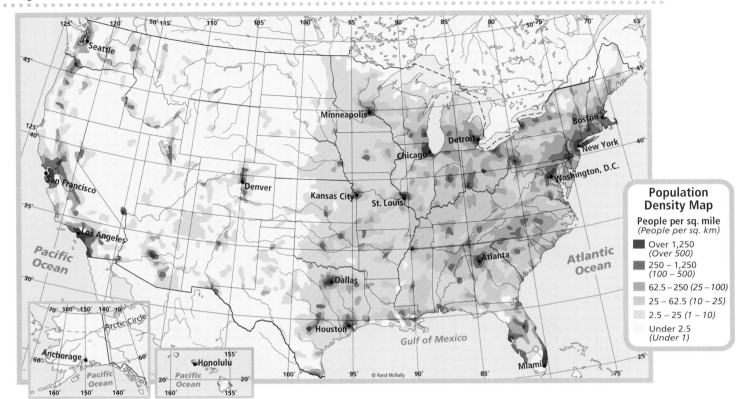

Population Density Map

People per sq. mile
(People per sq. km)

- Over 1,250 *(Over 500)*
- 250 – 1,250 *(100 – 500)*
- 62.5 – 250 *(25 – 100)*
- 25 – 62.5 *(10 – 25)*
- 2.5 – 25 *(1 – 10)*
- Under 2.5 *(Under 1)*

© Rand McNally

The United States has always been a nation of immigrants. It is one of the most culturally diverse countries in the world.

Approximately 81% of all Americans live in cities and towns.

Urban and Rural Population in the United States

1920

Rural 49% Urban 51%

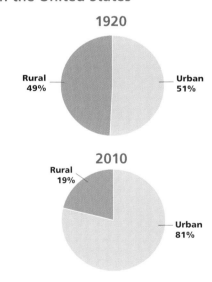

2010

Rural 19% Urban 81%

City Landmarks

Many cities have famous landmarks, such as buildings, bridges, and monuments. How many of these landmarks and their cities can you name? The answers are at the bottom of the page.

1
2
3
4
5
6

Answers: 1. The Gateway Arch in St. Louis, Missouri 2. The Space Needle in Seattle, Washington 3. The Alamo in San Antonio, Texas 4. The Golden Gate Bridge in San Francisco, California 5. The Empire State Building in New York, New York 6. The Corn Palace in Mitchell, South Dakota

Environments

Everything that surrounds you is your **environment**. The environments map shows the different types of environments found in the United States—what you would likely see if you visited any particular place.

Imagine that you could go back in time and see what the land looked like a few hundred years ago. You would find that many areas had different environments than they do now. For example, many areas that are now cropland were once grassland or forest.

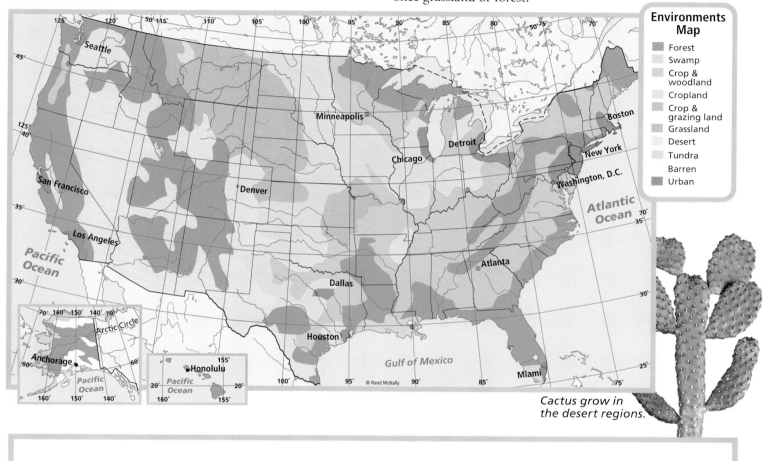

Environments Map

- Forest
- Swamp
- Crop & woodland
- Cropland
- Crop & grazing land
- Grassland
- Desert
- Tundra
- Barren
- Urban

Cactus grow in the desert regions.

Annual Precipitation Map

- Under 10 inches
- 10-20 inches
- 20-40 inches
- 40-60 inches
- 60-80 inches
- Over 80 inches

United States Regions

The United States can be divided into regions or areas with common characteristics. A single place can be part of several regions. For example, one city could be part of a mountain region, a cold region, and a forest region. The maps in the previous section show different kinds of regions. They show physical regions, political regions, and population regions, to name a few.

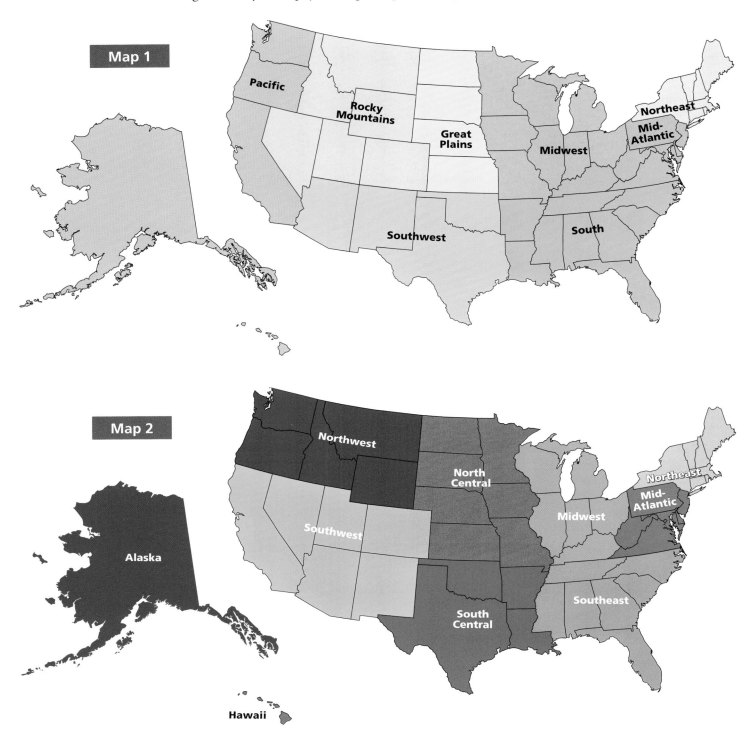

The 50 states can be grouped together into regions in many different ways. There are many opinions about what to call the different regions. There are also many opinions about where the boundary lines between regions belong. The pages that follow show information about the regions shown on Map 2. The regions are based on population, climate, landforms, land use, and location. Alaska and Hawaii are treated as two separate regions, because they are located apart from the other states and because they are so different from the other states, especially in their physical geography.

Comparing the Regions

The bar graphs below compare the 10 regions in two different ways. The graph on the left compares the regions by land area, or size. The graph on the right compares the regions by population. As you can see, some of the larger regions have relatively small populations. Similarly, some of the smaller regions have relatively large populations.

Land Area

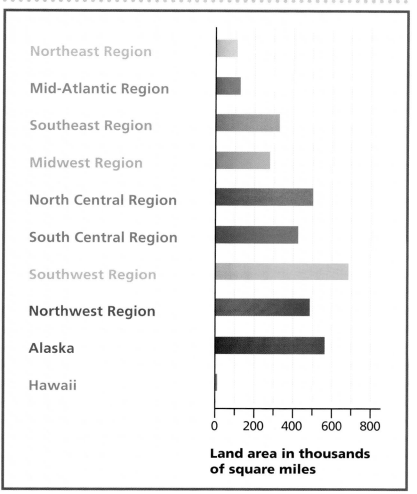

Northeast Region
Mid-Atlantic Region
Southeast Region
Midwest Region
North Central Region
South Central Region
Southwest Region
Northwest Region
Alaska
Hawaii

0   200   400   600   800

Land area in thousands of square miles

Population

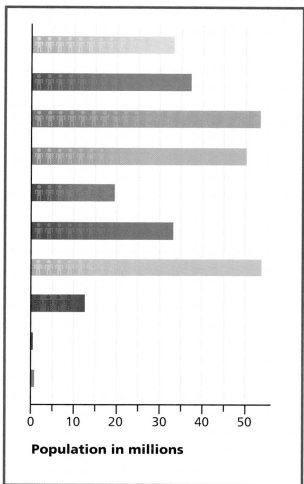

0   10   20   30   40   50

Population in millions

In the Northeast Region, New York City has a very large population compared to its small land area.

Looking at the Northeast Region

The Northeast Region is small in area but huge in population. It was settled by people from Western Europe. In fact, the six states east of New York are known as New England. The Northeast was the site of five of the original 13 American colonies. Most of the people live in an area that forms a broad band along the Atlantic coast, from Boston to New York City. This is called a **megalopolis,** a continuous urban area where the population centers all run together.

From early in the United States' history, people in this region have looked to the sea to meet their needs. Because much of the land is not suitable for farming, manufacturing has always been important in this region. Large cities are centers of business and trade. Today, ships from all over the world dock in the busy harbors of New York City and Boston, carrying goods to and from the country.

Vermont is known for its brilliant fall colors and its abundant dairy farms.

New York, New York, is the most populous city in the Northeast and in the United States.

States of the Northeast Region

Every state in the Northeast Region except Vermont borders the Atlantic Ocean. This lighthouse is in Maine.

State	Land Area (square miles)	Population	Capital
Connecticut	4,842	3,574,097	Hartford
Maine	30,843	1,328,361	Augusta
Massachusetts	7,800	6,547,629	Boston
New Hampshire	8,953	1,316,470	Concord
New York	47,126	19,378,102	Albany
Rhode Island	1,034	1,052,567	Providence
Vermont	9,217	625,741	Montpelier

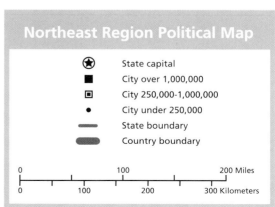

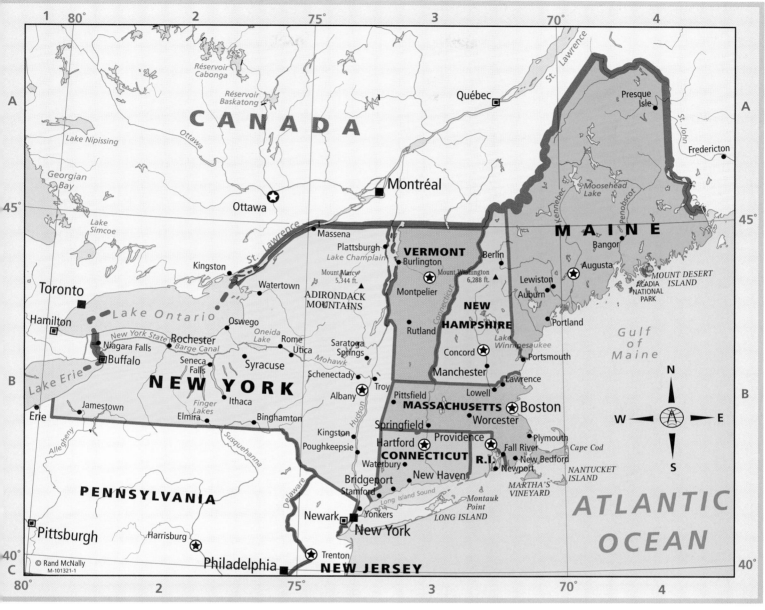

Map Labels

CANADA

Réservoir Cabonga
Réservoir Baskatong
Lake Nipissing
Ottawa
Georgian Bay
Lake Simcoe
Québec
Fredericton
St. Lawrence
Montréal
Ottawa
St. John
Moosehead Lake
Kingston
Massena
Plattsburgh
Lake Champlain
VERMONT
Berlin
Bangor
M A I N E
Augusta
Toronto
Lake Ontario
Watertown
Mount Marcy 5,344 ft.
Burlington
Montpelier
Mount Washington 6,288 ft.
Lewiston
ACADIA NATIONAL PARK
MOUNT DESERT ISLAND
Hamilton
Oswego
ADIRONDACK MOUNTAINS
Auburn
New York State Barge Canal
Rochester
Oneida Lake
Rome
NEW HAMPSHIRE
Portland
Gulf of Maine
Niagara Falls
Buffalo
Seneca Falls
Syracuse
Utica
Rutland
Lake Winnipesaukee
Concord
Portsmouth
Erie
Lake Erie
Jamestown
Finger Lakes
Ithaca
Mohawk
Schenectady
Manchester
Lawrence
NEW YORK
Elmira
Albany
Troy
Pittsfield
Lowell
Worcester
Boston
Binghamton
Hudson
Springfield
MASSACHUSETTS
Allegheny
Susquehanna
Kingston
Poughkeepsie
Hartford
Providence
Plymouth
Cape Cod
PENNSYLVANIA
Waterbury
CONNECTICUT
R.I.
Fall River
New Bedford
NANTUCKET ISLAND
Pittsburgh
Harrisburg
Bridgeport
Stamford
New Haven
New Haven
Newport
MARTHA'S VINEYARD
Newark
Yonkers
Long Island Sound
Montauk Point
New York
LONG ISLAND
Philadelphia
Trenton
NEW JERSEY
ATLANTIC OCEAN

© Rand McNally
M-101321-1

N W E S

The original Mayflower *ship brought 102 passengers from England to Massachusetts in 1620. Today, visitors can tour this replica in Plymouth, Massachusetts.*

Northeast Region Political Map

⊛ State capital
■ City over 1,000,000
▣ City 250,000–1,000,000
• City under 250,000
━ State boundary
━━ Country boundary

0		100		200 Miles
0	100	200	300 Kilometers	

The People of the Northeast

Most of the people in the Northeast live within 100 miles of the Atlantic coast. This is flatter land, so as cities grew, they were able to spread out in all directions. In some parts of the region, you can hardly tell where one city ends and another begins. New York City has the largest population of any city in the United States.

Comparing State Populations

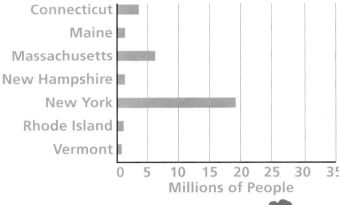

Climate Map

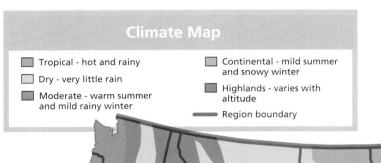

- Tropical - hot and rainy
- Dry - very little rain
- Moderate - warm summer and mild rainy winter
- Continental - mild summer and snowy winter
- Highlands - varies with altitude
- Region boundary

Boston

Climate

As the climate map shows, the Northeast has a continental climate. Winters are cold and snowy and summers are mild. At any time of the year, the Northeast can be hit with powerful storms. Sometimes snow falls for days, clogging roads and closing schools. A lot of precipitation falls during every month of the year!

Boston, Massachusetts: Continental Climate

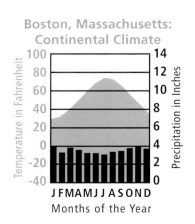

Temperature in Fahrenheit
Precipitation in Inches

J F M A M J J A S O N D
Months of the Year

Small towns, like this one in Vermont, dot the Northeast Region. The sugar maple trees of this region turn brilliant red with the cold temperatures of fall.

Working in the Northeast Region

Because of its rocky soil, the Northeast is not a major farming region. Instead, it has grown into a huge center for business. Many companies have their offices in the tall skyscrapers of New York City and Boston. Factories in the region produce goods such as helicopters and computers.

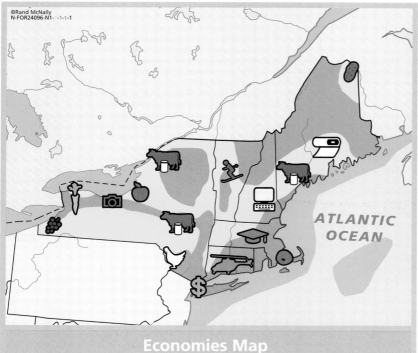

©Rand McNally
N-FOR24096-N1- -1-1-1

ATLANTIC OCEAN

Economies Map

Land Use	Economic Activity	
Agriculture	Apples	Grapes
Fishing	Cameras	Helicopters
Forestry	Cranberries	Paper
Manufacturing	Dairy cows	Potatoes
	Education	Poultry
	Electronics	Ski area
	Financial services	Vegetables

Lobster traps and buoys sit on a pier in Maine. Many people along Maine's coast make their living in the lobster industry.

The Boston area is a center of business and education. It is home to some of the country's top universities, including Harvard University and the Massachusetts Institute of Technology.

Land

A senator from Massachusetts once said, "The Northeast has a harsh climate, a rocky soil, a rough and stormy coast, and we love it." The Appalachian Mountains run through the region like a giant spine. Most of the land is very hilly. Rivers race down wooded slopes. Lakes are sprinkled across the lowlands. If you take a drive through the region, you can see why the Northeast is known for its beauty.

The moose is the state animal of Maine.

Dense forests blanket many of the mountainous areas of the Northeast Region, as shown in this photo of the Adirondack Mountains in New York.

Maine is not heavily populated, but its scenery draws visitors from all over the world.

The land and climate make skiing possible in the Northeast.

Niagara Falls, in New York and Canada, provide hydroelectric power to the Northeast.

A Threat to the Environment

Acid rain has become a problem in the Northeast. **Acid rain** refers to pollution in the air that falls as rain.

As you can see on the map, the Northeast is especially hard hit by acid rain. This is because of its factories and dense population. Cars and smokestacks in the Northeast spew out pollutants. Prevailing winds bring pollutants from cities in the Midwest, too. Over time, acid rain harms soils and lakes, which in turn harm forests and fish.

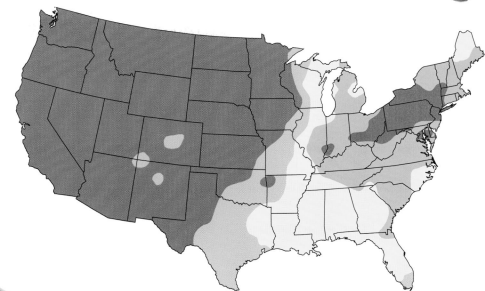

Cars can contribute to acid rain.

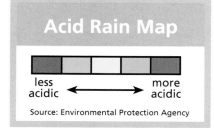

Acid Rain Map

less acidic ⟷ more acidic

Source: Environmental Protection Agency

©Rand McNally
N-FOR24000-X7- -1-1-1

How Acid Rain Occurs

Direction of prevailing winds

Pollutants enter the air

Pollutants mix with water droplets...

...and fall as rain

Acid Rain

Looking at the Mid-Atlantic Region

The Mid-Atlantic Region is small in size, but large in population. Most of the region's people live along or near the Atlantic Coast. The population thins out in the western part of the region. Oil, steel, and coal from this region fueled America's industry and power for many decades.

The Mid-Atlantic Region is home to the nation's capital, Washington, D.C., or the District of Columbia. The capital is not in any state. Instead, it is considered a federal district sandwiched between Maryland and Virginia. Many people in this area work in government offices.

The Senate and House of Representatives meet in the U.S. Capitol Building in Washington, D.C

Atlantic City, Cape May, and other resort cities draw millions of visitors to the New Jersey shore each year.

Philadelphia, Pennsylvania, is the most populous city in the Mid-Atlantic Region.

West Virginia is the most rural state in the Mid-Atlantic Region. This quaint scene is in Babcock State Park.

States of the Mid-Atlantic Region

State	Land Area (square miles)	Population	Capital
Delaware	1,949	897,934	Dover
Maryland	9,707	5,733,552	Annapolis
New Jersey	7,354	8,791,894	Trenton
Pennsylvania	44,743	12,702,379	Harrisburg
Virginia	39,490	8,001,024	Richmond
West Virginia	24,038	1,852,994	Charleston
Washington, D.C.*	61	601,723	— —

* The District of Columbia is not a state but a federal district.

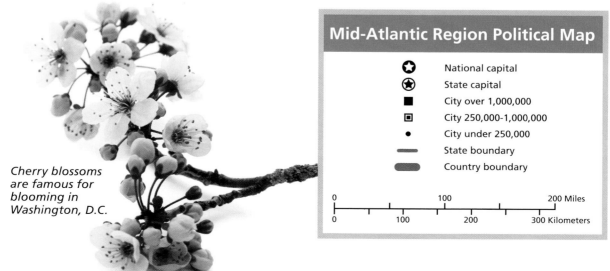

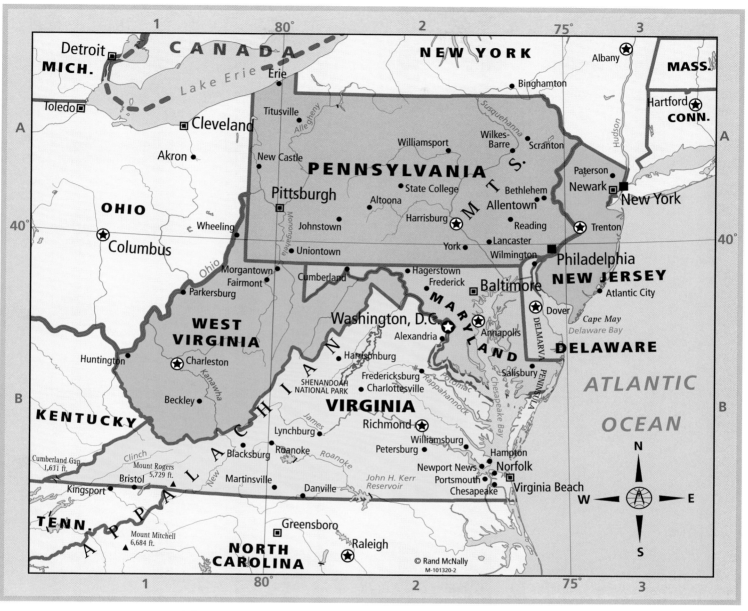

CANADA

Lake Erie

Detroit
MICH.
Toledo

NEW YORK
Albany
MASS.
Hartford
CONN.

Erie
Titusville
Cleveland
Akron
New Castle
PENNSYLVANIA
Williamsport
Wilkes-Barre
Scranton
Binghamton
Susquehanna
Paterson
Newark
New York
Pittsburgh
State College
Altoona
Bethlehem
Allentown
OHIO
Columbus
Wheeling
Johnstown
Harrisburg
Reading
Trenton
Uniontown
York
Lancaster
Wilmington
Philadelphia
NEW JERSEY
Morgantown
Fairmont
Parkersburg
Cumberland
Hagerstown
Frederick
Baltimore
MARYLAND
Atlantic City
Washington, D.C.
Alexandria
Annapolis
Dover
DELAWARE
WEST VIRGINIA
Huntington
Charleston
Harrisonburg
SHENANDOAH NATIONAL PARK
Fredericksburg
Charlottesville
Salisbury
Cape May
Delaware Bay
DELMARVA PENINSULA
Beckley
KENTUCKY
VIRGINIA
Richmond
Williamsburg
ATLANTIC
OCEAN
Lynchburg
Petersburg
Hampton
Cumberland Gap 1,631 ft.
Mount Rogers 5,729 ft.
Bristol
Blacksburg
Roanoke
Newport News
Norfolk
Kingsport
Martinsville
Danville
John H. Kerr Reservoir
Portsmouth
Chesapeake
Virginia Beach
TENN.
Greensboro
Mount Mitchell 6,684 ft.
NORTH CAROLINA
Raleigh
APPALACHIAN
MTS.
Allegheny
Monongahela
Ohio
Kanawha
Clinch
New
James
Roanoke
Rappahannock
Potomac
Chesapeake Bay
Hudson
© Rand McNally
M-101320-2

N
W E
S

Cherry blossoms are famous for blooming in Washington, D.C.

Mid-Atlantic Region Political Map

⊛ National capital
⊛ State capital
■ City over 1,000,000
▣ City 250,000–1,000,000
• City under 250,000
State boundary
Country boundary

0   100   200 Miles
0   100   200   300 Kilometers

The People of the Mid-Atlantic

Early in the United States history, settlements grew up along the Atlantic Coastal Plain. These factory towns could trade goods, along the rivers that flow into the Atlantic Ocean. Population patterns reflect that history today. Most people in the region still live east of the Appalachian Mountains.

Comparing State Populations

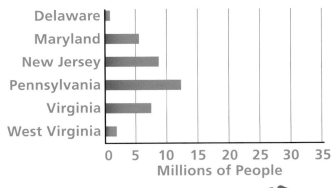

Climate Map

- Tropical - hot and rainy
- Dry - very little rain
- Moderate - warm summer and mild rainy winter
- Continental - mild summer and snowy winter
- Highlands - varies with altitude
- Region boundary

Climate

As the climate map shows, the Mid-Atlantic Region straddles the dividing line between continental and moderate climates. The climate is milder than in the Northeast. Temperatures often stay above freezing in the winter. This has made agriculture important in the region.

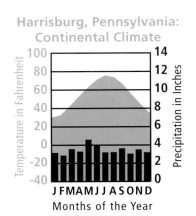

Harrisburg, Pennsylvania:
Continental Climate

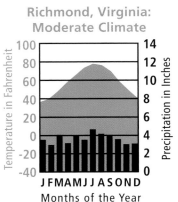

Richmond, Virginia:
Moderate Climate

The rolling hills of the Mid-Atlantic Region are dotted with farms. This scene is in the countryside of Maryland.

Working in the Mid-Atlantic Region

Work in this region is related to the physical geography. On the map below, notice the red band that runs from the center of the region to its northeast corner. This manufacturing area follows the fall line, which is discussed on page 73.

Coal mining is an important industry in the Appalachian Mountains. Coal is used to fuel many of the United States' industries, such as steel making. Steel production in this region allowed the United States to build and prosper in the 20th century.

The indented coastline and deep, protected harbors of the Mid-Atlantic make it an important shipping region. Ships are built in this area, and the United States Navy has several bases here.

Tobacco plant

This coal mine in West Virginia is one of many found in the Mid-Atlantic Region.

Many varieties of apples are grown in Virginia, including Granny Smith.

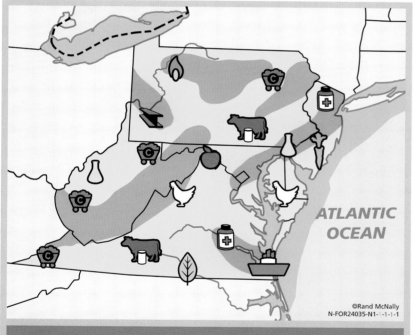

ATLANTIC
OCEAN

©Rand McNally
N-FOR24035-N1-1-1-1-1

Economies Map

Land Use

- ⬜ Agriculture
- ⬜ Fishing
- ⬜ Forestry
- ⬜ Manufacturing

Economic Activity

- 🍎 Apples
- ⚗️ Chemicals
- Coal
- Dairy cows
- Natural gas
- Pharmaceuticals
- 🐔 Poultry
- 🚢 Shipbuilding
- Steel
- Tobacco
- Vegetables

Boats sail through the waters of Chesapeake Bay.

Land

The physical geography of the Mid-Atlantic Region is similar to that of the Northeast. The Appalachian Mountains form the "backbone" of the Mid-Atlantic Region. On the east side of the mountains, the land slopes downhill through a hilly region called the **piedmont**. The green area on the map tells you that the land flattens into a low plain as it nears the ocean.

The White Pine tree is found along the Appalachian Mountains.

Much of the coast in the Mid-Atlantic Region is protected by barrier islands—long ridges of sand covered in grasses and laced with saltwater marshes.

New River Gorge National River, West Virginia

The Appalachians are old mountains that have been worn down by wind and rain. The photo above shows the weathered Seneca Rocks in West Virginia.

Working in the Southeast Region

Because of the region's warm, wet climate and expanse of low, flat plains, farmers in the Southeast grow a variety of crops—cotton, sugar cane, and oranges—that cannot be grown in colder regions. For this reason, many people in the Southeast live in **rural** areas and make their living in agriculture. Manufacturing and tourism are also important to the region's economy.

Ask any tourist what the Southeast is known for. The answer would probably be "sun." Beaches and warm, sunny weather draw tourists from all over the world.

A cotton farmer harvests his crop. Cotton grows well in the Southeast Region, because it needs a warm, humid climate.

Nashville, the capital of Tennessee, is known as Music City, U.S.A.

The Mississippi River is one of the nation's most important waterways.

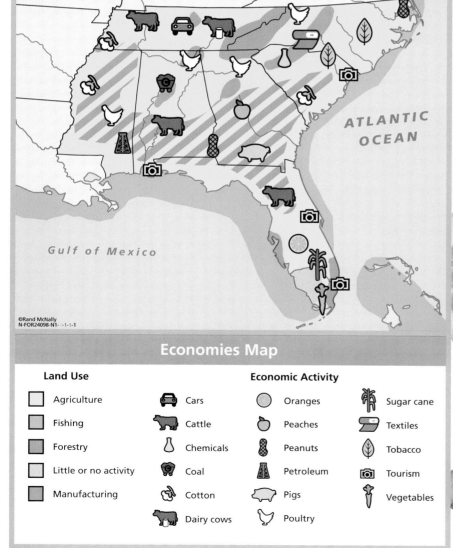

ATLANTIC OCEAN

Gulf of Mexico

©Rand McNally
N-FOR24098-N1-!-!-1-1-1

Economies Map

Land Use

- ☐ Agriculture
- ☐ Fishing
- ☐ Forestry
- ☐ Little or no activity
- ☐ Manufacturing

Economic Activity

- 🚗 Cars
- 🐻 Cattle
- ⚗ Chemicals
- Coal
- Cotton
- Dairy cows

- Oranges
- Peaches
- Peanuts
- Petroleum
- Pigs
- Poultry

- Sugar cane
- Textiles
- Tobacco
- Tourism
- Vegetables

Cotton, oranges, and sugar cane are grown in the warm climate of the Southeast.

Land

The Appalachian Mountains form an unbroken "wall" from the Northeast Region through the Mid-Atlantic Region. But in the Southeast Region, the mountains come to an end, and flat land takes their place. The physical map (page 44) shows the broad, low plains found along the coasts of the Atlantic Ocean and the Gulf of Mexico. Much of Florida is flat, swampy land that lies less than 50 feet above sea level.

The Everglades are a huge swamp in southern Florida. A swamp is land that is permanently wet. The waters of the Everglades are actually a vast river that spreads out over a flat plain.

Wide, sandy beaches outline much of the coastline in the Southeast Region. This beach is in Miami, Florida.

Spring in the North Carolina Appalachian Mountains.

In the Path of Hurricanes

Hurricanes form over oceans, usually in late summer when the temperature of the water is at its warmest. The warm water acts like a furnace, heating the air above it. When the winds are just right, rising heat may cause an ordinary storm to become a powerful hurricane.

The map of hurricane paths below shows how hurricanes seem to aim for the Southeast. Because of global wind currents, hurricanes tend to form off the coast of Africa and head across the Atlantic Ocean toward the United States. They die out when they hit land or cooler water. This is because they are no longer fueled by the heat energy of the warm water.

When hurricanes hit, people on the coastal plains often head for higher ground, away from the surging ocean and the powerful force of the wind and rain.

Hurricane Ike made landfall in September 2008.

This image of a hurricane approaching Florida was taken from a satellite high above the earth.

Diagram of the Common Paths of Hurricanes

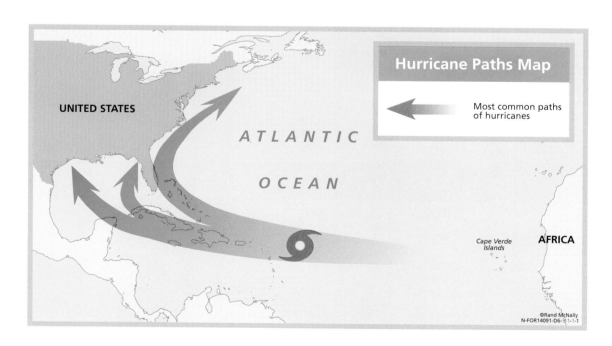

Hurricane Paths Map

Most common paths of hurricanes

UNITED STATES

ATLANTIC

OCEAN

Cape Verde Islands

AFRICA

©Rand McNally
N-FOR14091-D6- -1-1-1

Looking at the Midwest Region

The Midwest is often called "the Heartland" because of its location in the center of the country. Many of the region's cities are located on rivers and lakes and grew up as trade centers. Farm products were hauled to Chicago, for example, and shipped to other parts of the country on a network of waterways.

Later, cities such as Chicago, Detroit, and Cleveland became important manufacturing centers, and their populations soared. A growing network of transportation systems—highways, waterways, and rail lines—connected these cities to surrounding areas and other regions.

Away from the cities, the Midwest has some of the most fertile farmland in the United States. Farmers grow bountiful crops on land that was once covered by prairie and forests.

The Ohio River is a major transportation artery. Tugboats push barges filled with goods like grain and coal to distant places.

Chicago, Illinois, is the most populous city in the Midwest Region and the third most populous in the United States.

Cherries are grown in the Midwest.

States of the Midwest Region

State	Land Area (square miles)	Population	Capital
Illinois	55,519	12,830,632	Springfield
Indiana	35,826	6,483,802	Indianapolis
Kentucky	39,486	4,339,367	Frankfort
Michigan	56,539	9,883,640	Lansing
Ohio	40,861	11,536,504	Columbus
Wisconsin	54,158	5,686,986	Madison

1 · 90° · 2 · 85° · 3 · 80° · 4

CANADA

ISLE ROYALE NATIONAL PARK

Lake Superior

KEWEENAW PENINSULA

MINNESOTA

A

Duluth
Superior
Ashland
Marquette
Sault Ste. Marie
Sault Ste. Marie
Sudbury

Mille Lacs Lake

Rhinelander
Iron Mountain
Escanaba
BEAVER ISLAND
DOOR PENINSULA
Alpena

Georgian Bay

45°

WISCONSIN
Wausau
Eau Claire
Stevens Point
Green Bay
Appleton
Oshkosh
Manitowoc
Sheboygan
Traverse City
Ludington
MICHIGAN
Midland
Bay City
Saginaw
Saginaw Bay

Lake Huron

Minneapolis
St. Paul
Rochester
La Crosse
Lake Winnebago
Fond du Lac
Muskegon
Grand Rapids
Flint
Port Huron
Pontiac
London
Hamilton
Toronto
Lake Ontario

IOWA
B
Madison
Janesville
Beloit
Dubuque
Milwaukee
Racine
Kenosha
Holland
Kalamazoo
Battle Creek
Jackson
Lansing
Ann Arbor
Detroit
Windsor
Lake St. Clair
Lake Erie
Sarnia
Ashtabula
Erie
N.Y.

Cedar Rapids
Rockford
Waukegan
Evanston
Benton Harbor
Monroe
Toledo
Sandusky
Lorain
Cleveland
PA.

Des Moines
Davenport
Rock Island
Moline
Chicago
Gary
South Bend
Maumee
Findlay
Youngstown
Akron
Pittsburgh

Galesburg
Ottawa
Joliet
Kankakee
Fort Wayne
Lima
Marion
Mansfield
Canton
Steubenville

Peoria
Bloomington
INDIANA
Kokomo
Marion
OHIO
Newark
Wheeling
40°

Pekin
Lafayette
ILLINOIS
Danville
Anderson
Muncie
Columbus
Springfield
Dayton
Lancaster
Zanesville

Quincy
Decatur
Champaign
Indianapolis
Richmond
Hamilton
Chillicothe
Parkersburg

Springfield
Mattoon
Terre Haute
Bloomington
Columbus
Cincinnati
Portsmouth
WEST VIRGINIA

Columbia
St. Charles
Alton
East St. Louis
Vincennes
New Albany
Louisville
Frankfort
Lexington
Ashland
Huntington
Charleston

Jefferson City
St. Louis
Belleville
Centralia
Evansville
Owensboro
Richmond

MISSOURI
Carbondale
KENTUCKY
MAMMOTH CAVE NATIONAL PARK
VIRGINIA

Springfield
Cairo
Paducah
Lake Barkley
Hopkinsville
Bowling Green
Cumberland Gap 1,631 ft.
Lake Cumberland
NORTH CAROLINA

ARKANSAS
Nashville
TENNESSEE

© Rand McNally
M-101319-2

2 · 85° · 3 · 80°

Midwest Region Political Map

⊛ State capital
■ City over 1,000,000
▣ City 250,000–1,000,000
• City under 250,000
— State boundary
— Country boundary

0 · 100 · 200 Miles
0 · 100 · 200 · 300 Kilometers

Corn is abundant in the Midwest.

The People of the Midwest

As you can see on the political map on the previous page, people live in towns and cities all over the Midwest. However, the states in this region are not densely populated.

Comparing State Populations

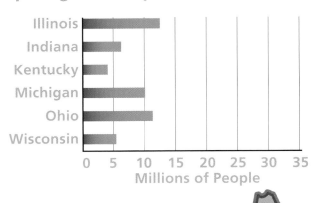

Climate Map

- ⬛ Tropical - hot and rainy
- ⬜ Dry - very little rain
- ⬛ Moderate - warm summer and mild rainy winter
- ⬛ Continental - mild summer and snowy winter
- ⬛ Highlands - varies with altitude
- ▬ Region boundary

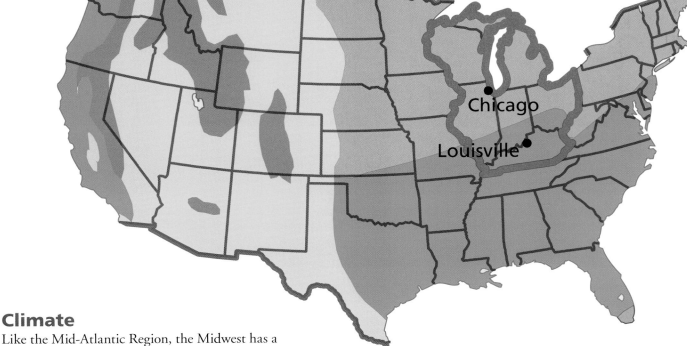

Chicago

Louisville

Climate

Like the Mid-Atlantic Region, the Midwest has a continental climate in the north and a moderate climate in the south. The areas that have a continental climate have longer, colder winters and shorter, milder summers than the areas that have a moderate climate.

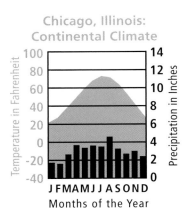

Chicago, Illinois: Continental Climate

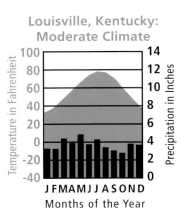

Louisville, Kentucky: Moderate Climate

The Midwest Region is home to many animals that can live in cold winters, such as foxes, raccoons, skunks, and deer. This photo shows a red fox.

Working in the Midwest Region

Manufacturing plays a big role in the region's economy. Large cities such as Chicago, Milwaukee, and Cleveland grew up as manufacturing centers along the shores of the Great Lakes. The largest of these areas stretches like a belt across the center of the region, connecting all the major cities that are located on the waterways. Manufactured goods are then carried to ports all over the world.

With some of the best farmland in the world, the Midwest is an important agricultural region. Outside the cities, farmers use the expanse of flat, fertile land for growing the nation's crops. Crops differ from north to south, depending on the length of the summer growing season.

Forestry is important in the northernmost part of the region. That's because it's too cold for farming, but perfect for some types of trees.

Soybeans and corn are two of the most important crops grown in the Midwest Region. This soybean field is in northern Indiana.

Wisconsin is a leading producer of dairy products such as cheese and milk.

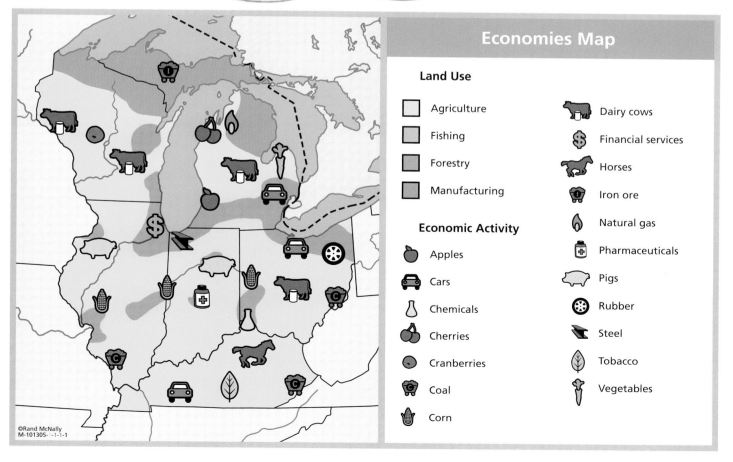

Economies Map

Land Use

- ☐ Agriculture
- ☐ Fishing
- ☐ Forestry
- ☐ Manufacturing

Economic Activity

- Apples
- Cars
- Chemicals
- Cherries
- Cranberries
- Coal
- Corn

- Dairy cows
- Financial services
- Horses
- Iron ore
- Natural gas
- Pharmaceuticals
- Pigs
- Rubber
- Steel
- Tobacco
- Vegetables

©Rand McNally
M-101305- -1-1-1

Land

Plains cover most of the Midwest Region. Flat or gently rolling land stretches in all directions as far as the eye can see. Why is the region so flat? Millions of years ago, the land was covered by a shallow sea. When the water drained away, the land left behind was generally flat. Over time, hills and valleys were sculpted by erosion. But later, huge glaciers plowed across the land and smoothed its surface.

Water frames the region. To the north are four of the five Great Lakes. They form part of the border with Canada. The Ohio River flows through the southern part of the region and forms part of its eastern boundary. The Mississippi River forms the region's western boundary. These huge lakes and rivers give the Midwest important outlets to the Gulf of Mexico and the Atlantic Ocean.

The northernmost part of this region is blanketed by forest and dotted with lakes. This photo shows Lake of the Clouds in northwestern Michigan.

The Great Blue Heron can be found on the shores of the Great Lakes.

Lake Superior is one of the Great Lakes north of the Midwest.

The Ohio river forms part of the eastern boundary of the Midwest.

The Mississippi river forms the western boundary of the Midwest.

Land Shaped by Glaciers

Thousands of years ago, vast sheets of ice, or glaciers, spread across much of this region. As they moved, the glaciers were like giant bulldozers. They picked up huge amounts of rock and soil and dragged it across the land. They scraped the tops off hills and filled in valleys. Land that was hilly became flat.

In other places, the glaciers created low hills. Some of these hills were formed when the glaciers melted and deposited rocks and soil along their edges. Others were created as rivers of meltwater beneath the glaciers deposited rocks and soil along their courses.

The glaciers scoured out enormous basins. When the glaciers melted, the basins filled with water. This is how the Great Lakes were created.

©Rand McNally
N-FOR24061-B4- -1-1-1

Glaciation Map

☐ Maximum extent of glaciation

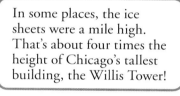

In some places, the ice sheets were a mile high. That's about four times the height of Chicago's tallest building, the Willis Tower!

Willis Tower

Glaciers like this sculpted the Midwest.

Looking at the North Central Region

The land in the North Central Region is mostly flat or gently rolling, but it rises steadily from east to west. Like the Midwest, the region is a center of our country's farming industry. Flat land and fertile soil make this the perfect place for growing crops and raising cattle on a large scale. Much of the country's wheat is grown on the Great Plains in the western part of the region.

Many of the people in the North Central Region live in small towns in farming areas. Cities in this region are smaller than those in other regions. Still, the region does have a few large cities, such as St. Louis, Missouri, and Minneapolis, Minnesota.

The Gateway Arch in St. Louis, Missouri, symbolizes the city's role as Gateway to the West.

Herds of buffalo roam the plains in parts of South Dakota.

DID YOU KNOW?

In the drier western half of this region, farmers make use of center-pivot irrigation systems, which tap into underground water.

Cattle are important to the economy of the North Central region.

States of the North Central Region

State	Land Area (square miles)	Population	Capital
Iowa	55,857	3,046,355	Des Moines
Kansas	81,759	2,853,118	Topeka
Minnesota	79,627	5,303,925	St. Paul
Missouri	68,741	5,998,927	Jefferson City
Nebraska	76,824	1,826,341	Lincoln
North Dakota	69,000	672,591	Bismarck
South Dakota	75,811	814,180	Pierre

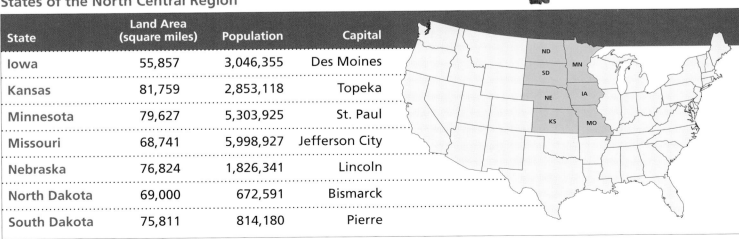

North Central Region Political Map

CANADA

NORTH DAKOTA
Williston • Minot • Devils Lake •
Dickinson • Bismarck ⊛ • Jamestown •
Grand Forks •
Moorhead •
Fargo •

Missouri
Souris
Lake Sakakawea
Devils Lake
Little Missouri
Yellowstone
Moreau
Lake Oahe

MONT.

MINNESOTA
International Falls •
Upper Red Lake
Lower Red Lake
Lake Winnibigoshish
Bemidji •
Virginia •
Hibbing •
Duluth •
Fergus Falls •
Brainerd •
Leech Lake
Mille Lacs Lake
St. Cloud •
Willmar •
St. Paul ⊛ ▣
Minneapolis ▣
Mankato •
Rochester •
Winona •
Albert Lea •
Austin •

Thunder Bay •
Lake Superior
MICHIGAN
WISCONSIN

Rainy Lake
Lake of the Woods
Red
MESABI RA.
St. Croix
Mississippi
Minnesota

SOUTH DAKOTA
Spearfish •
BLACK HILLS
Rapid City •
Harney Peak 7,242 ft. ▲
Pierre ⊛
Aberdeen •
Watertown •
Huron •
Brookings •
Mitchell •
Sioux Falls •

Lake Sharpe
White
Cheyenne
Lake Francis Case
James
Big Sioux

WYO.

NEBRASKA
Scottsbluff •
SAND HILLS
Valentine •
Norfolk •
North Platte •
Fremont •
Kearney •
Grand Island •
Omaha ▣
Council Bluffs •
Hastings •
Lincoln ⊛
McCook •
Beatrice •

Niobrara
North Platte
Lake McConaughy
Middle Loup
Platte
Republican
South Platte

GREAT PLAINS

IOWA
Mason City •
Fort Dodge •
Waterloo •
Dubuque •
Cedar Rapids •
Clinton •
Ames •
Marshalltown •
Iowa City •
Davenport •
Moline •
Rock Island •
Des Moines ⊛
Ottumwa •
Burlington •
Fort Madison •
Keokuk •

Iowa
Cedar
Des Moines

Sioux City •
Lewis and Clark Lake
Missouri

Madison ⊛
Milwaukee ▣
Rockford •
Peoria •
Wisconsin
Lake Winnebago
Illinois
ILLINOIS

COLORADO
Goodland •

N
W ⊛ E
S

KANSAS
Hays •
Salina •
Abilene •
Junction City •
Manhattan •
Topeka ⊛
Lawrence •
Kansas City ▣
Garden City •
Great Bend •
Hutchinson •
Dodge City •
Wichita ▣
Emporia •
Liberal •
Winfield •
Parsons •
Pittsburg •

Kansas
Arkansas
Neosho
FLINT HILLS

Atchison •
St. Joseph •
Leavenworth •
Kansas City ⊛ ▣
Sedalia •
Jefferson City ⊛
St. Charles •
St. Louis ▣
Hannibal •
Moberly •
Columbia •
Springfield ⊛
Kirksville •
Rolla •
Joplin •
Springfield •
Cape Girardeau •
Sikeston •
Poplar Bluff •

MISSOURI
Missouri
Chariton
Osage
Lake of the Ozarks
Harry S. Truman Reservoir
Mark Twain Lake
Bull Shoals Lake
Table Rock Lake
Black
Mississippi
Ohio

KY.
TENN.
OKLAHOMA
Tulsa ▣
Oklahoma City ⊛
ARKANSAS
Cimarron

© Rand McNally
M-101318-1

Legend

⊛ State capital
▣ City 250,000–1,000,000
• City under 250,000
— State boundary
— Country boundary

0   100   200 Miles
0 100 200 300 Kilometers

The People of the North Central

Fewer people live in this region. Cities tend to be smaller in population. The states that have the fewest people are in the western part of the region. North Dakota and South Dakota, for example, both rank among our country's five smallest states in population.

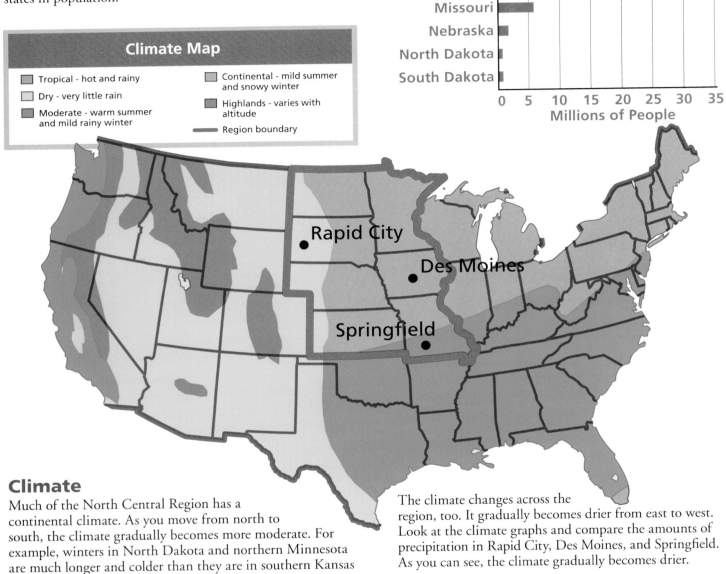

Comparing State Populations

Climate

Much of the North Central Region has a continental climate. As you move from north to south, the climate gradually becomes more moderate. For example, winters in North Dakota and northern Minnesota are much longer and colder than they are in southern Kansas and Missouri.

The climate changes across the region, too. It gradually becomes drier from east to west. Look at the climate graphs and compare the amounts of precipitation in Rapid City, Des Moines, and Springfield. As you can see, the climate gradually becomes drier.

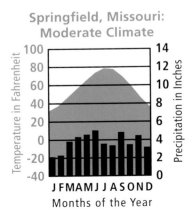

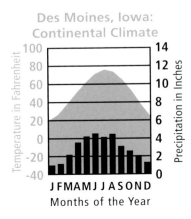

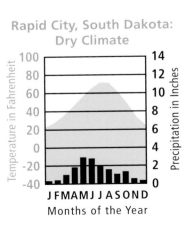

Working in the North Central Region

With such good soil and wide-open spaces, it's no wonder that the North Central Region is called our country's "breadbasket." Wheat is grown in the higher plains where the climate is cooler and drier. Corn tends to be grown at lower elevations where summers are hot and humid. The crops of the region feed our entire country and much of the world.

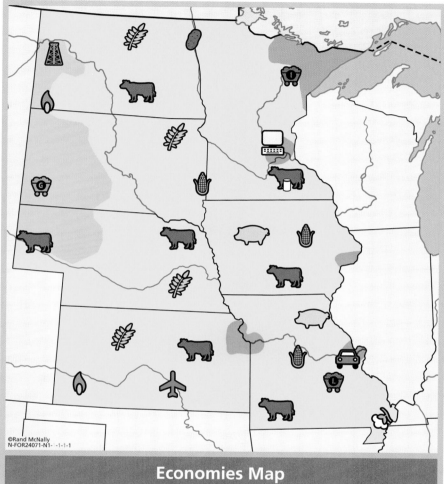

©Rand McNally
N-FOR24071-N1- -1-1-1

Economies Map

Land Use

- Agriculture
- Fishing
- Forestry
- Manufacturing
- Stock raising

Economic Activity

- Aircraft
- Cars
- Cattle
- Corn
- Cotton
- Dairy cows
- Electronics
- Gold
- Iron ore
- Lead
- Natural gas
- Petroleum
- Pigs
- Potatoes
- Wheat

The flat farmland of the North Central Region seems to go on forever, as in this scene in southern Minnesota.

Kansas City is located in two states—Kansas and Missouri. It grew up as a place where cattle were brought to be shipped to other parts of the country. Today, it is an important manufacturing city.

Land

Most of the land in the North Central Region is flat or gently rolling. The Great Plains at the region's western edge are about 2,000 feet higher than the plains at the eastern edge.

The highest mountains in the North Central Region are the Black Hills, which rise near the western edge of South Dakota.

Two of our country's greatest rivers are found in this region. The Mississippi River begins in Minnesota and forms most of the region's eastern boundary. The Missouri River begins its journey as melting snow in the Rocky Mountains. It flows eastward through the North Central Region and eventually joins the Mississippi.

The sculpted faces of four U.S. Presidents stare out from Mount Rushmore in the Black Hills of South Dakota.

Sunflowers grow on fertile prairie land in southeastern Minnesota.

Sylvan Lake in the Black Hills of South Dakota.

Roughly nine-tenths of the land in Iowa is used for farming.

Abandoned farms are a common sight in the western half of this region. Some areas have been losing population for decades.

In the Badlands of South Dakota, wind and water have sculpted the land into fantastic shapes.

Tornado Alley

The area known as "Tornado Alley" is hit by more twisters than any other part of the United States. Every year, hundreds of tornadoes tear through the North Central Region.

An invisible war between air masses takes place here. In the spring and early summer, air temperatures change as the seasons change. Hot, humid air flows north from the Gulf of Mexico. When it smashes into cool, dry air moving eastward from the Rocky Mountains, severe thunderstorms occur. Sometimes the air begins to rotate during a storm. When this happens, a spinning funnel cloud forms. White at first, tornadoes get blacker and blacker as they pick up soil and other objects from the ground.

This tornado struck a small town near Wichita, Kansas, on June 12, 2004. That year, 124 tornadoes hit Kansas alone!

Map of Tornado Alley

Tornado Alley Map

▪ Tornado Alley

Looking at the South Central Region

The South Central Region is similar to the North Central Region in many ways. From east to west, the land rises and the climate becomes drier. Farmers in this region grow crops such as wheat, cotton, and rice, and they raise cattle and sheep. Oil production is an important part of the economy.

Dallas and Houston, in Texas, are some of the biggest cities in the region—and in the country. Other cities in the region are smaller by comparison, but just as rich in history and culture. For example, New Orleans, Louisiana, is one of the country's oldest cities. It was founded almost three hundred years ago as a port city on the Mississippi River.

Suffolk Sheep

The Dallas-Fort Worth area is the fourth-largest metropolitan area in the United States.

New Orleans is home to many historic buildings in the French Quarter.

States of the South Central Region

State	Land Area (square miles)	Population	Capital
Arkansas	52,035	2,915,918	Little Rock
Louisiana	43,204	4,533,372	Baton Rouge
Oklahoma	68,595	3,751,351	Oklahoma City
Texas	261,231	25,145,561	Austin

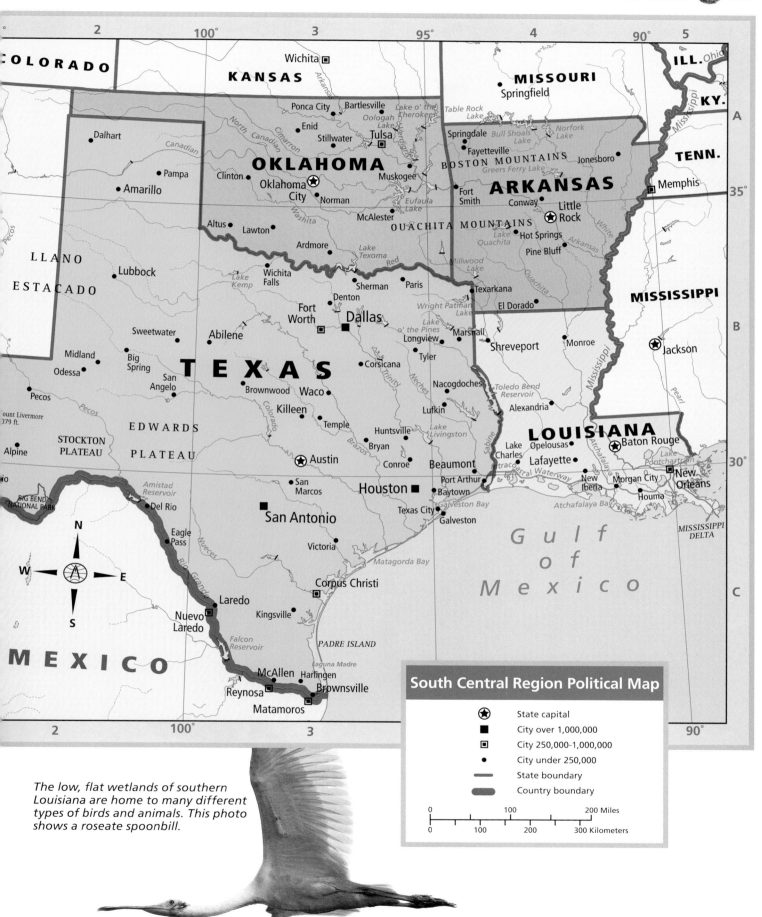

Map Labels

COLORADO

KANSAS
- Wichita
- Ponca City
- Bartlesville
- Enid
- Stillwater
- Tulsa

OKLAHOMA
- Dalhart
- Pampa
- Amarillo
- Clinton
- Oklahoma City
- Norman
- Muskogee
- Altus
- Lawton
- Ardmore
- McAlester
- Fort Smith

MISSOURI
- Springfield

ARKANSAS
- Springdale
- Fayetteville
- Jonesboro
- Conway
- Little Rock
- Hot Springs
- Pine Bluff
- El Dorado

ILL.
Ohio

KY.

TENN.
- Memphis

BOSTON MOUNTAINS

OUACHITA MOUNTAINS

MISSISSIPPI
- Jackson

TEXAS
- Lubbock
- Wichita Falls
- Sherman
- Paris
- Texarkana
- Denton
- Fort Worth
- Dallas
- Longview
- Marshall
- Sweetwater
- Abilene
- Corsicana
- Tyler
- Shreveport
- Monroe
- Midland
- Big Spring
- San Angelo
- Brownwood
- Waco
- Nacogdoches
- Odessa
- Killeen
- Lufkin
- Pecos
- Temple
- Alexandria
- Huntsville
- Bryan
- Alpine
- Austin
- Conroe
- Beaumont
- San Marcos
- Port Arthur
- Baytown
- Houston
- Del Rio
- San Antonio
- Texas City
- Galveston
- Eagle Pass
- Victoria
- Corpus Christi
- Laredo
- Nuevo Laredo
- Kingsville
- McAllen
- Harlingen
- Brownsville
- Reynosa
- Matamoros

LOUISIANA
- Opelousas
- Baton Rouge
- Lafayette
- Lake Charles
- New Iberia
- Morgan City
- Houma
- New Orleans

LLANO ESTACADO

EDWARDS PLATEAU

STOCKTON PLATEAU

MEXICO

BIG BEND NATIONAL PARK

MISSISSIPPI DELTA

Gulf of Mexico

Mount Livermore 8379 ft.

Lakes and rivers: Lake o' the Cherokees, Oologah Lake, Table Rock Lake, Bull Shoals Lake, Norfork Lake, Greers Ferry Lake, Eufaula Lake, Lake Texoma, Lake Kemp, Wright Patman Lake, Millwood Lake, Lake Ouachita, Lake o' the Pines, Toledo Bend Reservoir, Lake Livingston, Amistad Reservoir, Falcon Reservoir, Lake Pontchartrain, Atchafalaya Bay, Matagorda Bay, Galveston Bay, Laguna Madre

Rivers: Arkansas, Canadian, North Canadian, Cimarron, Verdigris, Washita, Red, Canadian, Pecos, Colorado, Trinity, Brazos, Neches, Sabine, Nueces, Rio Grande, Mississippi, White, Ouachita, Pearl, Ohio

PADRE ISLAND

Intracoastal Waterway

The low, flat wetlands of southern Louisiana are home to many different types of birds and animals. This photo shows a roseate spoonbill.

The People of the South Central

Most of the people in the South Central Region live in the eastern and central parts. The population thins out in the west, where the climate is drier. As you can tell from the bar graph, Texas is by far the largest state in the region in population. It has more people than the other three states combined. In fact, Texas has more people than any other state in the country except California.

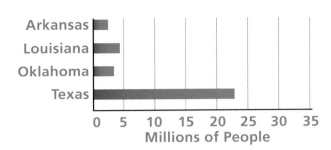

Comparing State Populations

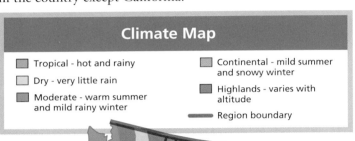

Climate Map

- Tropical - hot and rainy
- Dry - very little rain
- Moderate - warm summer and mild rainy winter
- Continental - mild summer and snowy winter
- Highlands - varies with altitude
- —— Region boundary

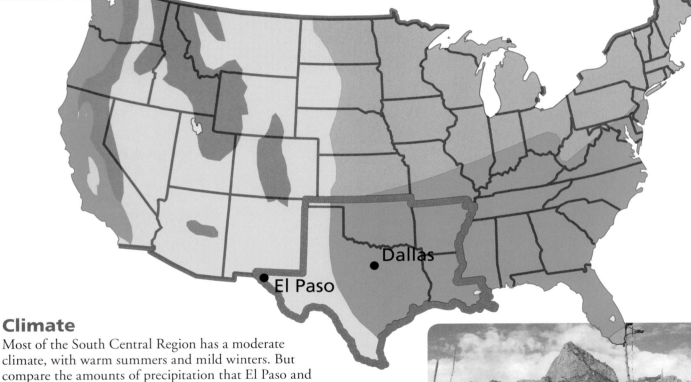

Climate

Most of the South Central Region has a moderate climate, with warm summers and mild winters. But compare the amounts of precipitation that El Paso and Dallas receive. As you can see, the western part of the region has a much drier climate. This affects how the land is used.

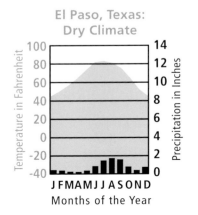

El Paso, Texas: Dry Climate

Dallas, Texas: Moderate Climate

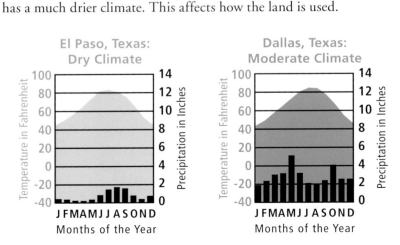

Only desert plants grow in this dry landscape in western Texas.

Working in the South Central Region

A few types of economic activity are especially important in this region. Can you tell what they are by looking at the economies map? Many of the people work in agriculture, stock raising, or businesses related to petroleum or natural gas.

Much of the region's land is used for agriculture. In the drier parts of the region, instead of farming, the land is used for raising livestock, such as cattle and sheep. That is because grazing animals don't need as much water as crops do.

On a rice farm in eastern Arkansas, huge grain silos tower above flooded fields. Arkansas leads the United States in rice production.

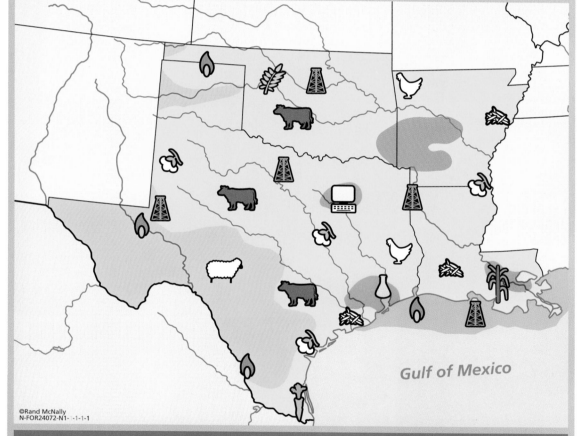

©Rand McNally
N-FOR24072-N1- -1-1-1

Gulf of Mexico

Economies Map

Land Use

Agriculture	
Fishing	
Forestry	
Manufacturing	
Stock raising	

Economic Activity

Cattle	Natural gas	Sheep	
Chemicals	Petroleum	Sugar cane	
Cotton	Poultry	Vegetables	
Electronics	Rice	Wheat	

Raising livestock is an important economic activity in Texas and Oklahoma.

Land

As you move west through the South Central Region, the land rises in a series of steps. The Great Plains in western Texas and Oklahoma are several thousand feet higher than the land near the Mississippi River and the Gulf of Mexico.

Alligators and crawfish live in the bayous of Louisiana.

Swamps and bayous cover much of southern Louisiana.

Canoeing, hiking, and other types of outdoor recreation are popular in the mountains of northwestern Arkansas.

The western half of this region is far more rugged than the eastern half. This photo is from Big Bend National Park in western Texas.

Riches of the Earth

Deposits of oil, or petroleum, are found across the South Central Region. From these deposits, oil companies produce about one-quarter of the oil the country uses.

Petroleum formed from ancient plants and animals that lived in the sea millions of years ago. When these living things died, they settled into the mud and sand on the seafloor. Over time, the ooze pressed into rock, and the living matter became petroleum. The word petroleum means "rock oil."

Today, petroleum is often found within layers of sandstone on coastal plains and along coasts. However, it is also found in areas once covered by seas but now located far inland, such as central Texas and central Oklahoma.

Looking like giant grasshoppers, oil pumps are found everywhere you look in the South Central Region, even in some urban areas.

Map of the South Central Oil Fields

COLORADO KANSAS MISSOURI KY.

OKLAHOMA

TENN.

NEW MEXICO

ARKANSAS

MISSISSIPPI

TEXAS

LOUISIANA

MEXICO

Gulf of Mexico

Oil Fields Map

☐ Oil field

© Rand McNally
N-FOR24059-F2-|-1-1-1

Looking at the Southwest Region

The Southwest Region is the largest region in both land area and population. This region stretches from the Great Plains in the east to the Pacific Ocean in the west. In between are high mountains, rugged canyonlands, barren deserts, and areas of rich farmland. In recent decades, the population has boomed in many parts of the region. It is home to 53 million people. That means that one out of every six people in the United States lives in the Southwest! Some of the cities in this region are very large. As you can see on the map, most of these cities are located in the coastal areas of California.

Much of this region has a Spanish flavor, which dates back to the colonial days when Spain controlled the area. If you study the map, you can see that many towns and cities have Spanish names, like Santa Fe, Los Angeles, and Las Vegas.

Los Angeles is the largest city in the Southwest Region.

The California poppy flourishes in dry climates. It is the state flower of California.

States of the Southwest Region

State	Land Area (square miles)	Population	Capital
Arizona	113,594	6,392,017	Phoenix
California	155,799	37,253,956	Sacramento
Colorado	103,642	5,029,196	Denver
Nevada	109,781	2,700,551	Carson City
New Mexico	121,298	2,059,179	Santa Fe
Utah	82,169	2,763,885	Salt Lake City

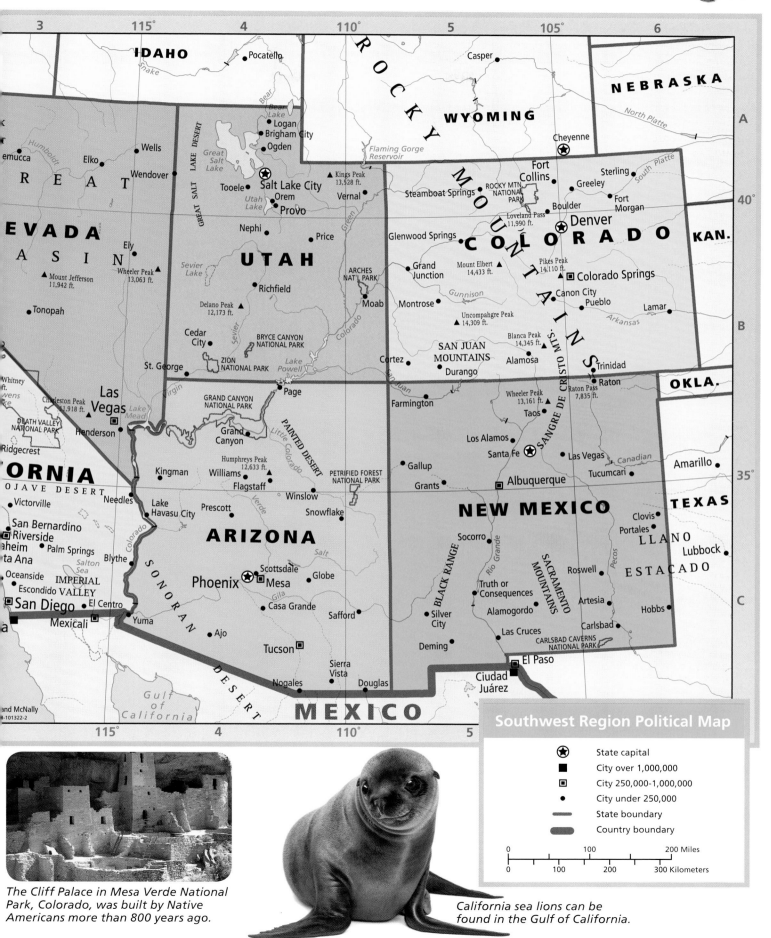

Southwest Region Political Map

IDAHO

WYOMING

NEBRASKA

3 · 115° · 4 · 110° · 5 · 105° · 6

Pocatello

Casper

ROCKY MOUNTAINS

Cheyenne

Snake

Bear

Flaming Gorge Reservoir

Logan
Brigham City
Ogden

Wells

Elko

emucca

Humboldt

Wendover

Great Salt Lake Desert

Great Salt Lake

Salt Lake City

Tooele

Kings Peak 13,528 ft.

Utah Lake

Orem
Provo

Vernal

Fort Collins

Sterling

ROCKY MTN. NATIONAL PARK

Steamboat Springs

Greeley

South Platte

Boulder

Fort Morgan

Loveland Pass 11,990 ft.

Denver

40°

A

NEVADA

BASIN

Ely

Mount Jefferson 11,942 ft.

Wheeler Peak 13,063 ft.

Nephi

Price

Sevier Lake

UTAH

Richfield

Delano Peak 12,173 ft.

Cedar City

Green

ARCHES NAT'L PARK

Moab

Colorado

Grand Junction

Montrose

Gunnison

COLORADO

Mount Elbert 14,433 ft.

Uncompahgre Peak 14,309 ft.

Glenwood Springs

Pikes Peak 14,110 ft.

Colorado Springs

Canon City

Pueblo

Lamar

Arkansas

KAN.

B

Tonopah

BRYCE CANYON NATIONAL PARK

ZION NATIONAL PARK

Sevier

Lake Powell

Blanca Peak 14,345 ft.

Cortez

SAN JUAN MOUNTAINS

Alamosa

SANGRE DE CRISTO MTS.

Whitney ft.

wens ke

Charleston Peak 11,918 ft.

St. George

Virgin

Durango

San Juan

Trinidad

Raton Pass 7,835 ft.

Raton

OKLA.

Las Vegas

Lake Mead

Henderson

DEATH VALLEY NATIONAL PARK

Ridgecrest

Page

Little Colorado

Farmington

Wheeler Peak 13,161 ft.

Taos

GRAND CANYON NATIONAL PARK

Grand Canyon

PAINTED DESERT

Los Alamos

Santa Fe

Las Vegas

Canadian

Amarillo

ORNIA

OJAVE DESERT

Victorville

Kingman

Williams

Humphreys Peak 12,633 ft.

Flagstaff

PETRIFIED FOREST NATIONAL PARK

Gallup

Grants

Albuquerque

Tucumcari

35°

San Bernardino
Riverside

Needles

Lake Havasu City

Prescott

Winslow

Snowflake

Verde

TEXAS

Clovis

Portales

Lubbock

LLANO ESTACADO

C

aheim
ta Ana

Palm Springs

Blythe

Colorado

Salton Sea

ARIZONA

Salt

Socorro

Rio Grande

Roswell

Pecos

Oceanside

IMPERIAL VALLEY

Escondido

San Diego

El Centro

Phoenix

Scottsdale
Mesa

Globe

Gila

Casa Grande

Safford

BLACK RANGE

Silver City

Truth or Consequences

Alamogordo

SACRAMENTO MOUNTAINS

Artesia

Hobbs

a

Mexicali

Yuma

Ajo

SONORAN DESERT

Tucson

NEW MEXICO

Deming

Las Cruces

Carlsbad

CARLSBAD CAVERNS NATIONAL PARK

Sierra Vista

Nogales

Douglas

El Paso

Ciudad Juárez

and McNally
4-101322-2

Gulf of California

MEXICO

115° · 4 · 110° · 5

Legend

- ⊛ State capital
- ■ City over 1,000,000
- ◫ City 250,000–1,000,000
- • City under 250,000
- ▬ State boundary
- ▬ Country boundary

0		100		200 Miles

0	100	200	300 Kilometers

The Cliff Palace in Mesa Verde National Park, Colorado, was built by Native Americans more than 800 years ago.

California sea lions can be found in the Gulf of California.

The People of the Southwest

California has by far the largest population of all the states in the Southwest Region. In fact, with more than 35 million people, California has the largest population of all the 50 states.

The five other states in the region have relatively small populations. All five rank among the least densely populated states in the nation. Population tends to be concentrated in urban centers, many of which are separated by large stretches of open space.

Comparing State Populations

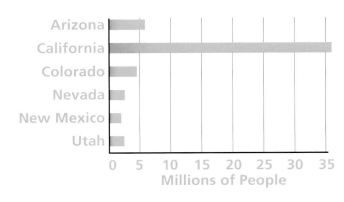

Climate Map

- ☐ Tropical - hot and rainy
- ☐ Dry - very little rain
- ☐ Moderate - warm summer and mild rainy winter
- ☐ Continental - mild summer and snowy winter
- ☐ Highlands - varies with altitude
- ── Region boundary

Climate

Hot sun and dry conditions give the Southwest a distinct character. Most of the region gets less than 10 inches of rain per year. But look at the climate graphs for Los Angeles and Boulder. As you can see, their climates are milder. Look at their locations. California is located on the Pacific Ocean, where moist, cool air blows in to air condition the land. Boulder is located in a mountainous area. There, temperatures get cooler as the elevation gets higher.

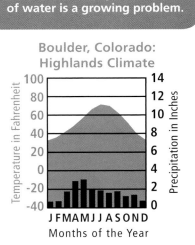

DID YOU KNOW?

Because of the dry climate, lack of water is a growing problem.

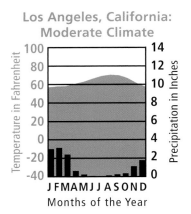

Los Angeles, California:
Moderate Climate

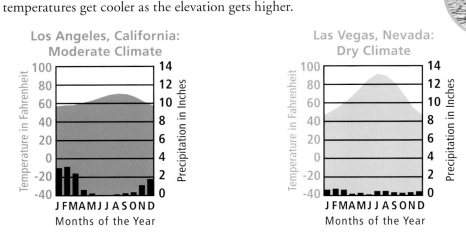

Las Vegas, Nevada:
Dry Climate

Boulder, Colorado:
Highlands Climate

Working in the Southwest Region

The work that people do in the Southwest Region is related to the land and climate patterns. You can see that forestry occurs in the mountainous areas. Now look at the climate map and the economies map. Stock raising takes place in the driest areas. Crops are grown only where farmers can irrigate in this dry region. Where that is not possible, the land can only be used for grazing.

Peaches are grown in central California.

Las Vegas is Nevada's economic center and largest city.

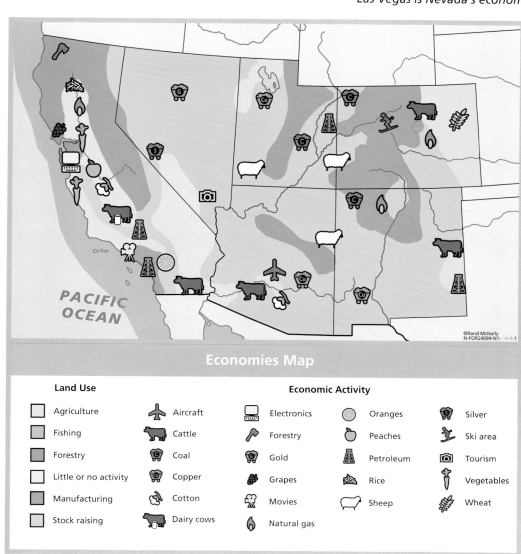

©Rand McNally
N-FOR24099-N1- -1-1-1

Economies Map

Land Use

☐	Agriculture
☐	Fishing
☐	Forestry
☐	Little or no activity
☐	Manufacturing
☐	Stock raising

Economic Activity

✈	Aircraft	💻 Electronics	🍊 Oranges	🅂 Silver
🐂	Cattle	🗡 Forestry	🍎 Peaches	⛷ Ski area
Ⓖ	Coal	🅖 Gold	🏭 Petroleum	📷 Tourism
🐑	Copper	🍇 Grapes	🌾 Rice	❦ Vegetables
🐇	Cotton	🎬 Movies	🐑 Sheep	🌿 Wheat
🐄	Dairy cows	🔥 Natural gas		

In the San Joaquin Valley in central California, irrigation canals make it possible to grow vegetables of all kinds in a dry area.

Land

Physical features make the Southwest different from other regions. Most of the region lies between two great mountain ranges: the Rocky Mountains in the east and the Sierra Nevada in the west. In between them lie the Great Basin and the Colorado Plateau. The Colorado Plateau has been eroded by wind and water into strange shapes. Deep canyons, like the Grand Canyon, were carved out by racing rivers.

Snowy peaks of the Rocky Mountains soar above a colorful valley in Colorado.

Rock formations called "hoodoos" rise majestically in Utah's Bryce Canyon National Park.

The Grand Canyon in Arizona was carved by the Colorado River over the course of millions of years.

San Francisco, California, is located on one of the world's finest natural harbors.

Lifeline of a Dry Region

From its source high in the Rocky Mountains, the Colorado River flows southwest for 1,450 miles. It is the major source of water in this desert land. Cities in the Southwest are growing rapidly, so all along the river's length, people tap this precious resource.

They have built canals to carry the water to distant places. The water is used for drinking as well as for making electricity and for irrigation. Irrigation allows farmers to grow crops in areas that otherwise would be too dry for farming.

The Colorado River once flowed into the Gulf of California. However, because people now use so much of its water, the river dries to a trickle in the desert miles from the Gulf.

The Colorado River snakes through Horseshoe Bend in Arizona.

Map of the Colorado River

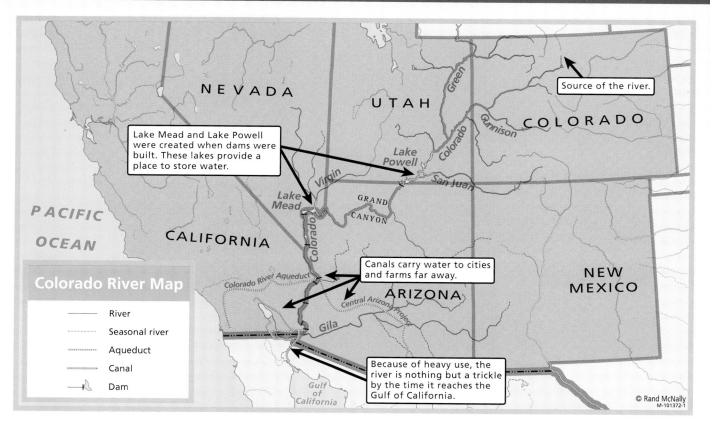

Source of the river.

Lake Mead and Lake Powell were created when dams were built. These lakes provide a place to store water.

Canals carry water to cities and farms far away.

Because of heavy use, the river is nothing but a trickle by the time it reaches the Gulf of California.

NEVADA

UTAH

COLORADO

Green

Gunnison

Colorado

Lake Powell

San Juan

Virgin

Lake Mead

GRAND CANYON

PACIFIC OCEAN

CALIFORNIA

Colorado

Colorado River Aqueduct

Central Arizona Project

ARIZONA

NEW MEXICO

Gila

Gulf of California

Colorado River Map

——	River
-----	Seasonal river
········	Aqueduct
≈≈≈≈	Canal
⊣	Dam

© Rand McNally
M-101372-1

Looking at the Northwest Region

The Northwest Region, like the Southwest Region, extends from the Great Plains in the east to the Pacific Ocean in the west. Much of the land is mountainous and thinly populated. Many of the region's people live near its western edge, between the Pacific Ocean and the Cascade Mountain Range.

The population of the entire Northwest Region—close to 14 million people—is less than the urban area population of Los Angeles, California. The region's largest city is Seattle, Washington. With a location on the Pacific Ocean, Seattle is an important port city. Over the last 50 years, trade across the Pacific Rim has increased. Goods move in and out of Seattle's busy harbor every day.

The Grand Teton Mountains were sculpted by glaciers and rise up like jagged peaks in western Wyoming.

DID YOU KNOW?

The city of Seattle, Washington, sits in the shadow of Mount Rainier, a volcano that last erupted in the 1840s.

Evergreen trees are abundant in the Northwest.

States of the Northwest Region

State	Land Area (square miles)	Population	Capital
Idaho	82,643	1,567,582	Boise
Montana	145,546	989,415	Helena
Oregon	95,988	3,831,074	Salem
Washington	66,455	6,724,540	Olympia
Wyoming	97,093	563,626	Cheyenne

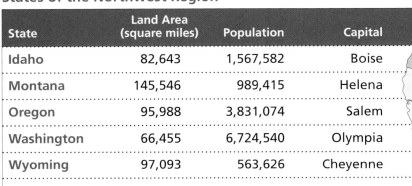

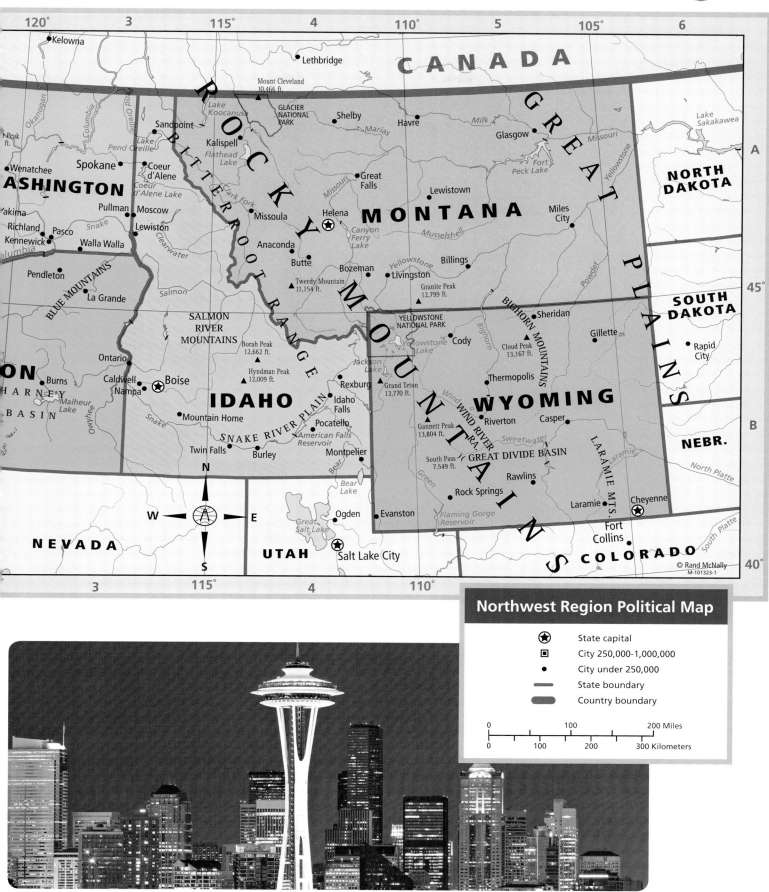

Northwest Region Political Map

★	State capital
▣	City 250,000–1,000,000
•	City under 250,000
—	State boundary
▬	Country boundary

0   100   200 Miles

0   100   200   300 Kilometers

Seattle, Washington, is a technology center and an important trading partner with nations across the Pacific Ocean.

The People of the Northwest

The region's two largest cities—Seattle and Portland—are located near the western edge of the Northwest Region. Most of the area east of the Cascades if more thinly populated. For example, Montana and Wyoming both rank among the 10 largest states in our country in land area, but they rank among the 10 smallest in population.

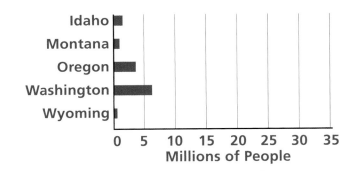

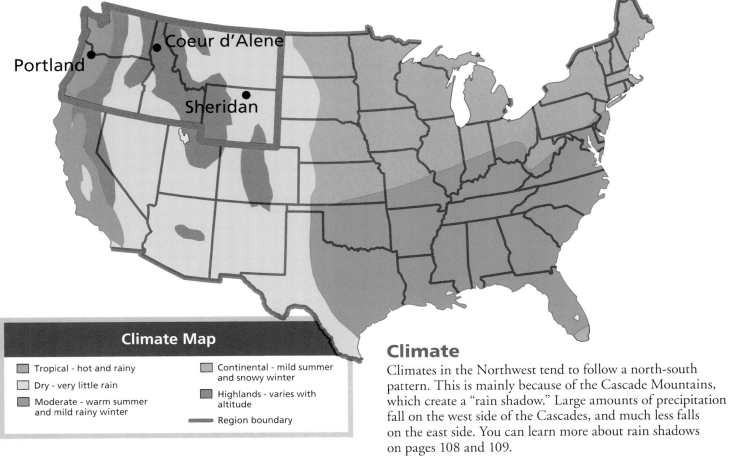

Climate Map

- Tropical - hot and rainy
- Dry - very little rain
- Moderate - warm summer and mild rainy winter
- Continental - mild summer and snowy winter
- Highlands - varies with altitude
- Region boundary

Climate

Climates in the Northwest tend to follow a north-south pattern. This is mainly because of the Cascade Mountains, which create a "rain shadow." Large amounts of precipitation fall on the west side of the Cascades, and much less falls on the east side. You can learn more about rain shadows on pages 108 and 109.

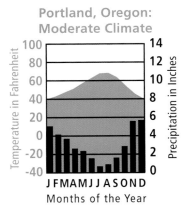

Portland, Oregon: Moderate Climate

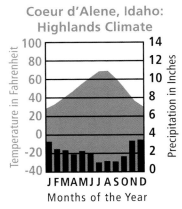

Coeur d'Alene, Idaho: Highlands Climate

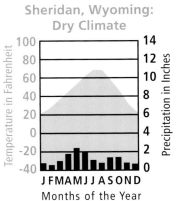

Sheridan, Wyoming: Dry Climate

Working in the Northwest Region

Compare the economies map below to the climate map on page 106. As you can see, stock raising takes place in the Northwest Region's driest areas, and forestry is important in its mountainous areas.

On the rolling land of eastern Washington, farms produce large amounts of wheat, barley, lentils, and peas.

Loggers use large equipment to move conifer trees in a log yard in Oregon.

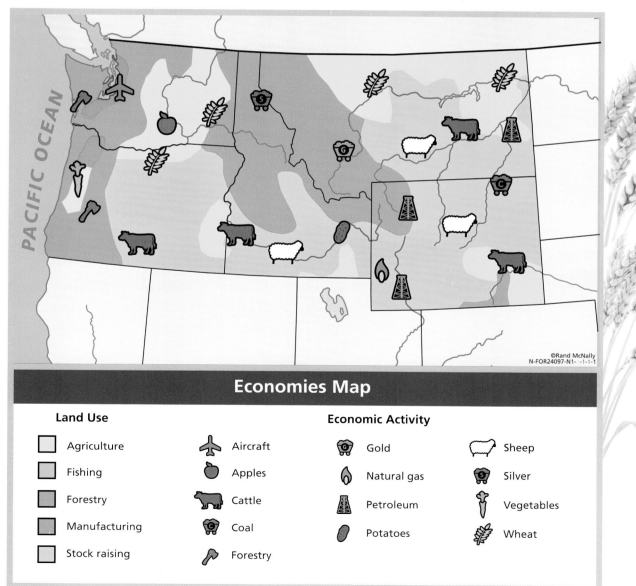

©Rand McNally
N-FOR24097-N1- -1-1-1

Economies Map

Land Use

- Agriculture
- Fishing
- Forestry
- Manufacturing
- Stock raising

Aircraft
Apples
Cattle
Coal
Forestry

Economic Activity

Gold
Natural gas
Petroleum
Potatoes

Sheep
Silver
Vegetables
Wheat

Land

Mountains are a major land feature in the Northwest Region. The Rocky Mountains cross the center of the region and the Cascade Range rises in the west. Between them lies the Columbia Plateau, where the land is lower, flatter, and drier. East of the Rockies, the land opens up into the Great Plains. This is known as Big Sky Country, where the whole expanse of the sky can be seen in any direction.

Oregon's Crater Lake lies in the crater of a dormant volcano.

Ice-chiseled peaks soar skyward in Montana's Glacier National Park.

Some of the richest agricultural land in the United States is found along the Snake River in Idaho. This photo shows rows of potato plants.

The Rain Shadow Effect

Mountains play a big part in shaping rainfall patterns in the Northwest Region. The mountains of the Cascade Range, the Coast Ranges, and the Olympic Mountains act like huge walls. Moist air blowing off the Pacific Ocean hits the "walls" and is forced upward. When air rises, it cools. Cool air cannot hold as much moisture as warmer air, so all that moisture falls to earth on the western side of the mountains as rain or snow. That leaves the other side of the mountains in a rain shadow, a region that gets very little rain.

South of this region, the Sierra Nevada and Coast Ranges of California also create a rain shadow. This explains why much of the western United States has a dry climate.

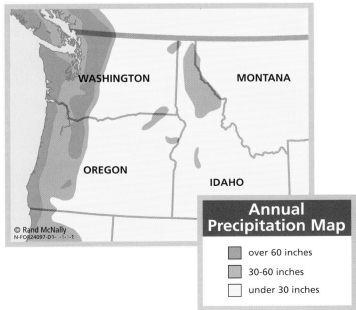

WASHINGTON

MONTANA

OREGON

IDAHO

© Rand McNally
N-FOR24097-D1- -1-1-1

Annual Precipitation Map

over 60 inches

30-60 inches

under 30 inches

A lush rain forest grows in Olympic National Park, Washington, on the western side of the Olympic Mountains.

This arid landscape in eastern Oregon shows the effect of the rain shadow.

Diagram of the Rain Shadow Effect

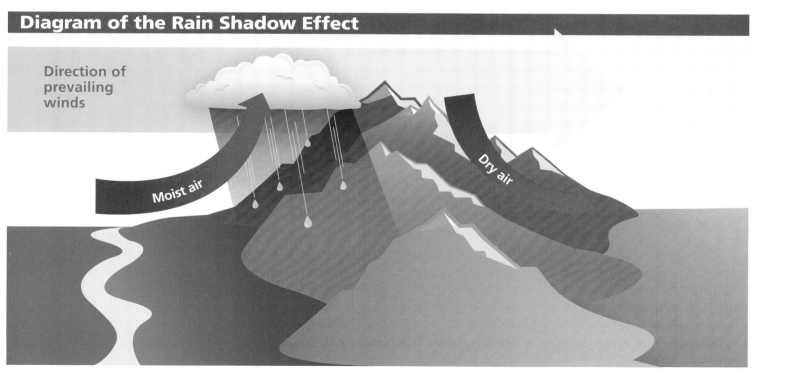

Direction of prevailing winds

Moist air

Dry air

Jagged mountains rise above a glacier and a valley filled with wildflowers in southeastern Alaska. Much of Alaska is pristine wilderness.

Alaska

Alaska lies hundreds of miles northwest of the lower 48 states. It is by far the largest of the 50 states. From its easternmost point to its westernmost point, in the Aleutian Islands, Alaska stretches about 2,400 miles. That is about the same as the distance between New York City and San Francisco.

Look at Alaska's location on the map. You can see that it is closer to Russia than it is to the rest of the United States. Flying from its capital city, Juneau, to Seattle, Washington, the nearest city in the lower 48 states, would take about four hours!

Because of its cold climate, it has a smaller population than all but three other states. Most Alaskans live in the southern part of the state. Alaska's landforms include broad plains, vast plateaus, and long mountain ranges.

Fireweed

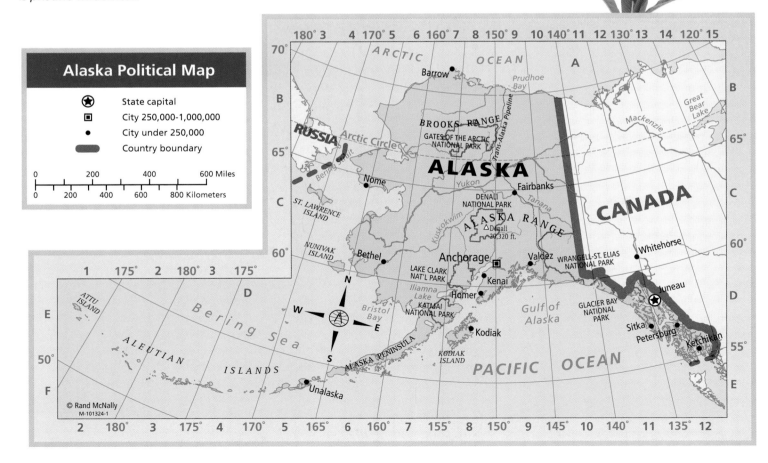

Alaska Political Map

⭐ State capital
▣ City 250,000–1,000,000
• City under 250,000
━ Country boundary

0   200   400   600 Miles
0 200 400 600 800 Kilometers

© Rand McNally
M-101324-1

Anchorage is Alaska's most populous city with more than one-third of Alaska's people.

The People of Alaska

With about 700,000 people, Alaska is the fourth smallest state in population. Comparing its population and area, Alaska has a population density of less than two people per square mile! Most Alaskans live near Anchorage, the largest city, located in the southern part of the state. Study the climate graphs below to find out why. As you can see, Anchorage has much milder temperatures than Barrow and is far less rainy than Juneau.

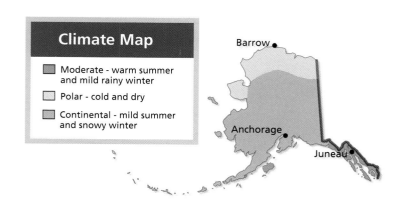

Climate

Three different climates are found in Alaska. The northern third of the state has a polar climate, with cold temperatures and little precipitation. Most of the rest of the state has a continental climate and is not as cold or dry. Southern Alaska is warmer because of its latitude and the warming effect of the ocean. The "panhandle," where Juneau is located, has a moderate climate but much greater rainfall than the rest of the state.

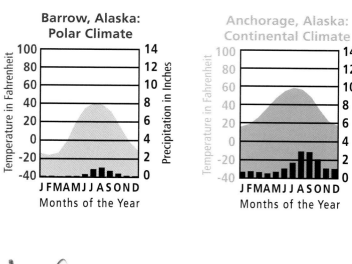

Polar bear

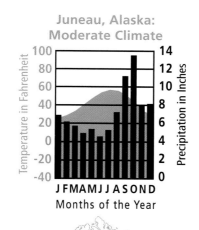

The Alaskan Malamute is a popular sledding dog in Alaska.

CANADA

State	Land Area (square miles)	Population	Capital
Alaska	570,641	710,231	Juneau

Working in Alaska

Because of its location on the Pacific Rim, Anchorage has become a transportation hub. Ships and planes from all over the world stop in Anchorage to refuel. As you can see on the economies map, hunting and fishing are the main economic activities over much of the state. Many Native Americans make their homes in Alaska. Their lifestyles fit their environment. They hunt seals and whales for food, depending on the season. Petroleum and natural gas production are important economic activities in the northernmost part of the state.

Soaring to 20,320 feet, Alaska's Denali is the highest peak in North America.

Land

Several mountain ranges tower over the Alaskan landscape. The highest mountains are found in the Alaska Range. This range was created over millions of years as two of the earth's tectonic plates crashed together in a slow-motion collision and forced the crust upward. Denali, rising nearly four miles into the sky, is the highest peak in North America.

Between Alaska's mountain ranges are vast plains and plateaus. North of the Brooks Range is a coastal lowland that is home to huge herds of caribou.

The mountainous Aleutian Islands extend in a long arc from the southwestern tip of the mainland.

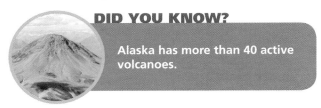

DID YOU KNOW?

Alaska has more than 40 active volcanoes.

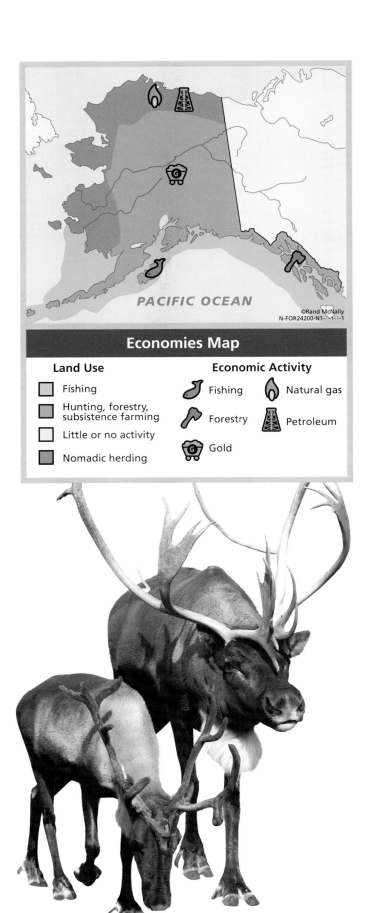

PACIFIC OCEAN

©Rand McNally
N-FOR24200-N1-1-1-1

Economies Map

Land Use

- Fishing
- Hunting, forestry, subsistence farming
- Little or no activity
- Nomadic herding

Economic Activity

- Fishing
- Forestry
- Gold
- Natural gas
- Petroleum

North of the Brooks Range lies a coastal lowland that is home to enormous herds of caribou.

Volcanic Islands

Like fireworks from the earth, volcanoes sometimes erupt in Alaska's Aleutian Islands. Earthquakes frequently shake the ground. This is because the islands are located along the tectonically active Ring of Fire.

Compare the physical map of Alaska on page 54 to the plate tectonics map on page 39. As you can see, the Aleutians line up along the boundary where the Pacific Plate rams under the North American Plate.

The diagram below shows how the edge of the Pacific Plate is forced downward. When that happens, pressure and friction cause magma to rise to the surface. Over time, eruptions of magma formed many of the islands in the Aleutian chain. These islands are really volcanoes that rise from the ocean floor. More than a dozen of the volcanoes have erupted in the past 100 years.

Flying over the Aleutian Islands is like looking down the "throats" of live volcanoes. Shishaldin Volcano is one of many in a long line of volcanic islands.

Map of the Volcanic Islands of Alaska

Aleutian Islands

Pacific Ocean

North American Plate

Pacific Plate

Magma

Some people call the island of Kaua'i the most beautiful of all the Hawai'ian Islands.

Hawaii

The island chain that makes up the state of Hawaii is located in the middle of the Pacific Ocean. It is made up of eight main islands, which are shown on the map below, and many smaller ones. The islands are actually the tops of volcanic mountains that rise from the ocean floor. Some of the volcanoes are still active.

Most of the islands have steep, forested mountains and lush, green valleys. On some islands there are brownish-black lava fields that look like huge rivers of spilled chocolate. Beaches ring the islands. Some are long expanses of white sand. Some are black sand made of ground-up lava. Because of Hawaii's warm, sunny climate, its beaches, and its spectacular scenery, the state is a popular destination for tourists from other states and from all over the world.

DID YOU KNOW?

Hawaii is the southernmost of the 50 states, and it is also the newest state. It did not become a state until 1959.

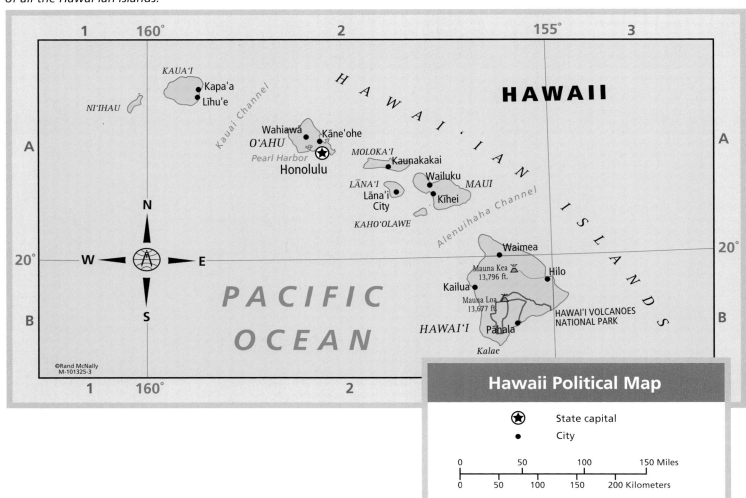

Hawaii Political Map

⊛   State capital

•   City

| 0 | 50 | 100 | 150 Miles |
| 0 | 50 | 100 | 150 | 200 Kilometers |

Honolulu is Hawaii's capital and main port. It is the most populous city, with more than 400,000 people! It stretches for about 10 miles along the coast of O'ahu.

The People of Hawaii

Hawaii is like a stepping stone in the middle of a big sea. For this reason, people have come to Hawaii from places all around the Pacific Ocean—from Japan, China, and Polynesia, to name a few. Many school children in Hawaii today still learn the languages and practice the traditions of their ancestors who came to the islands from far away.

Honolulu, on the island of O'ahu, is the only large city in Hawaii. Population thins out on the other islands, where most people live in small towns.

Climate

Hawaii is located at a latitude where the climate is always warm. The climate is also very rainy. Look at the climate graph for Hilo. This city's monthly rainfall ranges from about 7 inches to more than 14 inches. Mount Waialeale on the island of Kaua'i is the rainiest place in the world. Each year it receives about 460 inches of rainfall—that's more than 38 feet!

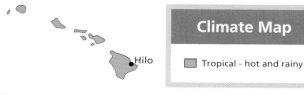

Hilo

Climate Map

⬜ Tropical - hot and rainy

Hawaii's pleasant climate is a result of its location in the tropics, the fact that it is surrounded by ocean, and the moderating effect of trade winds.

Thanks to abundant rainfall and mild temperatures, lush vegetation covers much of Hawaii. This rain forest is on the island of Hawai'i.

Hilo, Hawaii: Tropical Climate

Temperature in Fahrenheit / Precipitation in Inches

Months of the Year

J F M A M J J A S O N D

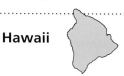

The tropical yellow hibiscus is the state flower of Hawaii.

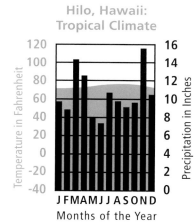

State	Land Area (square miles)	Population	Capital
Hawaii	6,423	1,360,301	Honolulu

Hawaii

Working in Hawaii

Hawaii draws tourists by the millions, so many Hawaiians work in the tourism industry. Because rain keeps the islands well-watered, Hawaii is also an important agricultural state. Tropical foods like pineapples and sugar cane are grown in its fertile, volcanic soil.

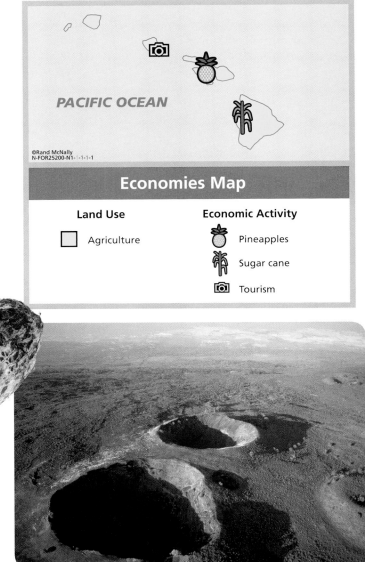

Economies Map

Land Use

☐ Agriculture

Economic Activity

🍍 Pineapples

🌴 Sugar cane

📷 Tourism

©Rand McNally
N-FOR25200-N1-1-1-1-1

Taro fields are a common sight in Hawaii. A staple food for many Hawaiians, taro grows well in areas that receive abundant rainfall.

Land

When you study Hawaii's physical map on page 54, you will notice that the Hawai'ian Islands are very mountainous. Most of the volcanoes are no longer active, but the island of Hawai'i has two volcanoes that continue to erupt: Mauna Loa and Kilauea.

Lava once poured from the craters of Hualalai, a volcano on the island of Hawai'i.

Rugged cliffs rise thousands of feet above the Pacific Ocean along the Na Pali Coast on the island of Kaua'i.

On the island of Hawai'i, lava flowing from Kilauea can close roads forever.

The Hawaiian Hot Spot

The Hawai'ian Islands formed over a hot spot, a vent where magma from the earth's mantle shoots up and melts the crust above it. As the crust of the Pacific Plate slowly moved across the hot spot, volcanoes grew into islands, one at a time. We know this because the islands are in order by age. The oldest island is at the northwest end of the chain, so it formed first.

The youngest is Hawai'i, "the Big Island." It formed last and is the only island that still has active volcanoes. Having moved off the hot spot, the volcanoes on the older islands are now extinct.

Located right over the hot spot, the volcanic Kilauea crater on the island of Hawai'i continues to be one of the most active volcanoes in the world.

Diagram of the Hot Spot

Direction of plate movement

Pacific Ocean

Pacific Plate

Hot Spot

SETTLEMENT OF THE UNITED STATES

Introduction

From its beginning, the United States has grown steadily larger—in both population and land area. The graph below shows the growth of the country's population. Compare it to events on the timeline to see when new lands were acquired.

The maps in this section show some important changes from early in our history to later times. As you look at these maps, you will see that our population is mixed. Native Americans were the first Americans, then came Europeans and Africans, then people from all over the world. But no matter where people came from, their lives were affected by geography. They settled where it was possible to survive and make a living. Landforms, climates, water bodies, and resources affected their choices.

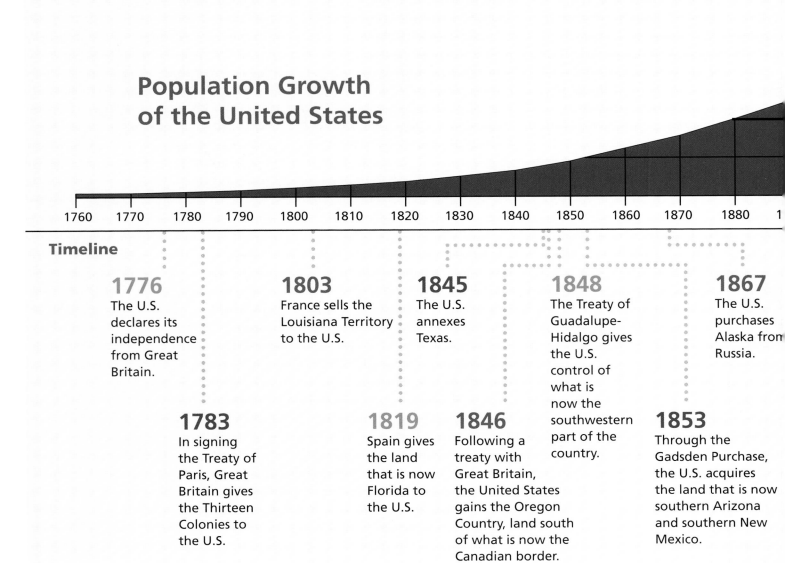

Population Growth of the United States

1760 1770 1780 1790 1800 1810 1820 1830 1840 1850 1860 1870 1880 1

Timeline

1776
The U.S. declares its independence from Great Britain.

1783
In signing the Treaty of Paris, Great Britain gives the Thirteen Colonies to the U.S.

1803
France sells the Louisiana Territory to the U.S.

1819
Spain gives the land that is now Florida to the U.S.

1845
The U.S. annexes Texas.

1846
Following a treaty with Great Britain, the United States gains the Oregon Country, land south of what is now the Canadian border.

1848
The Treaty of Guadalupe-Hidalgo gives the U.S. control of what is now the southwestern part of the country.

1853
Through the Gadsden Purchase, the U.S. acquires the land that is now southern Arizona and southern New Mexico.

1867
The U.S. purchases Alaska from Russia.

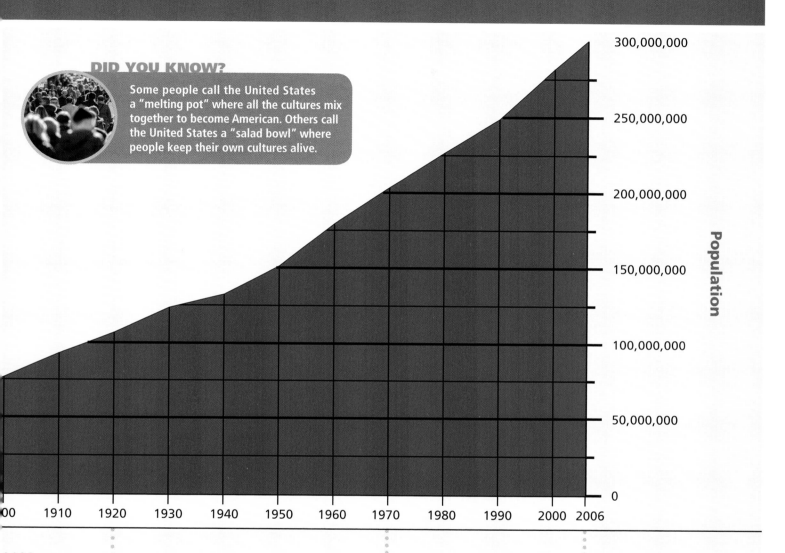

DID YOU KNOW?

Some people call the United States a "melting pot" where all the cultures mix together to become American. Others call the United States a "salad bowl" where people keep their own cultures alive.

Population

300,000,000

250,000,000

200,000,000

150,000,000

100,000,000

50,000,000

0

00 1910 1920 1930 1940 1950 1960 1970 1980 1990 2000 2006

1898
The U.S. annexes Hawaii.

1920
The population of the U.S. exceeds 100 million.

1970
The population of the U.S. exceeds 200 million.

2006
The population of the U.S. reaches 300 million.

THE FIRST PEOPLE

Native Americans

Native Americans were the first Americans. For thousands of years, they had made their homes in North America. They belonged to many different groups and spoke many different languages. They used the land in different ways, depending on the climate.

Some, like the Apache, spent their lives hunting and making camp in new places in the Southwestern desert. Others, like the Iroquois, who lived in the wooded Northeast, settled in one place for generations.

Native American Homelands

OASIS — Culture area

Blackfoot — Major tribe

Each culture area is shown in a different color.

© Rand McNally
N-FOR20000-V3- -1-1-1

Newcomers Arrive

By 1600, explorers from England, Spain, and France had journeyed to North America. Others followed and formed colonies. Over time, their settlements grew into towns and cities. With a warm, moist climate, the colonies in the southeast became farming regions. Many workers were needed. Africans were brought to the Americas as slaves to work in the fields. They did not come because they wanted to, but because they were forced to.

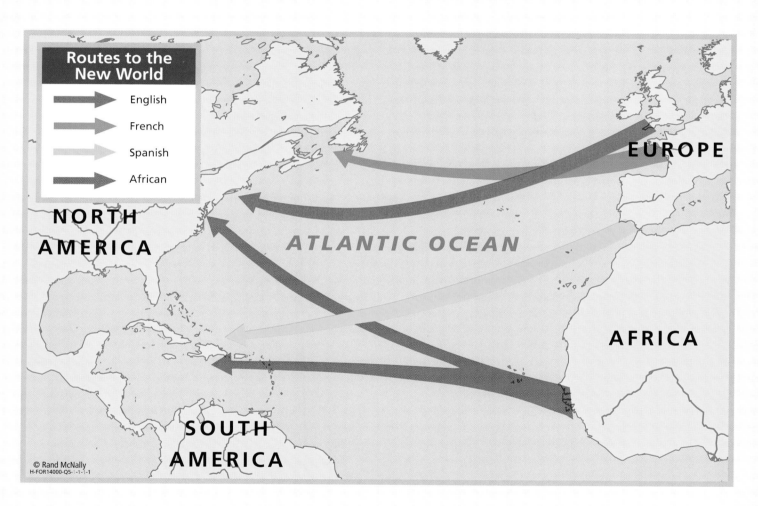

Routes to the New World

→ English
→ French
→ Spanish
→ African

NORTH AMERICA

ATLANTIC OCEAN

EUROPE

AFRICA

SOUTH AMERICA

© Rand McNally
H-FOR14000-Q5-1-1-1-1

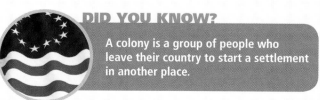

DID YOU KNOW?

A colony is a group of people who leave their country to start a settlement in another place.

THE COUNTRY GROWS

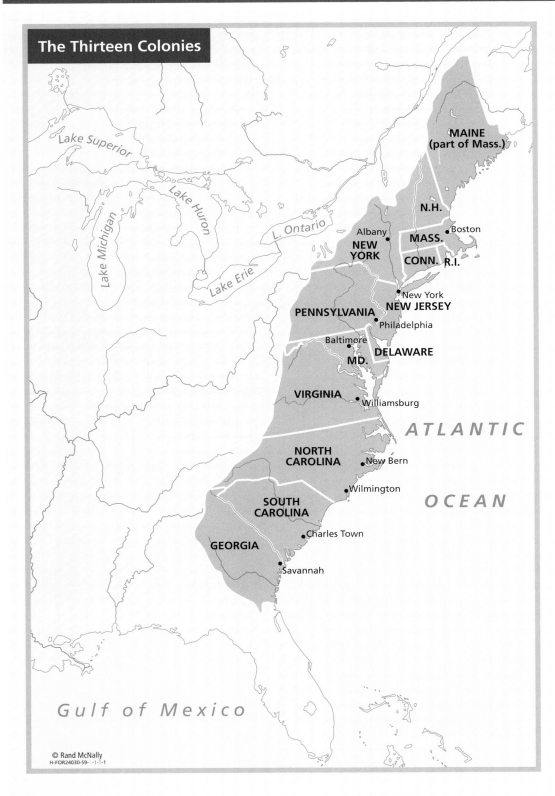

The Thirteen Colonies

MAINE
(part of Mass.)

N.H.

Albany • • Boston

MASS.

NEW
YORK

CONN. R.I.

• New York

NEW JERSEY

PENNSYLVANIA

• Philadelphia

Baltimore •

DELAWARE

MD.

VIRGINIA

• Williamsburg

ATLANTIC

NORTH
CAROLINA

• New Bern

• Wilmington

OCEAN

SOUTH
CAROLINA

GEORGIA

• Charles Town

• Savannah

Lake Superior

Lake Michigan

Lake Huron

L. Ontario

Lake Erie

Gulf of Mexico

© Rand McNally
H-FOR24030-59- -1-1-1

The Thirteen Colonies

The Thirteen Colonies were established in the period from 1607 to 1733. They were ruled by Great Britain, and the first people were British citizens. But the years passed. Three generations of people were born and raised on American soil. The people of these generations had never even seen Britain. They felt more American than they did British. With that strong feeling of patriotism for America, the colonists declared and fought for their own independence. They finally won it in 1783.

The United States Gains Land

In the 1700s and 1800s, the United States grew in land area as well as in population. Some of the territory, like the land between the original Thirteen Colonies and the Mississippi River, was added by treaty with Great Britain. Land in the Southwest was won after fighting a war with Mexico. Some land, like the vast Louisiana Territory, was purchased from France. When that happened, the United States gained full control of the Mississippi River. That meant that Americans could float their crops to the Gulf of Mexico and sell them around the world.

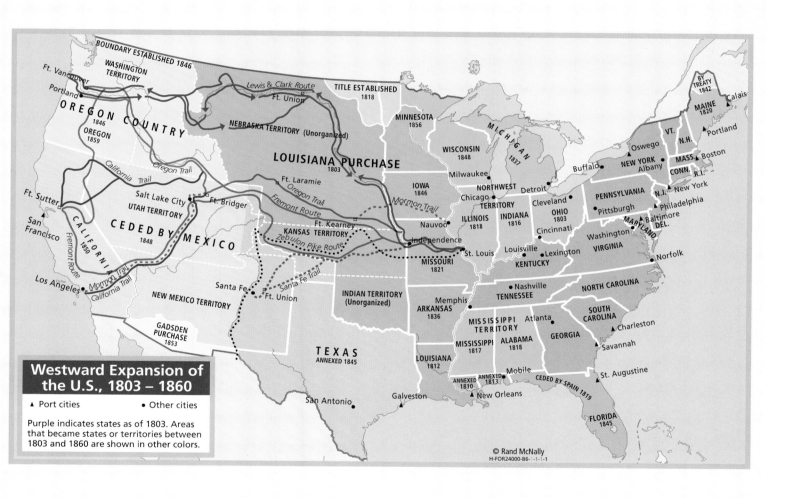

Westward Expansion of the U.S., 1803 – 1860

▲ Port cities • Other cities

Purple indicates states as of 1803. Areas that became states or territories between 1803 and 1860 are shown in other colors.

© Rand McNally
H-FOR24000-B6- -1-1-1

SETTLEMENT PATTERNS

Early Settlement and Roads

Map A shows settlement at the beginning of the 1800s. Most of the settled area lay between the Atlantic Ocean and the Appalachian Mountains. Roads connecting cities and towns were mud ruts. Traveling the length of what had been the Thirteen Colonies took nearly three months. Most east-west roads ended at the mountains.

Expanding Settlement and New Roads

Map B shows how settlement had spread west of the Appalachians by 1850. The U.S. government ordered roads built. The new roads connected farms to the towns along rivers, so businesses could grow. Canals were built to link the Ohio River and the Great Lakes with the Atlantic Ocean. That opened up a whole new direction of trade and made New York City boom.

Railroads and the Growth of the West

By 1890, railroads stretched across the country, as Map C shows. In the West, "cow towns" formed along the tracks. These were towns where cowboys would drive their herds to be loaded onto trains. People settled in the West in larger numbers. Businesses grew, and that drew even more people.

Map A

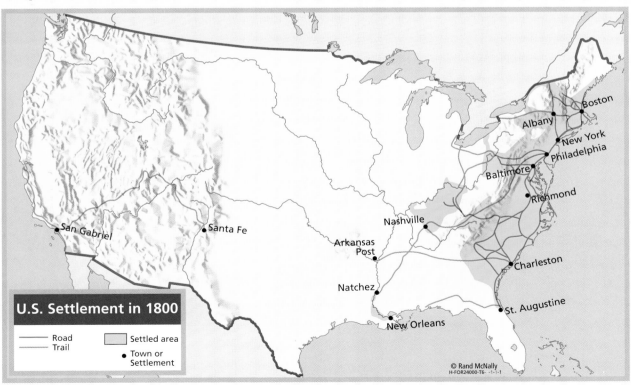

U.S. Settlement in 1800

— Road
— Trail
☐ Settled area
• Town or Settlement

© Rand McNally
H-FOR24000-T6- -1-1-1

Map B

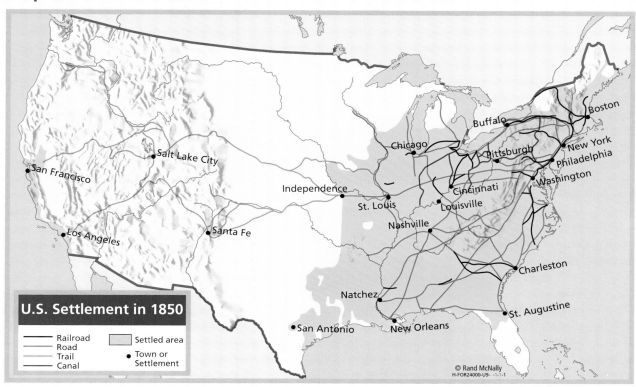

U.S. Settlement in 1850

Railroad
Road
Trail
Canal

Settled area

● Town or Settlement

© Rand McNally
H-FOR24000-U9- -1-1-1

Map C

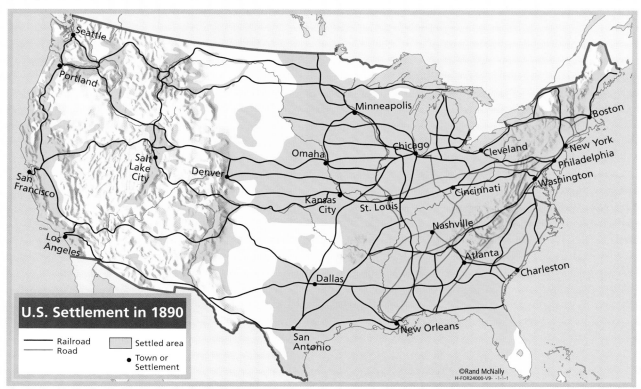

U.S. Settlement in 1890

Railroad
Road

Settled area

● Town or Settlement

©Rand McNally
H-FOR24000-V9- -1-1-1

WAVES OF IMMIGRATION

A Nation of Immigrants

The United States has always been a nation of immigrants. As Map A shows, a wave of immigration between 1820 and 1870 brought nearly 7 million people from northwestern and central Europe. In the period from 1880 to 1920, more than 20 million new immigrants came from these areas as well as from eastern and southern Europe, as shown on Map B.

Map C shows another large wave of immigrants that arrived in the United States between the 1960s and the 1990s. This time, most of the immigrants were from Asia, South America, Central America, and Mexico. Many of the people from Southeast Asia came to America to escape conflict. For all of these newcomers, America meant freedom and a chance to build better lives.

DID YOU KNOW?

Immigrants are people who move from one country to another to live.

Map A

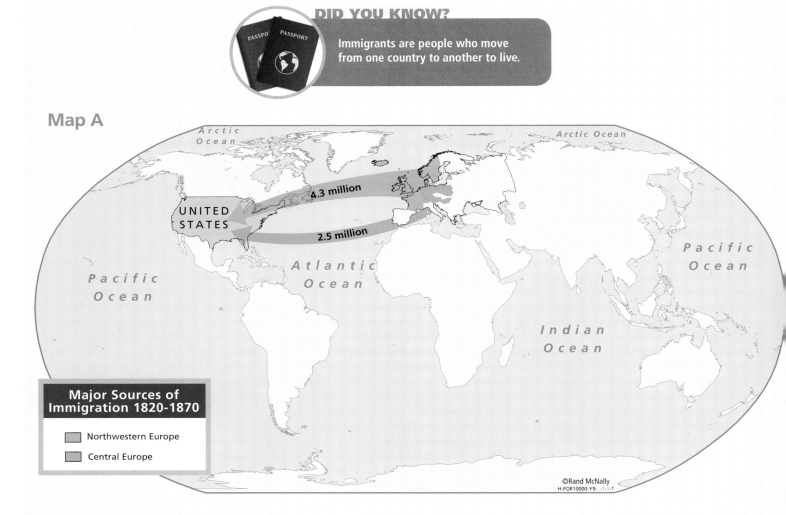

4.3 million

UNITED STATES

2.5 million

Arctic Ocean

Arctic Ocean

Pacific Ocean

Atlantic Ocean

Pacific Ocean

Indian Ocean

Major Sources of Immigration 1820-1870

- Northwestern Europe
- Central Europe

©Rand McNally
H-FOR10000-Y9- -1-1-1

Map B

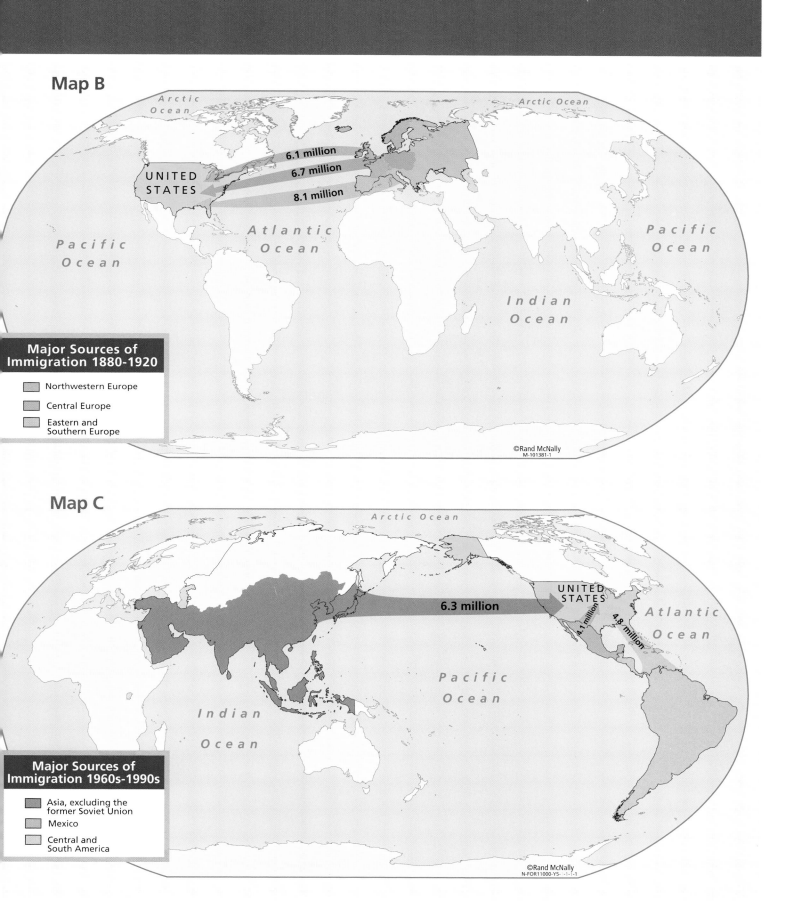

6.1 million

6.7 million

8.1 million

UNITED STATES

Arctic Ocean

Arctic Ocean

Pacific Ocean

Atlantic Ocean

Pacific Ocean

Indian Ocean

Major Sources of Immigration 1880-1920

Northwestern Europe

Central Europe

Eastern and Southern Europe

©Rand McNally
M-101381-1

Map C

Arctic Ocean

UNITED STATES

Atlantic Ocean

6.3 million

4.1 million

4.8 million

Pacific Ocean

Indian Ocean

Major Sources of Immigration 1960s-1990s

Asia, excluding the former Soviet Union

Mexico

Central and South America

©Rand McNally
N-FOR11000-Y5- -1-1-1

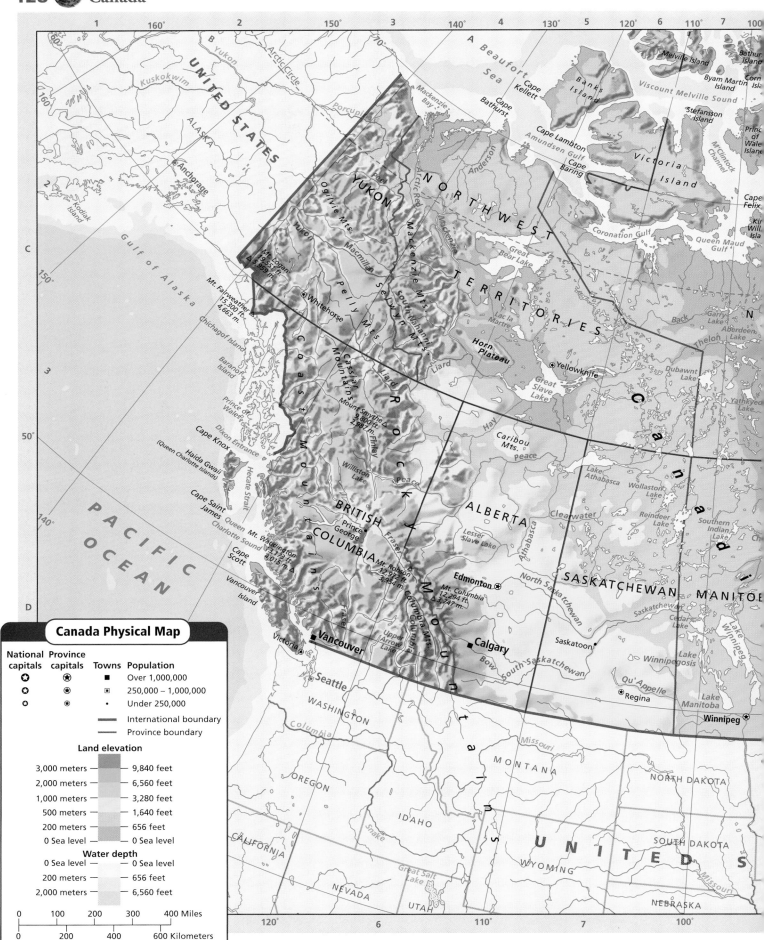

Canada Physical Map

National capitals	Province capitals	Towns	Population
✪	✪	■	Over 1,000,000
○	✪	◨	250,000 – 1,000,000
○	✪	•	Under 250,000

━━━ International boundary

─── Province boundary

Land elevation

3,000 meters —		— 9,840 feet
2,000 meters —		— 6,560 feet
1,000 meters —		— 3,280 feet
500 meters —		— 1,640 feet
200 meters —		— 656 feet
0 Sea level —		— 0 Sea level

Water depth

0 Sea level —		— 0 Sea level
200 meters —		— 656 feet
2,000 meters —		— 6,560 feet

0	100	200	300	400 Miles

0	200	400	600 Kilometers

9 80° 10 70° 11 60° 12 50° 13 40° 14 30° 15

Ellesmere Island
Jones Sound
Cape Parker
Devon Island
Lancaster Sound
Cape Liverpool
Bylot Island
Cape Adair
Baffin Bay

70°

Davis Strait

GREENLAND
(Denmark)

Arctic Circle

60°

30°

14

Cape Dyer

C

40°

Labrador Sea

ATLANTIC
OCEAN

13

Cumberland
Sound
Cape Mercy

ula
Gulf
of
Boothia
Melville
Peninsula
Prince Charles
Island
Cape
Wilson *Foxe*
Basin

Baffin Island

N U T

Cape
Dorchester
Foxe
Peninsula
Amadjuak
Lake
Iqaluit
Frobisher Bay
Resolution Island

Southampton
Island
Cape
Kendall
Seahorse
Point
Salisbury
Island
Nottingham
Island
Fair
Ness
Hudson Strait
Cap Hopes
Advance
Akpatok
Island
Killiniq Island

50°

Coats Island
Cape Southampton
Mansel
Island
Péninsule
d'Ungava
Ungava
Bay
Mt. d'Iberville
5,420 ft.
1,652 m.

N

E

S

Hudson
Bay

ape
hurchill
Cape Tatnam

Belcher
Islands

Feuilles

George

NEWFOUNDLAND AND LABRADOR

Cape Bauld

50°

Smallwood
Reservoir

Bonavista Bay

St. John's

50°

Cape
Henrietta
Maria
Pointe
Louis-XIV

Monts Otish

Newfoundland

Cape
Race

Akimiski
Island
James
Bay
Lac
Sakami
Rés.
Eastmain-
Opinaca
QUÉBEC
Réservoir
Manicouagan
Île d'Anticosti

ST. PIERRE AND
MIQUELON
(Fr.)

D

Severn

Lac
Mistassini

Monts Notre Dame

Cap
Gaspé
Gulf of
St. Lawrence
Cape
Ray

Albany
Missinaibi

S h

ONTARIO

i e

l d

Réservoir
Gouin

Les Laurentides

St. Lawrence

Îles de la
Madeleine

12

Lac
Seul
Lake
Nipigon
of
Woods

Réservoir
Cabonga

Québec

NEW
BRUNSWICK
Fredericton
PRINCE EDWARD
ISLAND
Charlottetown
Cape Breton
Island

NOVA SCOTIA

40°

Lake Superior

Ottawa

Montréal

MAINE

Halifax

SOTA

Ottawa

VT.

Bay of Fundy

Cape Sable

Manitoulin
Island
Georgian
Bay

N.H.

Gulf
of
Maine

WISCONSIN

Lake Michigan

Toronto
Lake Ontario

NEW YORK

MASS.

ATLANTIC

E

Minneapolis

T E S

Lake Huron

MICHIGAN

Niagara
Falls

Lake Erie

CONN. R.I.

OCEAN

Detroit

PENNSYLVANIA

New York

N.J.

© Rand McNally
Made in U.S.A.
M-100137-3

90° 9 80° 10 70° 11 60°

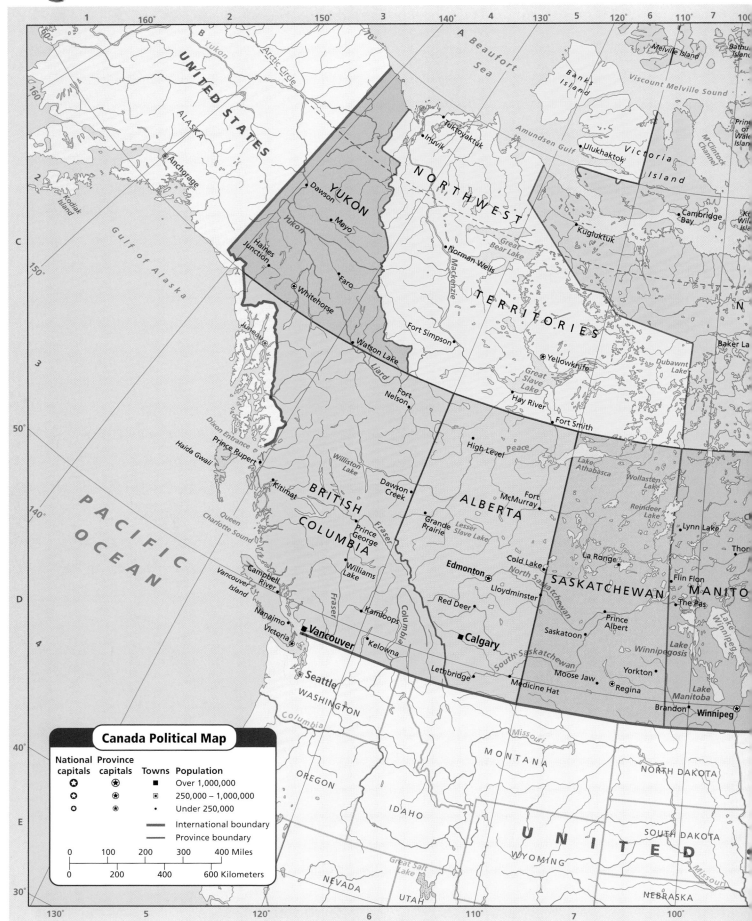

Canada Political Map

National capitals	Province capitals	Towns	Population
✪	✪	■	Over 1,000,000
✪	✪	⊡	250,000 – 1,000,000
✪	✪	•	Under 250,000

―― International boundary
―― Province boundary

0   100   200   300   400 Miles
0   200   400   600 Kilometers

Population

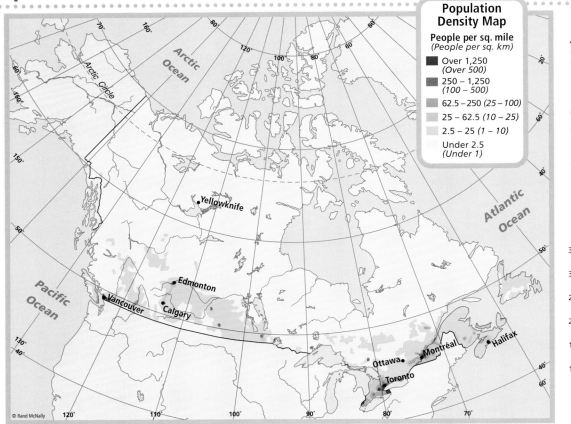

Population Density Map

People per sq. mile
(People per sq. km)

- ■ Over 1,250 *(Over 500)*
- ▨ 250 – 1,250 *(100 – 500)*
- ▨ 62.5 – 250 *(25 – 100)*
- ▨ 25 – 62.5 *(10 – 25)*
- ▨ 2.5 – 25 *(1 – 10)*
- □ Under 2.5 *(Under 1)*

© Rand McNally

Approximately 90% of Canada's population lives within 100 miles of the United States border.

Canada's Population Growth since 1851

Canada's population grew rapidly in the twentieth century when many immigrants arrived from other countries.

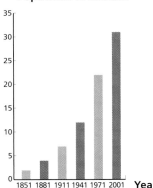

Population in millions

Year: 1851, 1881, 1911, 1941, 1971, 2001

Environments

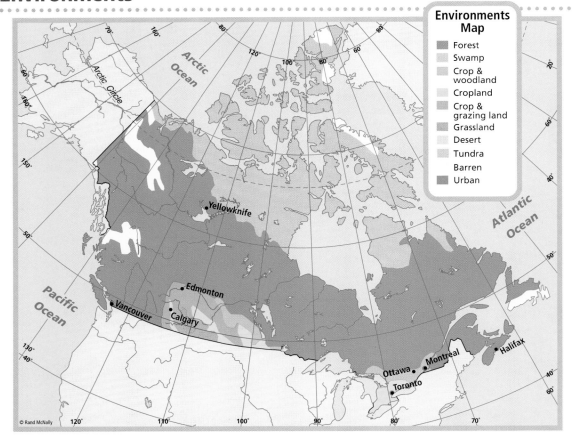

Environments Map

- ▨ Forest
- ▨ Swamp
- ▨ Crop & woodland
- ▨ Cropland
- ▨ Crop & grazing land
- ▨ Grassland
- ▨ Desert
- ▨ Tundra
- □ Barren
- ■ Urban

© Rand McNally

The Canadian Rocky Mountains extend through Alberta, British Columbia, and the Yukon territory.

The rocky plateau known as the Canadian Shield ends as headlands at the water's edge. Lighthouses help to guide ships away from the danger.

Transportation

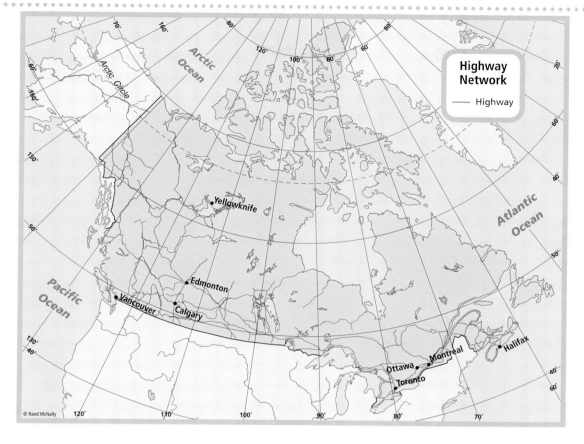

Scenic roads wind along the coasts of Canada's Maritime Provinces.

Canada's highways help to connect widely separated clusters of people across the country's vast expanse.

Economic Activities

Most of Canada's grain is grown in the "prairie provinces" of Alberta, Saskatchewan, and Manitoba.

Atlantic coast fishing is important to Canada's economy.

Toronto is Canada's financial center and the headquarters for many of the country's largest companies.

World Export of Oats

Oats are grains that are eaten by people and used for animal feed. On a global scale, Canada is a major oat producer. If Canadian weather interrupts oat growth, this can affect supply of oats across the world.

Canada's Economy

Services—such as banking, transportation, and government—account for more than two-thirds of Canada's economic output.

Agriculture 2%
Services 69%
Industry 29%

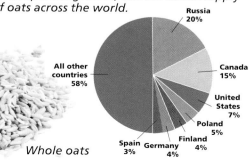

Whole oats

Russia 20%
All other countries 58%
Canada 15%
United States 7%
Poland 5%
Finland 4%
Germany 4%
Spain 3%

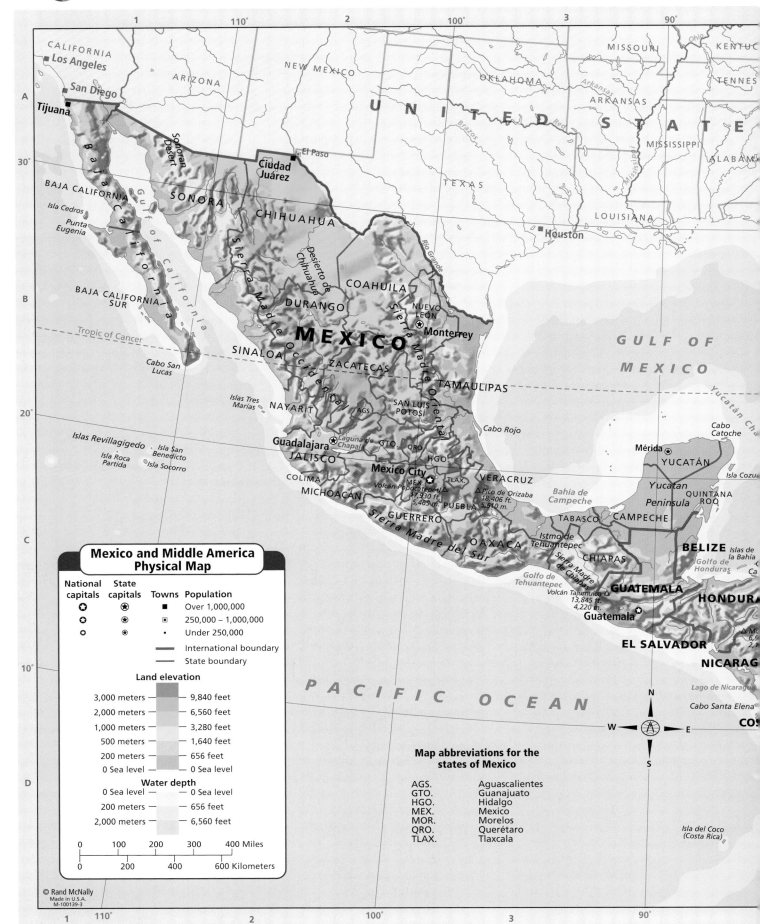

CALIFORNIA
■ Los Angeles
■ San Diego
Tijuana

ARIZONA
NEW MEXICO

OKLAHOMA

MISSOURI

KENTUC

ARKANSAS

TENNES

BAJA CALIFORNIA

Isla Cedros
Punta
Eugenia

Gulf of California

Sonoran
Desert

SONORA

El Paso
Ciudad
Juárez

CHIHUAHUA

Desierto de
Chihuahua

UNITED STATES

TEXAS

Rio Grande

MISSISSIPPI

ALABAM

LOUISIANA

Houston

BAJA CALIFORNIA
SUR

Tropic of Cancer

Cabo San
Lucas

SINALOA

Sierra Madre Occidental

COAHUILA

DURANGO

NUEVO
LEÓN

MEXICO

Monterrey

ZACATECAS

Sierra Madre Oriental

TAMAULIPAS

GULF OF

MEXICO

Yucatán Cha

Islas Tres
Marias

NAYARIT

AGS.

SAN LUIS
POTOSÍ

Cabo Rojo

Cabo
Catoche

Islas Revillagigedo
Isla Roca
Partida

Isla San
Benedicto
Isla Socorro

Guadalajara
JALISCO

Laguna de
Chapala

GTO.

QRO.

HGO.

Mérida

YUCATÁN

Isla Cozu

COLIMA

Mexico City
MEX.
Volcán Popocatépetl △
17,930 ft.
5,465 m.

TLAX.

△ Pico de Orizaba
18,406 ft.
5,610 m.

VERACRUZ

Yucatan
Peninsula

QUINTANA
ROO

PUEBLA

MICHOACÁN

GUERRERO

Sierra Madre del Sur

OAXACA

Bahía de
Campeche

TABASCO

CAMPECHE

Istmo de
Tehuantepec

Golfo de
Tehuantepec

CHIAPAS

Sierra Madre
de Chiapas

Volcán Tajumulco △
13,845 ft.
4,220 m.

GUATEMALA

BELIZE

Islas de
la Bahía

Golfo de
Honduras

Ca

HONDURA

PACIFIC OCEAN

Guatemala

EL SALVADOR

NICARAG

△ Mo
6,5
2,1

CO

Lago de Nicaragua

Cabo Santa Elena

N
W ⊕ E
S

Isla del Coco
(Costa Rica)

Mexico and Middle America Physical Map

	National capitals	State capitals	Towns	Population
	✪	✪	■	Over 1,000,000
	✪	✪	▣	250,000 – 1,000,000
	✪	✪	•	Under 250,000

International boundary
State boundary

Land elevation

3,000 meters —	— 9,840 feet
2,000 meters —	— 6,560 feet
1,000 meters —	— 3,280 feet
500 meters —	— 1,640 feet
200 meters —	— 656 feet
0 Sea level —	— 0 Sea level

Water depth

0 Sea level —	— 0 Sea level
200 meters —	— 656 feet
2,000 meters —	— 6,560 feet

0   100   200   300   400 Miles
0   200   400   600 Kilometers

Map abbreviations for the states of Mexico

AGS.	Aguascalientes
GTO.	Guanajuato
HGO.	Hidalgo
MEX.	Mexico
MOR.	Morelos
QRO.	Querétaro
TLAX.	Tlaxcala

© Rand McNally
Made in U.S.A.
M-100139-3

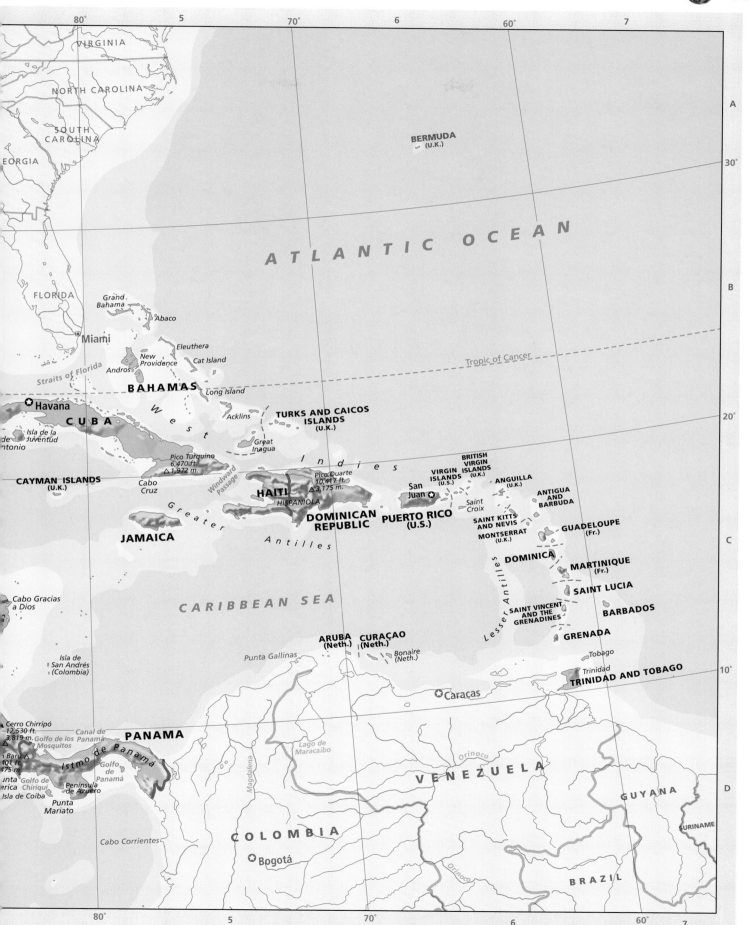

VIRGINIA

NORTH CAROLINA

SOUTH
CAROLINA

EORGIA

A

30°

ATLANTIC OCEAN

BERMUDA
(U.K.)

FLORIDA

B

Grand
Bahama
Abaco

Miami

Eleuthera

New
Providence   Cat Island

Andros

Straits of Florida

Tropic of Cancer

BAHAMAS   Long Island

Havana

CUBA

Isla de la
Juventud
ntonio

Acklins

Great
Inagua

West

TURKS AND CAICOS
ISLANDS
(U.K.)

20°

I n d i e s

Pico Turquino
6,470 ft.
△1,972 m.

CAYMAN ISLANDS
(U.K.)

Cabo
Cruz

Windward Passage

Pico Duarte
10,417 ft.
△3,175 m.

HAITI

HISPANIOLA

San
Juan

VIRGIN
ISLANDS
(U.S.)

BRITISH
VIRGIN
ISLANDS
(U.K.)

ANGUILLA
(U.K.)

ANTIGUA
AND
BARBUDA

G r e a t e r

DOMINICAN
REPUBLIC

PUERTO RICO
(U.S.)

Saint
Croix

SAINT KITTS
AND NEVIS

MONTSERRAT
(U.K.)

GUADELOUPE
(Fr.)

C

JAMAICA

A n t i l l e s

DOMINICA

MARTINIQUE
(Fr.)

Cabo Gracias
a Dios

CARIBBEAN SEA

SAINT LUCIA

L e s s e r   A n t i l l e s

SAINT VINCENT
AND THE
GRENADINES

BARBADOS

Isla de
San Andrés
(Colombia)

GRENADA

ARUBA
(Neth.)

CURAÇAO
(Neth.)

Bonaire
(Neth.)

Tobago

Punta Gallinas

Trinidad

TRINIDAD AND TOBAGO

10°

Cerro Chirripó
12,530 ft.
3,819 m. Golfo de los
Mosquitos

PANAMA

Canal de
Panamá

Caracas

Baru △
401 ft.
75 m.

Istmo de Panamá

Golfo
de
Panamá

Lago de
Maracaibo

Orinoco

unta
rica Golfo de
Chiriqui

Isla de Coiba

Peninsula
de Azuero

Punta
Mariato

VENEZUELA

GUYANA

D

Magdalena

COLOMBIA

SURINAME

Cabo Corrientes

Bogotá

Orinoco

BRAZIL

80°   5   70°   6   60°   7

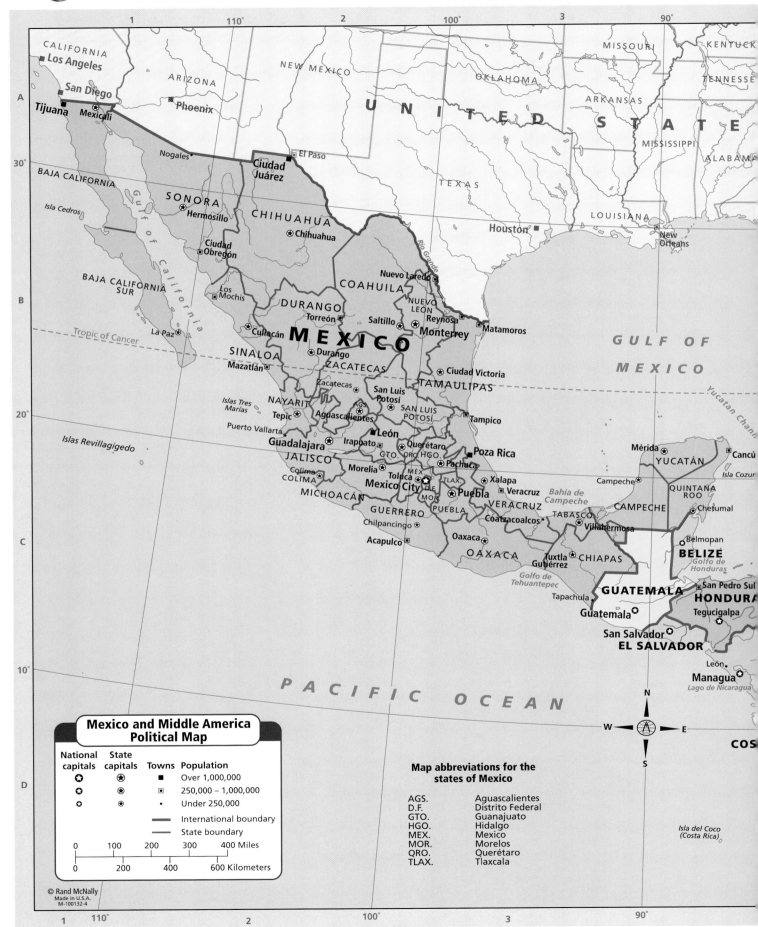

Mexico and Middle America Political Map

National capitals
- ⊛ (Over 1,000,000)
- ⊚
- ⊙

State capitals
- ⊛
- ⊛
- ⊛

Towns | Population
- ■ Over 1,000,000
- ⊡ 250,000 – 1,000,000
- • Under 250,000

— International boundary
— State boundary

0 100 200 300 400 Miles
0 200 400 600 Kilometers

© Rand McNally
Made in U.S.A.
M-100132-4

Map abbreviations for the states of Mexico

AGS.	Aguascalientes
D.F.	Distrito Federal
GTO.	Guanajuato
HGO.	Hidalgo
MEX.	Mexico
MOR.	Morelos
QRO.	Querétaro
TLAX.	Tlaxcala

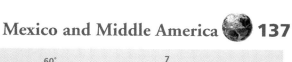

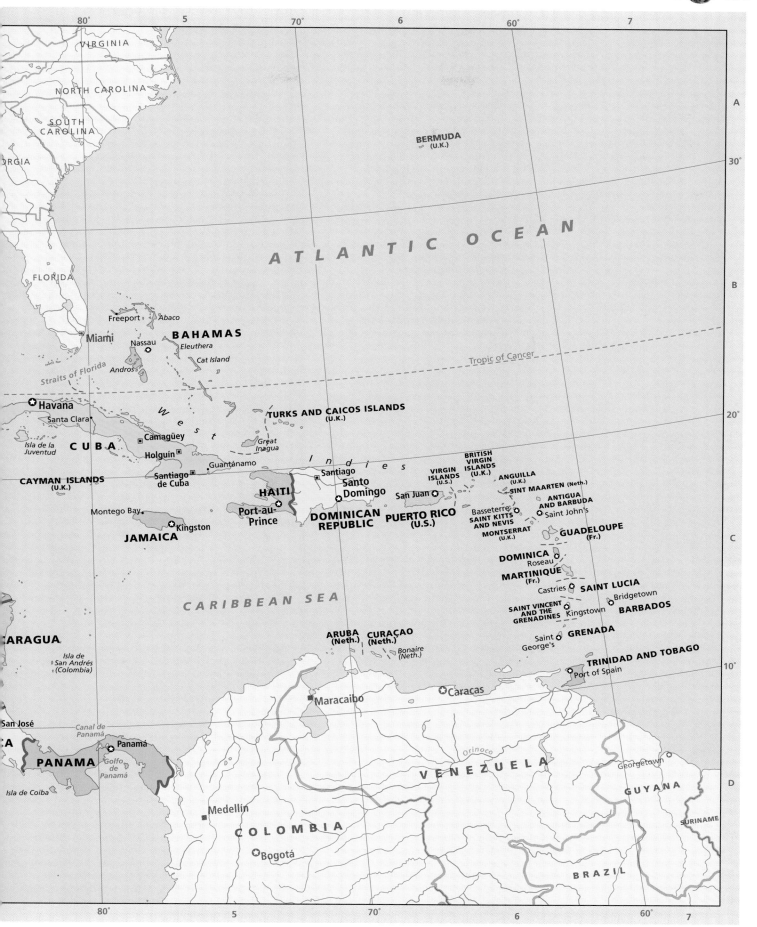

VIRGINIA

NORTH CAROLINA

SOUTH CAROLINA

ORGIA

FLORIDA

A T L A N T I C   O C E A N

BERMUDA
(U.K.)

A

30°

B

Straits of Florida

Freeport · Ábaco

Miami

Nassau

BAHAMAS

Eleuthera

Cat Island

Andros

Tropic of Cancer

Havana

Santa Clara

Isla de la Juventud

CUBA

Camagüey

Holguín

TURKS AND CAICOS ISLANDS
(U.K.)

Great Inagua

20°

West

Indies

CAYMAN ISLANDS
(U.K.)

Santiago de Cuba

Guantánamo

Santiago

Santo Domingo

VIRGIN ISLANDS
(U.S.)

BRITISH VIRGIN ISLANDS
(U.K.)

ANGUILLA
(U.K.)

SINT MAARTEN (Neth.)

ANTIGUA AND BARBUDA

Montego Bay

Kingston

JAMAICA

HAITI

Port-au-Prince

DOMINICAN REPUBLIC

San Juan

PUERTO RICO
(U.S.)

Basseterre

SAINT KITTS AND NEVIS

MONTSERRAT
(U.K.)

Saint John's

GUADELOUPE
(Fr.)

C

DOMINICA

Roseau

MARTINIQUE
(Fr.)

C A R I B B E A N   S E A

Castries

SAINT LUCIA

Bridgetown

SAINT VINCENT AND THE GRENADINES

Kingstown

BARBADOS

ARAGUA

Isla de San Andrés
(Colombia)

ARUBA
(Neth.)

CURAÇAO
(Neth.)

Bonaire
(Neth.)

Saint George's

GRENADA

TRINIDAD AND TOBAGO

10°

Port of Spain

San José

Canal de Panamá

Panamá

Maracaibo

Caracas

Orinoco

PANAMA

Golfo de Panamá

VENEZUELA

Georgetown

GUYANA

D

Isla de Coiba

Medellín

SURINAME

COLOMBIA

Bogotá

B R A Z I L

Population

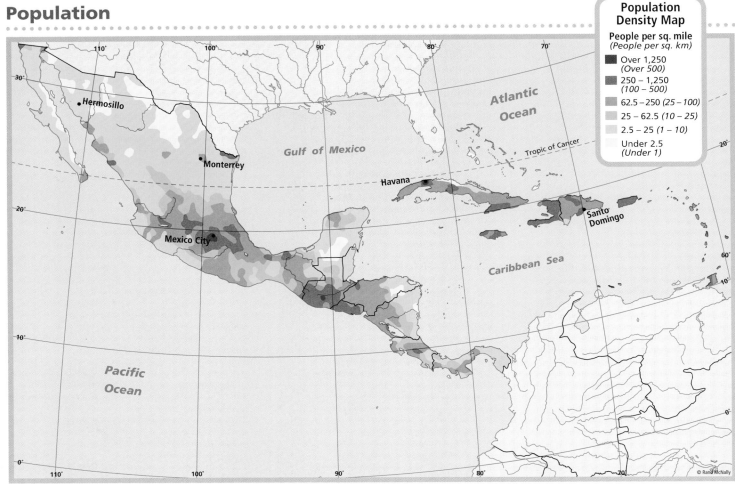

Population Density Map

People per sq. mile
(People per sq. km)

- Over 1,250 (Over 500)
- 250 – 1,250 (100 – 500)
- 62.5 – 250 (25 – 100)
- 25 – 62.5 (10 – 25)
- 2.5 – 25 (1 – 10)
- Under 2.5 (Under 1)

© Rand McNally

Comparing Urban and Rural Population

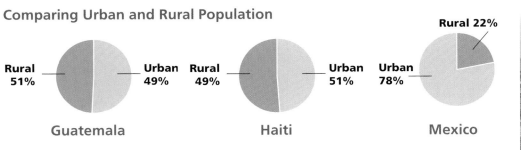

Guatemala
Rural 51%
Urban 49%

Haiti
Rural 49%
Urban 51%

Mexico
Urban 78%
Rural 22%

Mexico City is home to nearly one-fifth of Mexico's people.

A Timeline of Mexico City, Mexico

1500 B.C.E.
Native Americans settle in farm villages along the shores of Lake Texcoco.

1325 C.E.
Aztecs build the city of Tenochtitlán on an island in Lake Texcoco.

1521
Spaniards capture and destroy Tenochtitlán. They drain the lake, fill it with land, and build a new city they call Mexico City.

1960
Mexico City's population reaches 7 million.

1985
An earthquake does extensive damage, partly because Mexico City is built on soft, spongy soil.

2000
Mexico City's population reaches 18 million.

2010
Mexico City becomes the eighth richest metropolitan area in the world. The rating is based on the value of goods and services provided by the city in one year.

Economies

Per capita income is one way of measuring the relative wealth of countries. This graph compares the per capita income of six countries in Middle America. It shows how greatly wealth varies across the region, from relatively rich countries like Aruba to poor countries like Haiti.

Annual per capita income (in U.S. dollars)

Puerto Rico	$26,000
Aruba	$23,000
Mexico	$9,000
Cuba	$5,700
Jamaica	$4,900
Haiti	$600

Cactuses grow in the hot, dry climate of Baja California, Mexico.

Tropical rain forest covers much of Central America.

Palm trees flourish in the warm climate of the Caribbean Sea.

Transportation

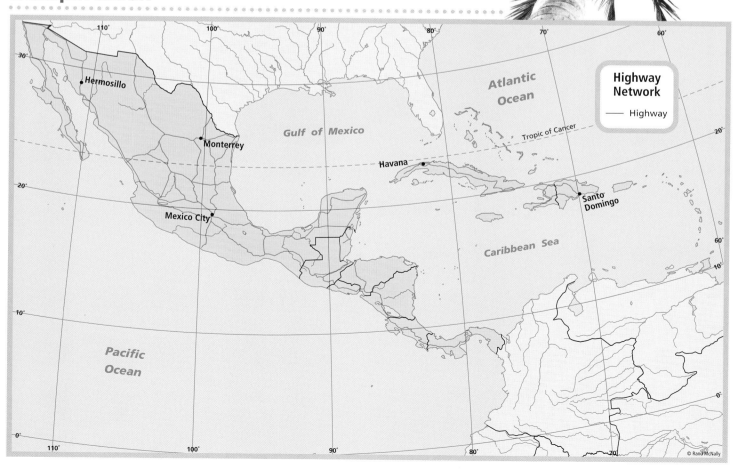

SOUTH AMERICA

South America is a continent of extremes. The Andes Mountains stretch 4,500 miles (7,200 kilometers) from north to south. They form the longest mountain chain in the world. Lake Titicaca, on the Peru-Bolivia border, is the highest lake in the world used for transportation. Arica, Chile, experienced the longest dry period ever recorded: No rain fell there for more than 14 years!

The Amazon River has the greatest volume of water of any river in the world. The Amazon discharges so much water into the Atlantic that it changes the color of the ocean's water for more than 100 miles (160 kilometers) off the shore.

Most South Americans live in cities that are major ports or are near major ports. São Paulo and Rio de Janeiro, Brazil, and Buenos Aires, Argentina, are among the world's largest cities. Altogether, almost 367 million people live in South America.

Iguassu Falls on the Brazil-Argentina border is among the most spectacular sights in South America.

Colorful buildings in Buenos Aires, Argentina

Giant tortoises on Ecuador's Galapagos Islands

A Historical Look At South America

Circa C.E. 600
Tiahuanaco civilization prospers along the shore of Lake Titicaca.

1498
Christopher Columbus reaches the Orinoco River.

1438-1535
The Inca Empire controls the Andes and the Pacific Coast.

1530s
The Portuguese establish sugar plantations in Brazil.

Rain Forests

A rain forest is a dense forest that receives at least 100 inches (250 centimeters) of rain a year. The Amazon rain forest is rich in plant and animal life, and new species are discovered almost daily. Scientists have learned that many of the plants can be used to produce life-saving drugs.

However, the rain forest is becoming smaller. Mining, logging, and industrial developments such as hydroelectric factories, are attracting people to the rain forest. From 2000 to 2010, the Amazon population has grown 23%. These people are looking for a place to work, and they also need a place to live. As a result, land is cleared of trees and other plants. Clearing and settling the land lead to deforestation. Nearly 20% of rain forest has been lost to deforestation.

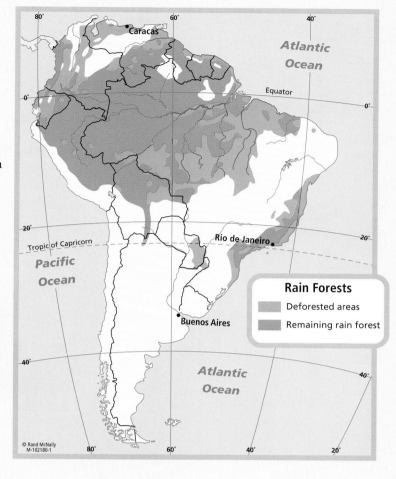

Rain Forests
- Deforested areas
- Remaining rain forest

DID YOU KNOW?

The Amazon River is the world's largest river by volume. Some scientists believe that this river is the longest river in the world, too. But other scientists believe that the Nile River is the longest.

Sights of the Andes Mountains

More than 40 peaks in the Andes rise 20,000 feet (6,000 meters) or higher. Mining is important in the Andes, and tourism is a growing industry.

The ancient Incan city of Machu Picchu, Peru

Lake Titicaca on the Peru-Bolivia border

A jagged peak along the Argentina-Chile border

The South American llama, a relative of the camel

1580
Spaniards found the city of Buenos Aires in Argentina.

1726
The first coffee plantation is established in Brazil.

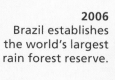

2004
South America's population reaches 365 million.

2006
Brazil establishes the world's largest rain forest reserve.

South America Physical Map

National capitals
- ☆ Over 1,000,000
- ✪ 250,000 – 1,000,000
- ✪ Under 250,000

Towns **Population**
- ■ Over 1,000,000
- ▣ 250,000 – 1,000,000
- • Under 250,000

—— International boundary

Land elevation

3,000 meters —	9,840 feet
2,000 meters —	6,560 feet
1,000 meters —	3,280 feet
500 meters —	1,640 feet
200 meters —	656 feet
0 Sea level —	0 Sea level

Water depth

0 Sea level —	0 Sea level
200 meters —	656 feet
2,000 meters —	6,560 feet

0   200   400   600   800   1000 Miles
0   300   600   900   1200 1500 Kilometers

© Rand McNally
Made in U.S.A.
M-100306-2

South America Political Map

National capitals
- ✪ Over 1,000,000
- ✪ 250,000 – 1,000,000
- ✪ Under 250,000

Towns
- ■
- ▫
- •

Population
- Over 1,000,000
- 250,000 – 1,000,000
- Under 250,000

━━━ International boundary

200 400 600 800 1000 Miles

300 600 900 1200 1500 Kilometers

© Rand McNally
Made in U.S.A.
M-100129-3

Natural Hazards

Natural Hazards Map

- • Earthquakes*
- Δ Volcanoes*
- \ Tsunamis
- ◤ Tropical storm tracks *(over 5 per year)*

*Since 1900

© Rand McNally
M-102181-1

Climate

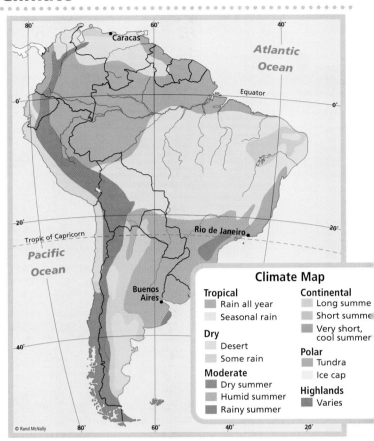

Climate Map

Tropical
- Rain all year
- Seasonal rain

Dry
- Desert
- Some rain

Moderate
- Dry summer
- Humid summer
- Rainy summer

Continental
- Long summe
- Short summe
- Very short, cool summer

Polar
- Tundra
- Ice cap

Highlands
- Varies

© Rand McNally

Environments

Environments Map

- Forest
- Swamp
- Crop & woodland
- Cropland
- Crop & grazing land
- Grassland
- Desert
- Tundra
- Barren
- Urban

© Rand McNally

The Amazon rain forest supports almost half of Earth's animal and plant species.

WHAT IF?

? What could happen if all of the rain forests in South America are destroyed?

Population

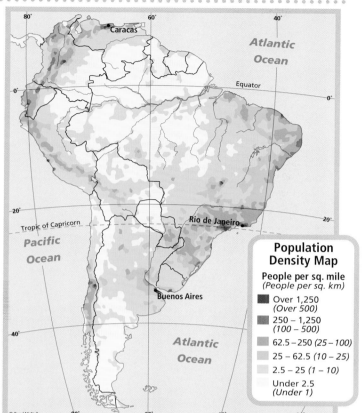

Population Density Map

People per sq. mile
(People per sq. km)

- Over 1,250 (Over 500)
- 250 – 1,250 (100 – 500)
- 62.5 – 250 (25 – 100)
- 25 – 62.5 (10 – 25)
- 2.5 – 25 (1 – 10)
- Under 2.5 (Under 1)

© Rand McNally

Most Brazilians live in large cities such as Rio de Janeiro.

Roughly three out of five people living in Brazil are under the age of 29.

DID YOU KNOW?

São Paulo, Brazil, is South America's most populous city.

Cusco, Peru, was once capital of the Incan empire.

The forest in the Amazon River Basin is so thick in parts that sunlight cannot reach the ground.

Economic Activities

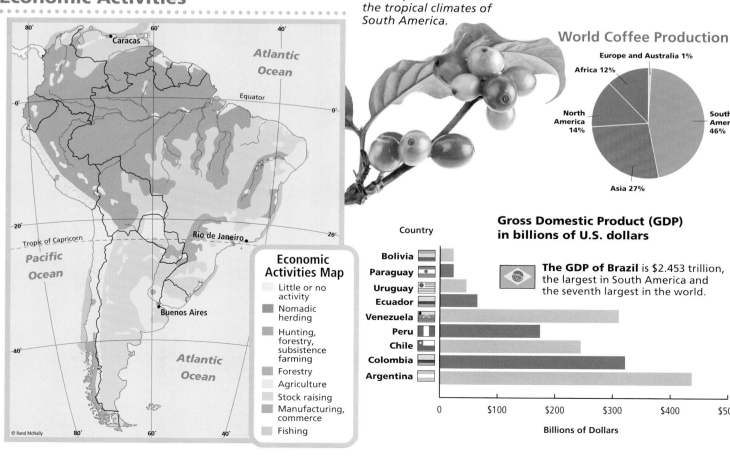

Economic Activities Map

- Little or no activity
- Nomadic herding
- Hunting, forestry, subsistence farming
- Forestry
- Agriculture
- Stock raising
- Manufacturing, commerce
- Fishing

© Rand McNally

Coffee plants thrive in the tropical climates of South America.

World Coffee Production

- Europe and Australia 1%
- Africa 12%
- North America 14%
- South America 46%
- Asia 27%

Gross Domestic Product (GDP) in billions of U.S. dollars

Country

- Bolivia
- Paraguay
- Uruguay
- Ecuador
- Venezuela
- Peru
- Chile
- Colombia
- Argentina

0   $100 $200 $300 $400 $500

Billions of Dollars

The GDP of Brazil is $2.453 trillion, the largest in South America and the seventh largest in the world.

EUROPE

Prague, Czech Republic

Do you know what a *lago* is? A *lac*? A *loch*? These are just some of the words for "lake" in Europe. Europe is the world's second-smallest continent, but it has many countries and many languages.

Only the giant continents of Asia and Africa have more people than Europe. Because more than 729,000,000 live in the small continent of Europe, it is one of the most densely populated regions in the world.

The two smallest countries in the world are in Europe. Vatican City and Monaco are each less than one square mile (2.6 square kilometers) in size.

In recent decades, there have been great changes in Europe. East and West Germany were reunited in 1990 after being separated for 45 years. In 1991, the Soviet Union split up into 15 different countries. The following year, Czechoslovakia peacefully divided into two new countries: the Czech Republic and Slovakia.

Slovenia, Croatia, Macedonia, and Bosnia and Herzegovina broke away from Yugoslavia in 1991-92 to become independent countries. In 2003, Yugoslavia changed its name to Serbia and Montenegro. Then, in 2006, Montenegro split from Serbia to become an independent country. In 2008, a region known as Kosovo declared its independence from Serbia.

Church in the Alps of Austria

Hilltop village in Spain

Donkey and farmhouse, Aran Islands, Ireland

DID YOU KNOW?

Five European countries—Iceland, Norway, Sweden, Finland, and Russia—lie partly within the Arctic Circle.

A Historical Look At Europe

Circa 2200 B.C.E.
Erecting of Stonehenge pillars begins in Great Britain.

776 B.C.E.
The first recorded Olympic Games are held in Greece.

753 B.C.E.
Rome is founded.

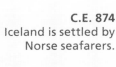

C.E. 874
Iceland is settled by Norse seafarers.

The European Union

Twenty-eight nations have joined the European Union
to form a single, powerful market for business and trade.

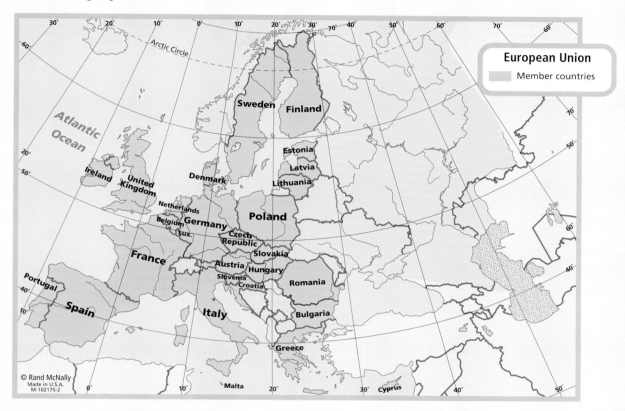

European Union
Member countries

Arctic Circle
Atlantic Ocean
Sweden Finland
Estonia
Latvia
Lithuania
Ireland United Kingdom Denmark
Netherlands
Belgium Germany
Lux. Czech Republic
France Slovakia
Austria Hungary
Slovenia Croatia
Portugal Romania
Spain Italy
Bulgaria
Greece
Malta Cyprus

© Rand McNally
Made in U.S.A.
M-102175-2

The headquarters of the European Union is in Brussels, Belgium.

Some countries of the European Union use the euro as their currency.

Because Europe has so many languages, there are 24 official languages of the European Union.

The European Union has its own passports. Citizens of all countries can move freely around the entire area.

1163–1200
The great gothic Notre Dame Cathedral is built in Paris.

1300s–1500s
The period known as the Renaissance marks a rebirth in art and science.

Circa 1750
The Industrial Revolution begins in England.

2007
Romania and Bulgaria join the European Union.

Europe Physical Map

National capitals
- ⊕ Over 1,000,000
- ⊕ 250,000 – 1,000,000
- ⊕ Under 250,000

Towns   Population
- ■ Over 1,000,000
- ▣ 250,000 – 1,000,000
- • Under 250,000

— International boundary

Land elevation

3,000 meters	9,840 feet
2,000 meters	6,560 feet
1,000 meters	3,280 feet
500 meters	1,640 feet
200 meters	656 feet
0 Sea level	0 Sea level

Water depth

0 Sea level	0 Sea level
200 meters	656 feet
2,000 meters	6,560 feet

0   100   200   300   400 Miles
0   200   400   600 Kilometers

ICELAND
Horn
Surtsey
Fontur

ATLANTIC OCEAN

FAROE ISLANDS (Den.)

NORWEGIAN SEA
Lofoten Islands
Vestfjorden
Kebnekaise 6,926 ft. 2,111 m.

SWEDEN
NORWAY
Galdhøpiggen 8,100 ft. 2,469 m.
Glåma
Dalälven
Vänern
Vättern
Gulf of

Arctic Circle

Shetland Islands
Orkney Islands
Hebrides
Moray Firth
Kinnaird Head
Ben Nevis 4,406 ft. 1,343 m.
Grampian Mts.

British Isles

UNITED KINGDOM
Firth of Forth
Cheviot Hills

IRELAND
Irish Sea
Mizen Head
St. George's Channel
Great Britain
Land's End

NORTH SEA

DENMARK
Skagerrak
Kattegat
Sjælland
Gotland
Öland
BALTIC
Bornholm (Den.)
RUS

NETHERLANDS
English Channel
Strait of Dover
London
Thames

BELGIUM
LUX.

Europe
Elbe
North
Berlin ⊕
Oder
GERMANY
POLAND
Warsaw ⊕
Rhine
Ore Mts.
Sudeten
CZECH REPUBLIC
Bohemian Forest
Danube

Paris ⊕
Paris Basin
Loire
Seine
Saône
Black Forest
Lake Constance
Lake Geneva
SWITZERLAND
LIECH.
AUSTRIA
Grossglockner 12,457 ft. 3,797 m.
HUNGARY
Great Alf

FRANCE

Cabo Finisterre
Cantabrian Mts.
Aquitaine Basin
Dordogne
Pyrenees
ANDORRA
Massif Central
Mont Blanc 15,771 ft. 4,807 m.
ALPS
Po
SLOVENIA
CROATIA
Dinaric Alps
Drava
Balk

Bay of Biscay

Douro
Duero
Iberian Mts.
Ebro
Golfe du Lion
MONACO
Ligurian Sea
SAN MARINO
Apennines
BOSNIA AND HERZEGOVINA
SE
MONTENEGRO
KOS
M

PORTUGAL
Sistema Central
Tagus
Iberian Peninsula
SPAIN
Sierra Morena
Mulhacén 11,424 ft. 3,482 m.
Balearic Islands
Eivissa
Mallorca
Menorca
Cap de la Nao
Corsica (Fr.)
Sardinia (It.)
Vesuvius 4,203 ft. 1,281 m.
ITALY
Rome ⊕
ADRIATIC SEA
ALBANIA
Pind

Cabo de São Vicente
Strait of Gibraltar
GIBRALTAR (U.K.)

MEDITERRANEAN
TYRRHENIAN SEA
Monte Etna 10,902 ft. 3,323 m.
Sicily
Capo Passero
IONIAN SEA

AFRICA
MOROCCO
ALGERIA
TUNISIA
MALTA

SEA

70°   7   40°   8   50°   9   60°   10   70°   11   80°

Murmansk

Kola
Peninsula

Ponoy

Timan ridge

Pechora

Gora Narodnaya △
6,214 m.
1,894 m.

WHITE SEA

Ob'

Mezen

Severnaya Dvina

Sukhona

Severnyye Uvaly
(Hills)

Kama

Kama
Resevoir

Irtysh

B

Lake
Onega

Onega

Ural Mountains

Lake
Ladoga

Rybinsk
Res.

Gorki
Res.

Kuybyshev
Res.

50°

FINLAND

70°

f. Finland

Lake
Peipus

Volga

Oka

R U S S I A

A S I A

C

ONIA

LATVIA

Valdai
Hills

Moscow

Kuybyshev
Res.

Volga

UANIA

ain

Central
Russian
Upland

Don

Oka-Don Plain

Khopr

Volga
Upland

Volgograd
Res.

Ural

KAZAKHSTAN

Aral Sea

Neman

BELARUS

Caspian Depression

UZBEKISTAN

Prypjac'

Dnieper Lowland

Kiev

Donets Basin

Tsymlyansk
Res.

Volga

Amu Darya

40°

UKRAINE

Dnieper

60°

MOLDOVA

Sea of Azov

CASPIAN   SEA

TURKMENISTAN

nister

Crimean
Peninsula

MANIA

anian Alps

Caucasus

BLACK   SEA

Gora El'brus
18,510 ft.
5,642 m.

GEORGIA

AZERBAIJAN

D

Danube

ninsula

ARMENIA

AZER.

BULGARIA

Rhodope Mts.

İstanbul

Sea of
Marmara

TURKEY

IRAN

ympus
ft.
m.

AEGEAN SEA

IRAQ

ECE

Tigris

30°

Sea of Crete

Rhodes

SYRIA

Euphrates

Crete

CYPRUS

LEBANON

6   30°   7   40°   8   50°   9

ICELAND
Reykjavík

Arctic Circle

NORWEGIAN SEA

FAROE ISLANDS (Den.)

N
W E
S

Trondheim

Umeå
SWEDEN

Kiru

NORWAY

Bergen

Oslo

Stockholm
Göteborg

Skagerrak
Vänern   Vättern

DENMARK
Copenhagen

BALTIC SE

LITHUA

Kaliningrad
Gdańsk

RU

Europe Political Map

National capitals	State capitals	Towns	Population
⚙	✪	■	Over 1,000,000
⚙	✪	▫	250,000 – 1,000,000
⚙	✪	·	Under 250,000

International boundary
State boundary

0   100   200   300   400 Miles
0   200   400   600 Kilometers

ATLANTIC OCEAN

SCOTLAND   Aberdeen
Glasgow
Edinburgh

UNITED
KINGDOM

NORTH SEA

Hamburg

Berlin

Szczecin

POLAND
Warsaw

Łódź

NORTHERN IRELAND
Belfast

IRELAND
Dublin

Cork

Liverpool   Manchester
WALES
Birmingham
ENGLAND
Cardiff

Irish Sea

St. George's Channel

Plymouth

Thames

London

Strait of Dover

English Channel

Le Havre

Brest

Nantes

Loire

FRANCE

Paris

Strasbourg

NETHERLANDS
Amsterdam
The Hague

Antwerp
Brussels
BELGIUM
LUX.

Luxembourg

GERMANY

Essen
Cologne
Bonn
Frankfurt

Dresden
Wrocław
Katowice
Krak

Prague
CZECH REPUBLIC

SLOVAKI

Bordeaux

Toulouse

Bay of Biscay

A Coruña
Gijón
Bilbao

Valladolid

Ebro

Zaragoza

Madrid

PORTUGAL
Porto

Lisbon

Tagus

SPAIN

Córdoba

Seville

Málaga

GIBRALTAR (U.K.)

Strait of Gibraltar

ANDORRA

València

Alacant

Palma

Barcelona

Marseille
Golfe du Lion

MONACO

Nice

Genoa

Turin

Milan

Venice

Bologna

Corsica

Sardinia

Cagliari

Stuttgart
Munich

Zurich
Bern
Geneva
SWITZERLAND

Lyon

Rhône

LIECH.

Vienna
AUSTRIA
Graz

Bratislava

Budapest
HUNGARY

SLOVENIA
Ljubljana

Zagreb

CROATIA

SAN MARINO

Florence

Rome

VATICAN CITY

ITALY

Naples

Bari

ADRIATIC SEA

Split

BOSNIA AND HERZEGOVINA
Sarajevo

MONTENEGRO
Podgorica

SER

Belgr

KO

ALBANIA
Tiranë

Pri

Skoj

M

RU

LIGURIAN SEA

TYRRHENIAN SEA

Palermo
Sicily
Messina
Catania

MEDITERRANEAN SEA

IONIAN SEA

GRE

MALTA

Algiers

AFRICA

MOROCCO   ALGERIA   TUNISIA

Danube

Rhine

Seine

Vistula

Oder

Elbe

Po

Vänern

Gulf of Bo

Hamme

Tan

Kartegat

Kra

FINLAND

WHITE SEA

70°
7
40°
8
50°
9
60°
10
70°
11
80°

Murmansk

Arkhangel'sk

Syktyvkar

Ukhta

Pechora

RUSSIA

Berezniki

B

80°

Petrozavodsk
Lake
Onega

Kirov

Perm'

50°

Helsinki

Lake
Ladoga

Izhevsk

Naberezhnye
Chelny

Ufa

70°

of Finland

Saint Petersburg

Cherepovets
Rybinsk
Res.

Gorki
Res.

Nizhniy
Novgorod

Kuybyshev
Res.

ESTONIA

Lake
Peipus

Yaroslavl'

Ivanovo

Kazan'

ASIA

Riga

Tver'

Oka

Samara

LATVIA

Moscow

Ryazan'

Penza

Volga

Vicebsk

Vilnius

Tula

Bryansk

Don

Lipetsk

Saratov

Volgograd
Res.

C

Minsk

Homel'

Voronezh

Ural

KAZAKHSTAN

Aral Sea

BELARUS

Chornobyl'

Kiev

Kharkiv

Volgograd

Atyraū

UZBEKISTAN

L'viv

Vinnytsia

UKRAINE

Dnieper

Dnipro-
petrovs'k

Luhans'k

Tsymlyansk
Res.

Volga

Astrakhan'

CASPIAN

40°

Dniester

Donets'k

Rostov-na-Donu

MOLDOVA

Kryvyi Rih

Zaporizhzhia

Mariupol'

TURKMENISTAN

60°

Iaşi

Chişinău

Sea of Azov

Stavropol'

SEA

Cluj-Napoca

Odesa

Krasnodar

ROMANIA

Galaţi

Simferopol'

Vladikavkaz

Sevastopol'

BLACK SEA

GEORGIA

Tbilisi

Baku

D

Craiova

Bucharest

Constanţa

ARMENIA

AZERBAIJAN

Danube

BULGARIA

Varna

AZER.

Sofia

Plovdiv

Yerevan

Tehran

İstanbul

Sea of
Marmara

IRAN

Thessaloníki

AEGEAN

Ankara

TURKEY

30°

Athens

SYRIA

IRAQ

Baghdad

Crete

CYPRUS

LEBANON

© Rand McNally
Made in U.S.A.
M-100128-4

6
30°
7
40°
8
50°
9

Climate

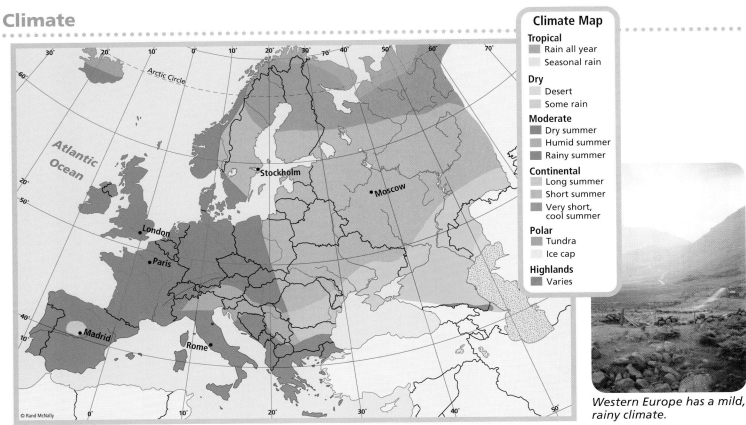

Climate Map

Tropical
- Rain all year
- Seasonal rain

Dry
- Desert
- Some rain

Moderate
- Dry summer
- Humid summer
- Rainy summer

Continental
- Long summer
- Short summer
- Very short, cool summer

Polar
- Tundra
- Ice cap

Highlands
- Varies

Western Europe has a mild, rainy climate.

Population

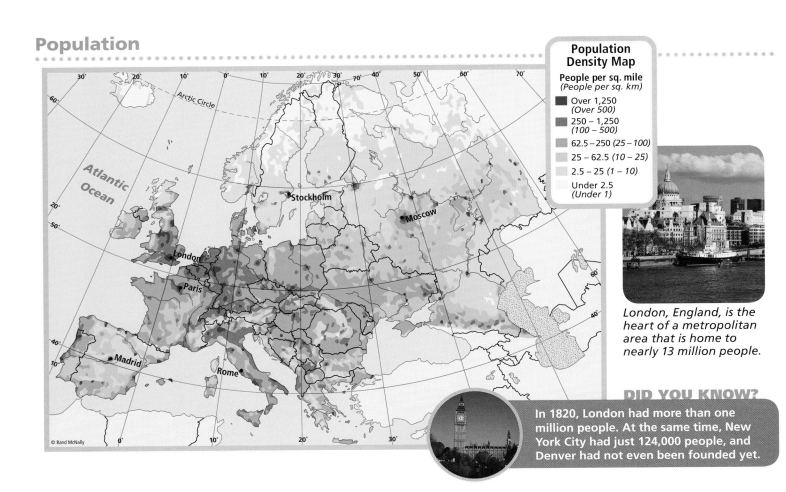

Population Density Map

People per sq. mile
(People per sq. km)

- Over 1,250 *(Over 500)*
- 250 – 1,250 *(100 – 500)*
- 62.5 – 250 *(25 – 100)*
- 25 – 62.5 *(10 – 25)*
- 2.5 – 25 *(1 – 10)*
- Under 2.5 *(Under 1)*

London, England, is the heart of a metropolitan area that is home to nearly 13 million people.

DID YOU KNOW?

In 1820, London had more than one million people. At the same time, New York City had just 124,000 people, and Denver had not even been founded yet.

Environments

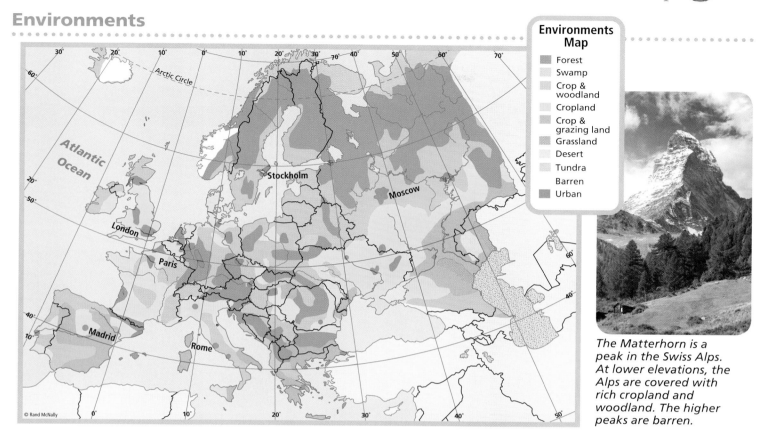

Environments Map

- Forest
- Swamp
- Crop & woodland
- Cropland
- Crop & grazing land
- Grassland
- Desert
- Tundra
- Barren
- Urban

The Matterhorn is a peak in the Swiss Alps. At lower elevations, the Alps are covered with rich cropland and woodland. The higher peaks are barren.

Economic Activities

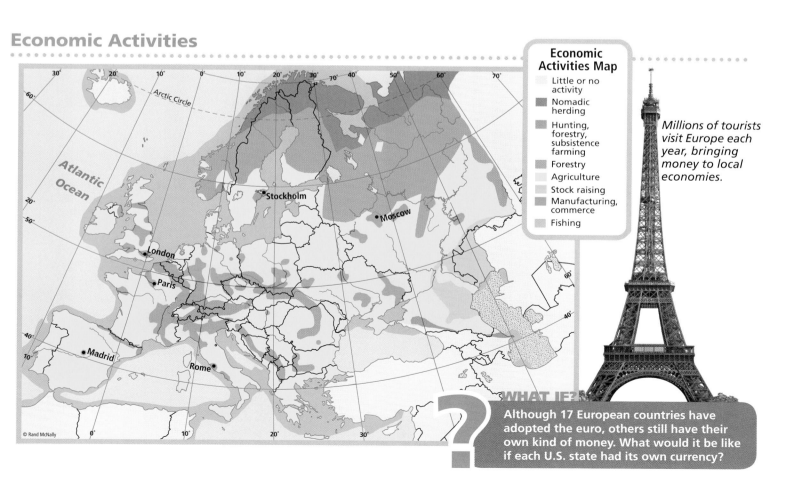

Economic Activities Map

- Little or no activity
- Nomadic herding
- Hunting, forestry, subsistence farming
- Forestry
- Agriculture
- Stock raising
- Manufacturing, commerce
- Fishing

Millions of tourists visit Europe each year, bringing money to local economies.

WHAT IF?

Although 17 European countries have adopted the euro, others still have their own kind of money. What would it be like if each U.S. state had its own currency?

Natural Hazards

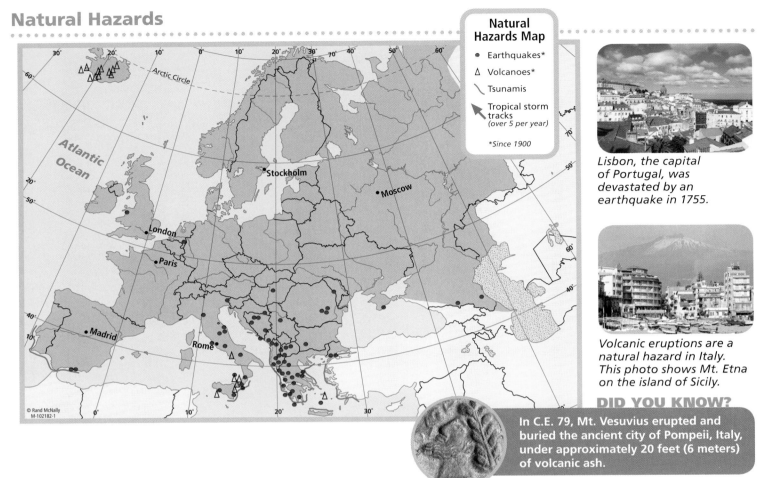

Natural Hazards Map

- • Earthquakes*
- Δ Volcanoes*
- ╲ Tsunamis
- ◤ Tropical storm tracks *(over 5 per year)*

*Since 1900

Atlantic Ocean

Stockholm
Moscow
London
Paris
Madrid
Rome

© Rand McNally
M-102182-1

Lisbon, the capital of Portugal, was devastated by an earthquake in 1755.

Volcanic eruptions are a natural hazard in Italy. This photo shows Mt. Etna on the island of Sicily.

DID YOU KNOW?

In C.E. 79, Mt. Vesuvius erupted and buried the ancient city of Pompeii, Italy, under approximately 20 feet (6 meters) of volcanic ash.

Transportation

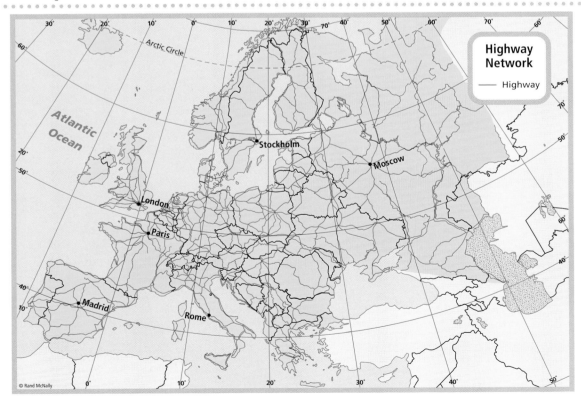

Highway Network

— Highway

Atlantic Ocean

Stockholm
Moscow
London
Paris
Madrid
Rome

© Rand McNally

A canal boat is a modern means of transportation in Amsterdam, the Netherlands.

High-speed rail systems connect many European cities.

Energy

Energy Plants Map

- ▪ Nuclear
- ● Hydroelectric
- ▽ Geothermal

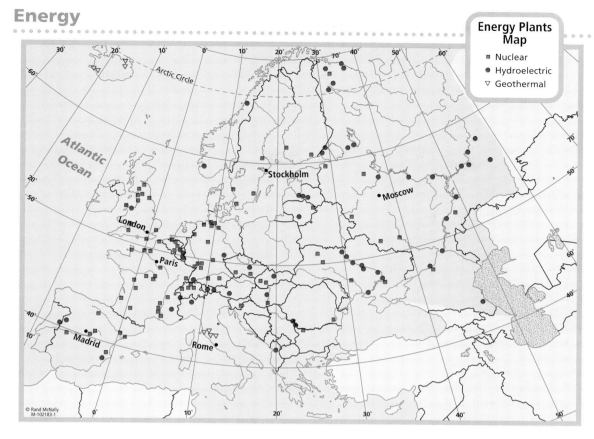

Atlantic Ocean

Arctic Circle

Stockholm

Moscow

London

Paris

Madrid

Rome

© Rand McNally
M-102183-1

In Iceland, water from hot springs heats homes and fuels geothermal plants.

Hydroelectric power is important in some parts of Europe. This dam is in Switzerland.

Mineral Fuel Deposits Map

- ◤ Coal
- ▲ Petroleum
- △ Natural gas

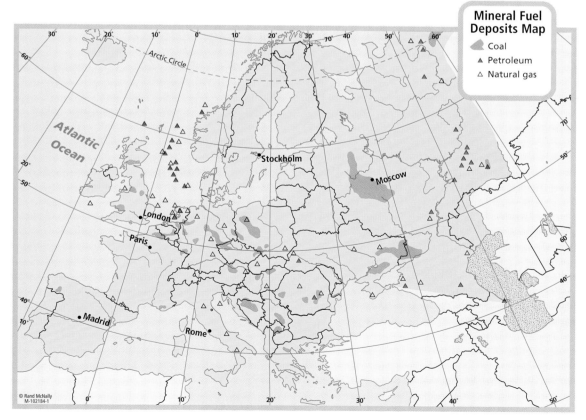

Atlantic Ocean

Arctic Circle

Stockholm

Moscow

London

Paris

Madrid

Rome

© Rand McNally
M-102184-1

North Sea oil and gas are important sources of energy for the United Kingdom and Norway.

Coal was the first fuel for modern factories, but today it is less favored because it is so polluting.

African elephant

Africa is a huge continent. It is larger than every other continent except Asia. More than 1 billion people live in Africa, and the population is growing fast.

The Sahara, the largest desert in the world, covers most of northern Africa. South of the Sahara is the Sahel, an area of dry grasslands. The Sahel expands and recedes with changes in climate.

The tropical rain forests of central Africa provide a natural habitat for gorillas, chimpanzees, and monkeys. North and south of the rain forests and in eastern Africa are vast grassy plains, or savannas. These plains are home to herds of grazing animals, as well as elephants, lions, and other animals most of us see only in zoos.

During the late 19th and early 20th centuries, European countries occupied and governed most of Africa. Today, almost every country in Africa is independent. Africa has 54 countries, the most of any continent.

Many of Africa's people are poor, and they face great challenges in health care, literacy, and life expectancy. Terrible civil wars have torn apart several nations.

Nevertheless, Africa has many possibilities. Hydroelectric power from the Congo and other rivers, minerals such as iron and copper, and improved farming methods offer the hope of better lives to many Africans.

DID YOU KNOW?

Tectonic forces are slowly tearing Africa into two parts. The Rift Valley in eastern Africa marks the dividing line.

A Historical Look At Africa

Circa 140,000 B.C.E.
The first people live in Africa.

Circa 8000 B.C.E
Permanent fishing communities are established along many lakes and rivers.

3000 B.C.E.–400 C.E.
The Nile River valley is home to thriving civilizations.

500–1076
The kingdom of Ghana flourishes in the Sahel.

African Independence

In the late 19th and early 20th centuries, European countries colonized in almost all of Africa. As recently as 1950, only four African countries were independent: Egypt, Ethiopia, Liberia, and South Africa. During the following decades, anti-colonial movements gathered strength across the continent. By the end of the 1970s, a total of 43 countries had become independent. Today, the only African country that is not independent is Western Sahara, which is under the control of Morocco.

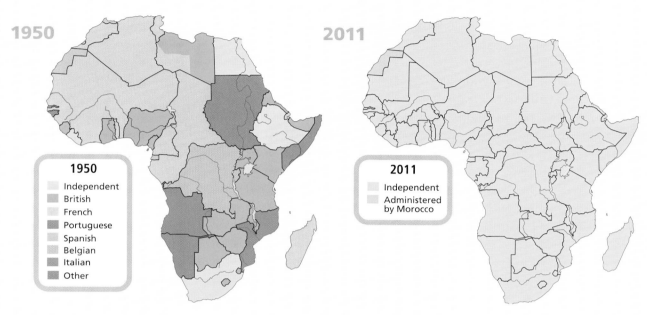

1950

1950
- Independent
- British
- French
- Portuguese
- Spanish
- Belgian
- Italian
- Other

2011

2011
- Independent
- Administered by Morocco

The People of Africa

There are more than 800 ethnic groups in Africa. It is estimated that the people of Africa speak between 800 and 1,600 different languages.

Girl from Egypt

Children from Ethiopia

Children from South Africa

Shepherd from the Sahel

1847
Liberia, founded as a refuge for freed slaves returning to Africa, gains independence.

1950–1979
Most African countries become independent.

2011
South Sudan gains independence.

1885
European countries divide Africa into colonies.

1991
South Africa ends apartheid, the official policy of racial segregation.

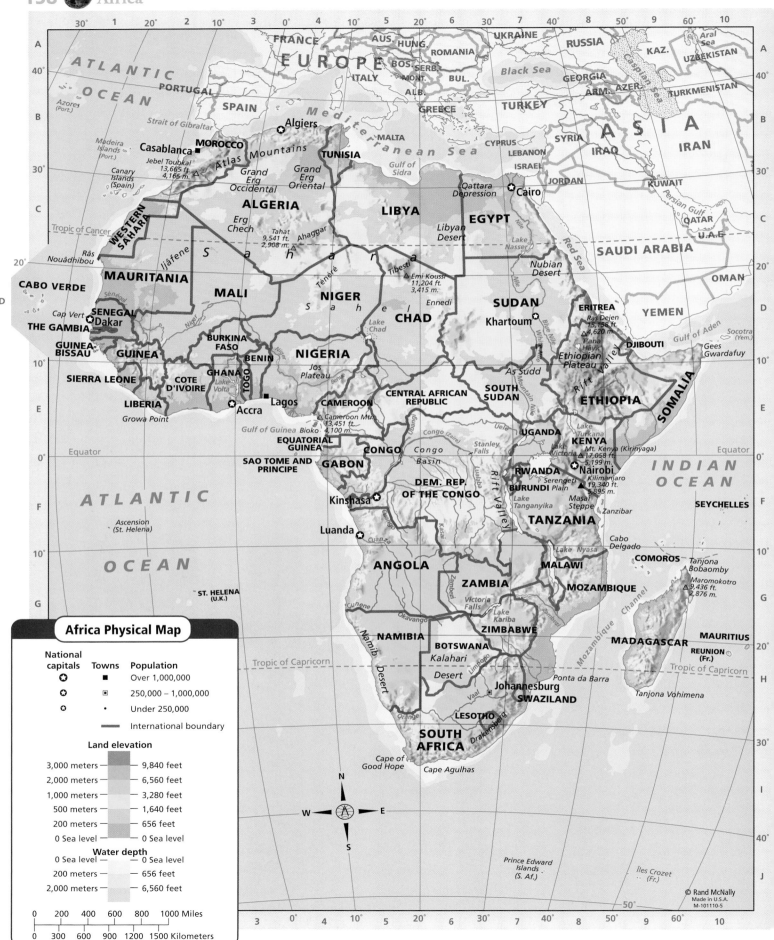

Africa Physical Map

National capitals
⊛ Over 1,000,000
⊛ 250,000 – 1,000,000
⊛ Under 250,000

Towns
■ Over 1,000,000
▣ 250,000 – 1,000,000
• Under 250,000

Population

International boundary

Land elevation

3,000 meters	9,840 feet
2,000 meters	6,560 feet
1,000 meters	3,280 feet
500 meters	1,640 feet
200 meters	656 feet
0 Sea level	0 Sea level

Water depth

0 Sea level	0 Sea level
200 meters	656 feet
2,000 meters	6,560 feet

0   200   400   600   800   1000 Miles
0   300   600   900   1200   1500 Kilometers

© Rand McNally
Made in U.S.A.
M-101110-5

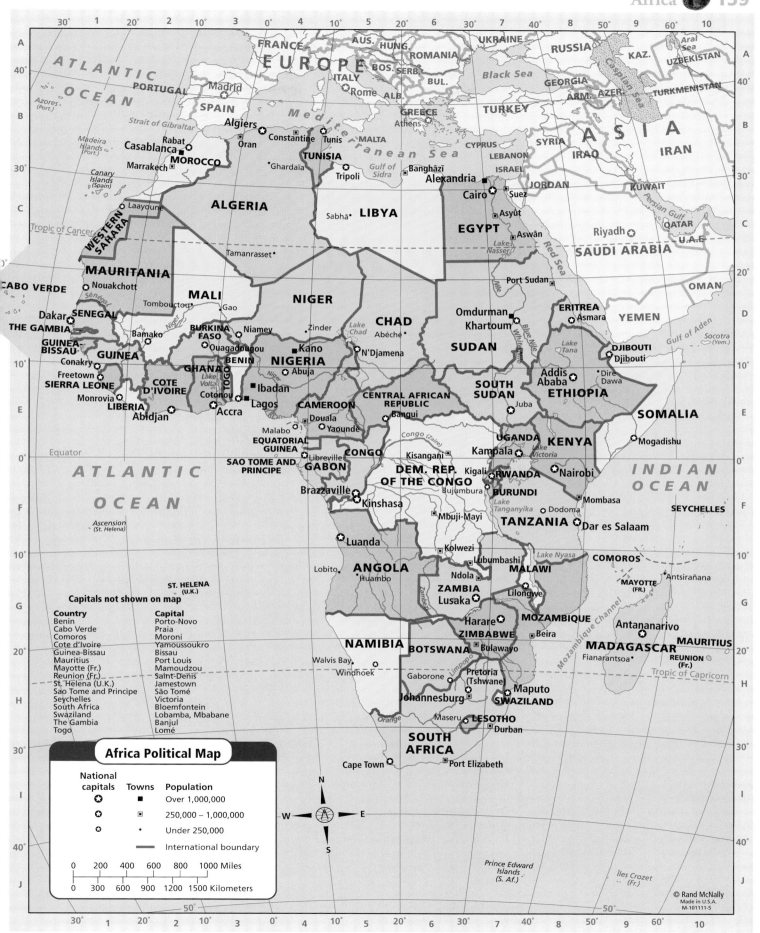

Africa Political Map

National capitals
- ⊛ Over 1,000,000
- ⊛ 250,000 – 1,000,000
- ⊛ Under 250,000

Towns   **Population**
- ■ Over 1,000,000
- ▫ 250,000 – 1,000,000
- • Under 250,000
- ── International boundary

Scale
0 200 400 600 800 1000 Miles
0 300 600 900 1200 1500 Kilometers

Capitals not shown on map

Country	Capital
Benin	Porto-Novo
Cabo Verde	Praia
Comoros	Moroni
Cote d'Ivoire	Yamoussoukro
Guinea-Bissau	Bissau
Mauritius	Port Louis
Mayotte (Fr.)	Mamoudzou
Reunion (Fr.)	Saint-Denis
St. Helena (U.K.)	Jamestown
Sao Tome and Principe	São Tomé
Seychelles	Victoria
South Africa	Bloemfontein
Swaziland	Lobamba, Mbabane
The Gambia	Banjul
Togo	Lomé

© Rand McNally
Made in U.S.A.
M-101111-5

Environments

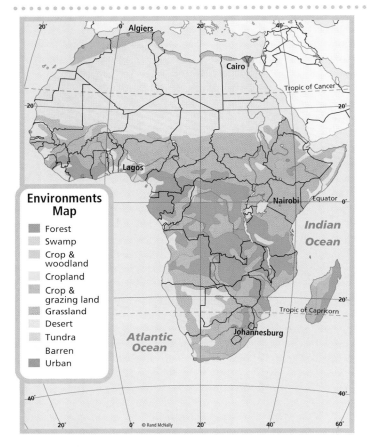

Environments Map

- Forest
- Swamp
- Crop & woodland
- Cropland
- Crop & grazing land
- Grassland
- Desert
- Tundra
- Barren
- Urban

© Rand McNally

Tropical rain forests of central Africa are hot and humid. Jungles are areas of dense, tangled plant growth in these forests.

An erg is a large area of sand dunes in a desert. Deserts cover about one-third of Africa.

Savannas, areas of grassland with few trees, cover about two-fifths of Africa's land area. Similar areas in North America are called prairies.

The region known as the Sahel borders the Sahara on the south. Overfarming, overgrazing, and droughts have caused parts of the Sahel to become desert.

An oasis in a desert is found where underground water comes to the surface.

Although many Africans still live in the countryside, Africa has large, modern cities. This is a view of Johannesburg, South Africa.

Africa's most fertile cropland is found along its rivers. This farm is in Egypt's Nile River valley.

Climate

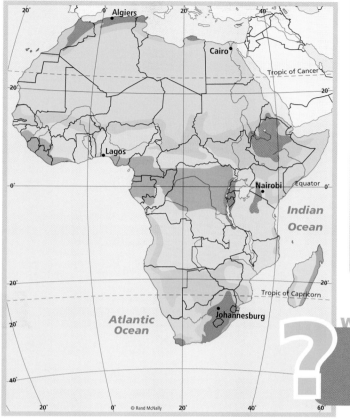

Climate Map

Tropical
- Hot with rain all year
- Hot with seasonal rain

Dry
- Desert
- Some rain

Moderate (Rainy Winter)
- Hot, dry summer
- Hot, humid summer
- Mild, rainy summer

Continental (Snowy Winter)
- Long, warm, humid summer
- Short, cool, humid summer
- Very short, cool, humid summer

Polar
- Tundra – very cold and dry
- Ice cap

Highlands
- Varies with altitude

© Rand McNally

? WHAT IF?

Scientists believe that the Sahara expands, recedes, and expands again. What happens if people settle on fertile land that turns back into desert?

The Sahara

The Sahara is the largest hot desert in the world. It covers about 3.3 million square miles (about 8.5 million square kilometers). The name *Sahara* comes from the Arabic word for desert.

The highest temperature ever recorded in the world was in the Sahara: 136°F (58°C). But the Sahara can be very cold at night, because the dry air does not hold much heat. The daytime and nighttime temperatures can differ by as much as 100°F (56°C).

On average, rainfall in the Sahara is less than 10 inches (25 centimeters) per year. There may be no rain at all for years at a time.

Besides sand, the Sahara has vast areas of gravel, rocky plateaus, and volcanic mountains.

Animals of the Savanna

African elephants

Lion

Thomson's gazelles

White rhinoceroses

Zebras

Cheetah and cub

Natural Hazards

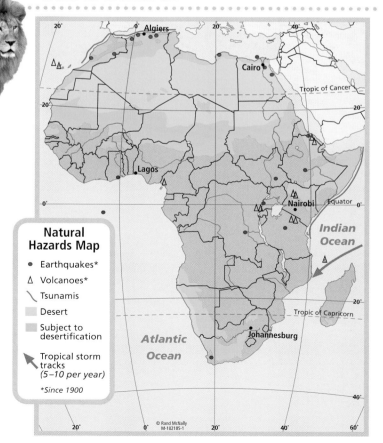

Natural Hazards Map
- • Earthquakes*
- △ Volcanoes*
- \ Tsunamis
- Desert
- Subject to desertification
- ↙ Tropical storm tracks (5–10 per year)

*Since 1900

© Rand McNally
M-102185-1

Population

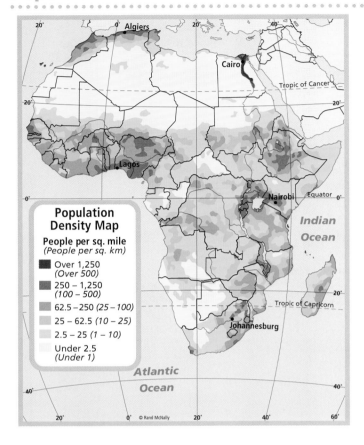

Population Density Map

People per sq. mile
(People per sq. km)

- Over 1,250 *(Over 500)*
- 250 – 1,250 *(100 – 500)*
- 62.5 – 250 *(25 – 100)*
- 25 – 62.5 *(10 – 25)*
- 2.5 – 25 *(1 – 10)*
- Under 2.5 *(Under 1)*

© Rand McNally

Life Expectancy

Life expectancy varies widely across Africa. In recent decades, the deadly disease AIDS has shortened the average life span of people in many African countries, especially those south of the Sahara Desert.

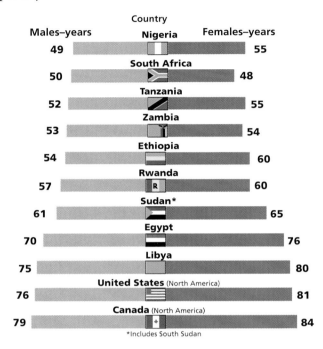

Males–years	Country	Females–years
49	**Nigeria**	55
50	**South Africa**	48
52	**Tanzania**	55
53	**Zambia**	54
54	**Ethiopia**	60
57	**Rwanda**	60
61	**Sudan***	65
70	**Egypt**	76
75	**Libya**	80
76	**United States** (North America)	81
79	**Canada** (North America)	84

*Includes South Sudan

Transportation

DID YOU KNOW?

During the 1967 war with Israel, Egypt sank ships in the Suez Canal to block traffic. The canal stayed closed for eight years.

Fewer than 10% of the roads in Africa are paved.

Camels are still used to transport goods across the desert. Their heavy-lidded eyes and closeable nostrils offer protection in sandstorms, and they can travel long distances without water.

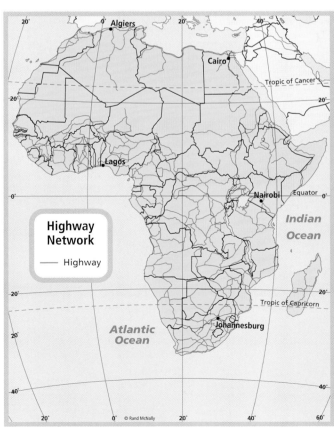

Highway Network

— Highway

© Rand McNally

Economic Activities

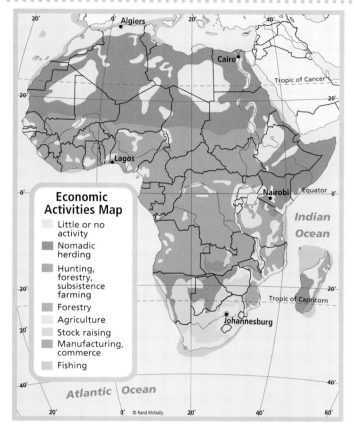

Economic Activities Map

- Little or no activity
- Nomadic herding
- Hunting, forestry, subsistence farming
- Forestry
- Agriculture
- Stock raising
- Manufacturing, commerce
- Fishing

Per Capita Income

Per capita income measures the relative wealth of countries. Most African countries have per capita incomes far below those of the three wealthy non-African countries included in this graph: Canada, Sweden, and the United States.

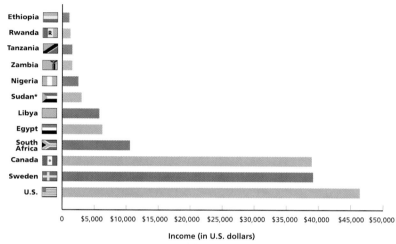

Income (in U.S. dollars)

*Includes South Sudan

In many parts of Africa, nomadic herding is the way of life for most people.

The monuments of ancient Egypt attract millions of visitors each year. Tourism revenue is an important contributor to Egypt's economy.

About 65% of all Africans make a living by farming.

World Gold Production

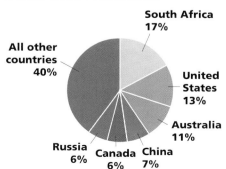

- South Africa 17%
- All other countries 40%
- United States 13%
- Australia 11%
- Russia 6%
- Canada 6%
- China 7%

World Platinum Production

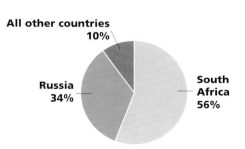

- All other countries 10%
- Russia 34%
- South Africa 56%

World Diamond Production

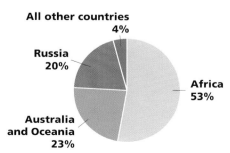

- All other countries 4%
- Russia 20%
- Africa 53%
- Australia and Oceania 23%

One reason for the high annual per capita income for South Africa is that it is rich in gold, platinum, and diamonds. Discovery of these precious mineral resources in the 1800s brought many Europeans to settle in South Africa.

ASIA

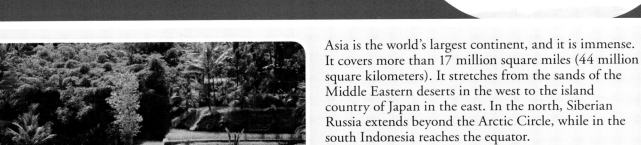

Terraced rice field in Bali, Indonesia

Asia is the world's largest continent, and it is immense. It covers more than 17 million square miles (44 million square kilometers). It stretches from the sands of the Middle Eastern deserts in the west to the island country of Japan in the east. In the north, Siberian Russia extends beyond the Arctic Circle, while in the south Indonesia reaches the equator.

Asia is home to some of the world's oldest civilizations. Farming, cities, and writing began in Mesopotamia, in the Indus River valley, and in China thousands of years ago. Asians also invented many things that we use today, such as the idea of zero, paper, the printing press, and the magnetic compass.

Many countries in Asia are working to develop their economies, and their people still have difficult lives. Other Asian countries such as Japan, Taiwan, and Singapore are economic powers. The fortunes of the oil-rich countries of the Middle East depend on the value of their oil exports.

Asia has more people than any other continent: 4.2 billion, which is about 60% of the world's people. China alone has 1.3 billion people, and India has passed one billion. Eastern China is as densely populated as the New York City urban area.

Oil drums

Mt. Fuji in Japan

Limestone pinnacles along the Li River in China

A Historical Look At Asia

Circa 3500 B.C.E.
Sumerian civilization begins in Mesopotamia (modern Iraq).

403 B.C.E.
Construction of the Great Wall of China begins.

C.E. 618-907
The T'ang Dynasty rules China.

1631-1648
The Taj Mahal is built in India.

The Regions of Asia

Asia has six distinct regions. Use the political map on pages 168 and 169 to determine the countries in each region.

Use the political map on pages 168 and 169

Central Asia
Central Asia is rugged and dry. Farming in most places is difficult, and many people make a living as nomadic herders. The region has large deposits of oil.

Southwest Asia
Most of Southwest Asia is desert and semi-desert. The region has the world's richest deposits of oil.

South Asia
India and neighboring countries make up South Asia. The Himalayas border the northeastern part of this region.

North Asia
North Asia has long, bitterly cold winters. Despite its mineral resources, fewer people live in North Asia than in any other part of the continent.

East Asia
Eastern China and its neighbors make up East Asia. About one quarter of the world's people live in East Asia.

Southeast Asia
The southeast part of the Asian mainland and many islands make up Southeast Asia. Most of the region has a tropical climate.

DID YOU KNOW?

The highest point in the world (Mt. Everest) and the lowest point (the Dead Sea) are both in Asia.

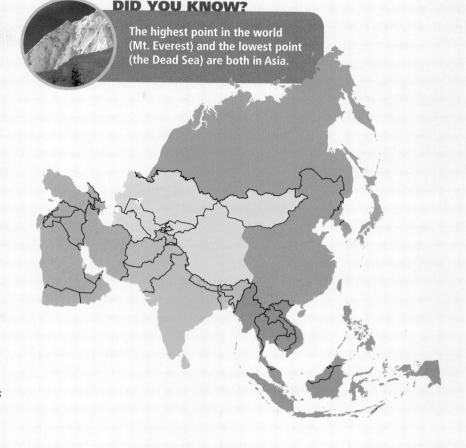

Central Asia

Southwest Asia

South Asia

North Asia

East Asia

Southeast Asia

1854
Japan begins trading with the United States.

Circa 1900
Britain begins developing oil fields in southwestern Iran.

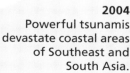
1947
India is divided into two countries, India and Pakistan, and both become independent from British rule.

2004
Powerful tsunamis devastate coastal areas of Southeast and South Asia.

Mt. Everest, which rises along the border between Nepal and China, is the world's highest mountain. It is 29,028 feet (8,848 meters) high.

The Dead Sea, located between Israel and Jordan, is the lowest point on Earth. Its shore is 1,339 feet (408 meters) below sea level.

Lake Baikal in Russia is the deepest lake in the world. Its greatest depth is slightly more than a mile.

Russia's Kamchatka Peninsula is one of the most volcanically active places in the world.

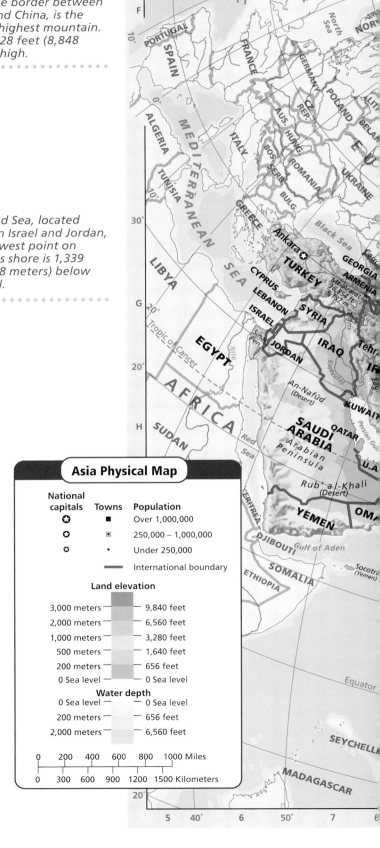

Asia Physical Map

National capitals	Towns	Population
✪	■	Over 1,000,000
✪	▣	250,000 – 1,000,000
✪	•	Under 250,000
	▬	International boundary

Land elevation

3,000 meters	9,840 feet
2,000 meters	6,560 feet
1,000 meters	3,280 feet
500 meters	1,640 feet
200 meters	656 feet
0 Sea level	0 Sea level

Water depth

0 Sea level	0 Sea level
200 meters	656 feet
2,000 meters	6,560 feet

0   200   400   600   800   1000 Miles

0   300   600   900   1200   1500 Kilometers

ARCTIC OCEAN

North Pole

SWEDEN
FINLAND
BARENTS SEA
Novaya Zemlya
Yamal Pen.
KARA SEA
Severnaya Zemlya
New Siberian Islands
LAPTEV SEA
EAST SIBERIAN SEA
Aleutian Islands (U.S.)

Ural Mountains
North Siberian Lowland
Central Siberian Plateau
RUSSIA
West Siberian Plain
Verkhoyansk Mts.
Kolyma
Kamchatka Peninsula
Mys Lopatka
BERING SEA

Novosibirsk
Angara
Lake Baikal
Stanovoy Mountains
Amur
SEA OF OKHOTSK
Sakhalin
Kuril Islands

Caspian Depression
KAZAKHSTAN
Kazakh Hills
Altay Mountains
Sayan Mountains
Selenge
Yablonovy Range
Greater Khingan Range
Manchuria
Sikhote-Alin (Mts.)
Tatar Strait
Hokkaidō

Aral Sea
Üstirt (Plateau)
UZBEKISTAN
Lake Balkhash
Dzungarian Basin
MONGOLIA
Gobi Desert
Honshū
JAPAN
Tōkyō

TURKMENISTAN
KYRGYZSTAN
Tien Shan
NORTH KOREA
SEA OF JAPAN (EAST SEA)
Fuji-san 12,388 ft. 3,776 m.

TAJIKISTAN
Pamirs (Mts.)
Tarim Pendi (Basin)
Qilian Shan (Mts.)
Beijing
Bo Hai
SOUTH KOREA
Korea Strait
Shikoku
Kyūshū
PACIFIC OCEAN

AFGHANISTAN
Hindu Kush
K2 (Qogir Feng) 28,250 ft. 8,611 m.
Altun Shan (Mts.)
Qaidam Pendi (Basin)
CHINA
Huang (Yellow)
YELLOW SEA

PAKISTAN
Kunlun Mts.
Plateau of Tibet
Qin Ling (Mts.)
Shanghai
EAST CHINA SEA
Tropic of Cancer
NORTHERN MARIANA ISLANDS (U.S.)

New Delhi
NEPAL
Mt. Everest 29,028 ft. 8,848 m.
Himalayas
BHUTAN
Szechwan Basin
Yangtze
Plateau of Yunnan
Nan Ling (Mts.)
Wuyshan (Hills)
Taiwan Strait
Philippine Sea
GUAM (U.S.)

Great Indian Desert
Indus
Brahmaputra
Ganges
BANGLA-DESH
Kolkata (Calcutta)
Ayeyarwady
Luzon Strait
Luzon

Gulf of Oman
Kāthiāwār Peninsula
Mumbai (Bombay)
Godāvari
INDIA
Deccan (Plateau)
Western Ghats
Eastern Ghats
MYANMAR
LAOS
Salween
Mekong
Red
Gulf of Tonkin
Hainan Dao
Manila
PHILIPPINES

ARABIAN SEA
Bay of Bengal
THAILAND
Bangkok
CAMBODIA
VIETNAM
SOUTH CHINA SEA
Mindanao
PALAU

Lakshadweep (India)
Andaman Islands (India)
Gulf of Thailand
Mui Ca Mau (Cape)
Sulu Sea

Cape Comorin
SRI LANKA
Dondra Head
Nicobar Islands (India)
Andaman Sea
MALAY PENINSULA
BRUNEI
Celebes Sea
Moluccas
New Guinea
Puncak Jaya 16,503 ft. 5,030 m.

MALDIVES
Str. of Malacca
MALAYSIA
MALAYSIA
Celebes
Ceram
Banda Sea
Arafura Sea

SINGAPORE
Borneo
TIMOR-LESTE

INDIAN OCEAN
N W E S
Sumatra
Greater Sunda Islands
Java Sea
INDONESIA
Lesser Sunda Is.
Timor
Gulf of Carpentaria
AUSTRALIA

Jakarta
Java
Timor Sea

© Rand McNally
Made in U.S.A.
M-101114-6

Indonesia is an island nation located in Southeast Asia. It has a larger population than all but three of the world's countries: China, India, and the United States.

China is the world's most populous country. It is home to more than 1.3 billion people.

Kyrgyzstan is located in Central Asia. It became a country when the Soviet Union broke up in 1991.

Turkey is Asia's westernmost country. Istanbul, Turkey's largest city, lies along the Bosporus Strait, which divides Asia and Europe.

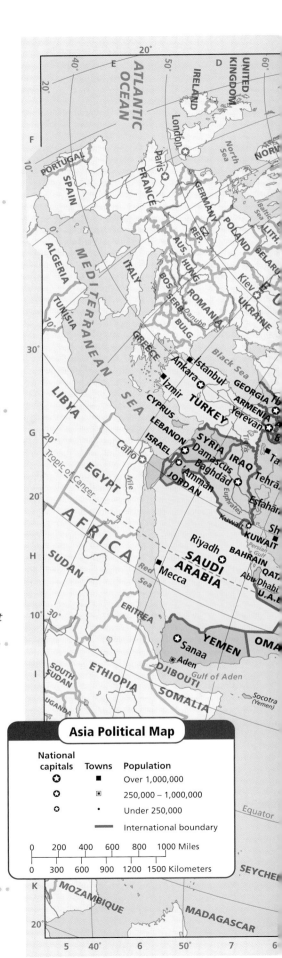

Asia Political Map

National capitals	Towns	Population
✪	■	Over 1,000,000
✪	▣	250,000 – 1,000,000
✪	•	Under 250,000
—		International boundary

0 200 400 600 800 1000 Miles
0 300 600 900 1200 1500 Kilometers

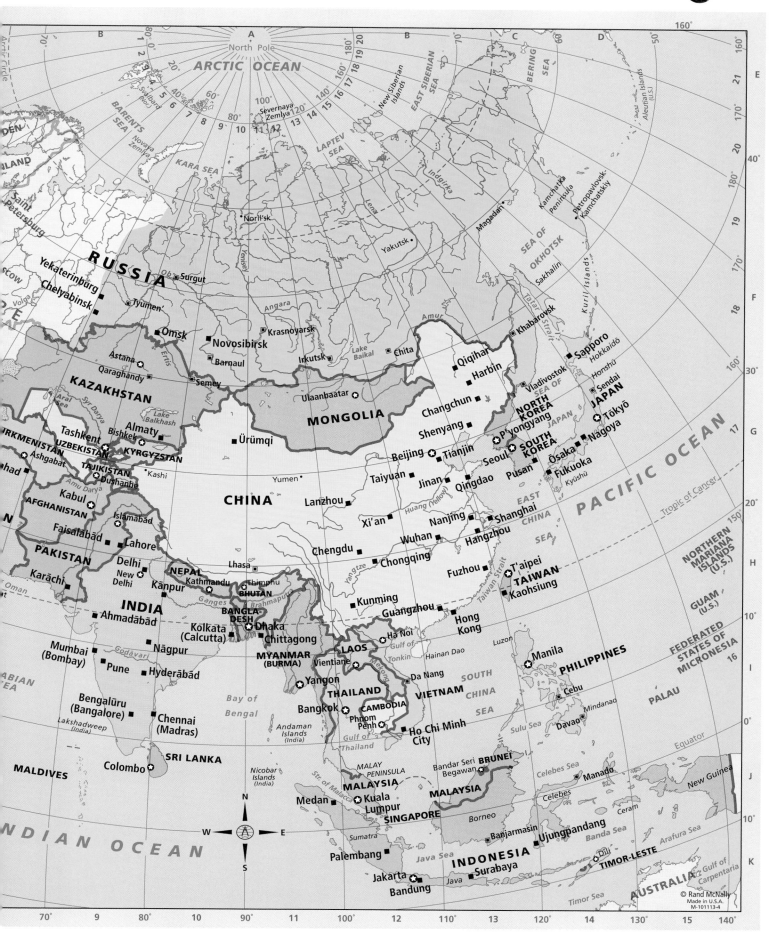

Asia

North Pole

ARCTIC OCEAN

BARENTS SEA

KARA SEA

LAPTEV SEA

EAST SIBERIAN SEA

BERING SEA

Novaya Zemlya

Severnaya Zemlya

New Siberian Islands

Kamchatka Peninsula

Petropavlovsk-Kamchatskiy

Aleutian Islands (U.S.)

Svalbard (Nor.)

DEN

LAND

Saint Petersburg

stow

Volga

PE

RUSSIA

Yekaterinburg

Chelyabinsk

Tyumen'

Omsk

Ob

Surgut

Noril'sk

Yenisey

Angara

Krasnoyarsk

Novosibirsk

Barnaul

Irkutsk

Lena

Yakutsk

Lake Baikal

Chita

Amur

Khabarovsk

Indigirka

Magadan

SEA OF OKHOTSK

Sakhalin

Tatar Strait

Kuril Islands

Sapporo

Hokkaidō

Honshū

Sendai

JAPAN

Tōkyō

Nagoya

PACIFIC OCEAN

Astana

Qaraghandy

KAZAKHSTAN

Aral Sea

Syr Darya

Lake Balkhash

Almaty

Bishkek

Tashkent

KYRGYZSTAN

Ürümqi

MONGOLIA

Ulaanbaatar

Qiqihar

Harbin

Changchun

Shenyang

NORTH KOREA

Pyongyang

Vladivostok

SEA OF JAPAN

SOUTH KOREA

Seoul

Pusan

Ōsaka

Fukuoka

Kyūshū

RKMENISTAN

UZBEKISTAN

Ashgabat

had

TAJIKISTAN

Dushanbe

Amu Darya

Kashi

Yumen

CHINA

Lanzhou

Beijing

Tianjin

Taiyuan

Jinan

Qingdao

Huang (Yellow)

EAST CHINA SEA

Tropic of Cancer

NORTHERN MARIANA ISLANDS (U.S.)

Kabul

AFGHANISTAN

Islamabad

Faisalabad

Lahore

PAKISTAN

Karāchi

Delhi

New Delhi

Kānpur

NEPAL

Kathmandu

Thimphu

BHUTAN

Lhasa

Chengdu

Yangtze

Xi'an

Chongqing

Wuhan

Nanjing

Shanghai

Hangzhou

Fuzhou

T'aipei

TAIWAN

Kaohsiung

Taiwan Strait

GUAM (U.S.)

FEDERATED STATES OF MICRONESIA

INDIA

Ahmadābād

Ganges

Brahmaputra

BANGLA-DESH

Dhaka

Kolkata (Calcutta)

Chittagong

Kunming

Guangzhou

Hong Kong

Ha Noi

Gulf of Tonkin

Hainan Dao

Luzon

Manila

PHILIPPINES

PALAU

Mumbai (Bombay)

Godāvari

Nāgpur

Pune

Hyderābād

MYANMAR (BURMA)

Vientiane

LAOS

Da Nang

VIETNAM

SOUTH CHINA SEA

Cebu

Mindanao

Davao

Yangon

THAILAND

Bengalūru (Bangalore)

Chennai (Madras)

Lakshadweep (India)

Bay of Bengal

Andaman Islands (India)

Bangkok

CAMBODIA

Phnom Penh

Ho Chi Minh City

Mekong

Sulu Sea

MALDIVES

Colombo

SRI LANKA

Nicobar Islands (India)

Gulf of Thailand

MALAY PENINSULA

Bandar Seri Begawan

BRUNEI

Celebes Sea

Manado

New Guinea

ABIAN EA

Str. of Malacca

MALAYSIA

Medan

Kuala Lumpur

SINGAPORE

MALAYSIA

Borneo

Celebes

Ceram

NDIAN OCEAN

Sumatra

Palembang

Java Sea

INDONESIA

Surabaya

Java

Banjarmasin

Ujungpandang

Banda Sea

Dili

TIMOR-LESTE

Arafura Sea

Timor Sea

AUSTRALIA

Gulf of Carpentaria

Jakarta

Bandung

Taiyuan

Jinan

N

W

E

S

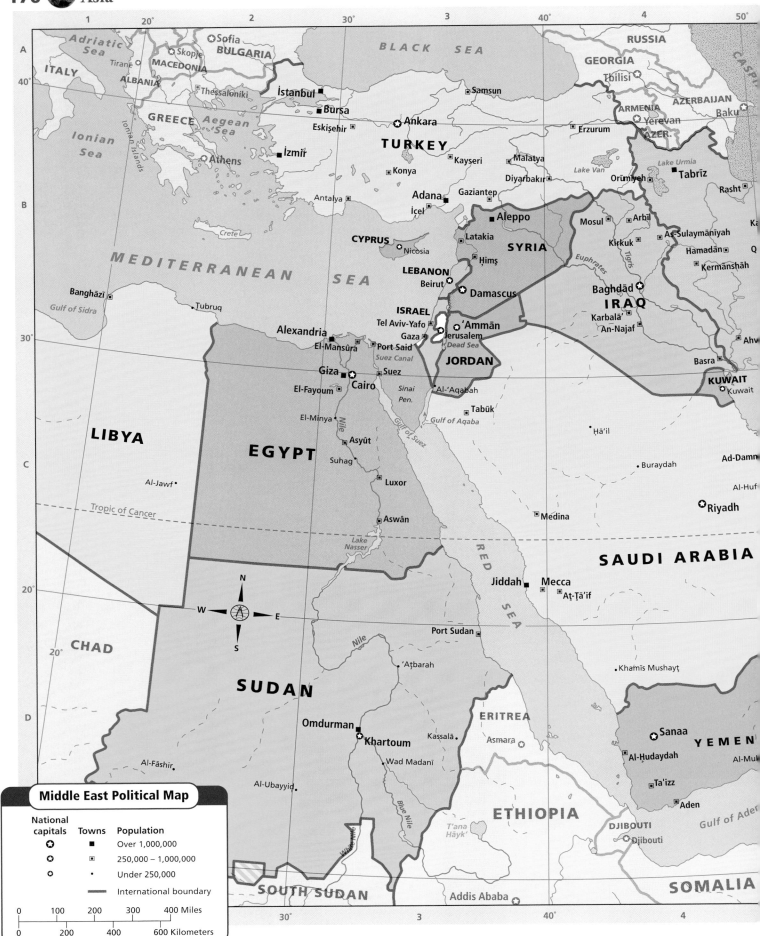

Middle East Political Map

National capitals	Towns	Population
✪	■	Over 1,000,000
✪	▣	250,000 – 1,000,000
✪	•	Under 250,000
	━━	International boundary

0 100 200 300 400 Miles

0 200 400 600 Kilometers

The Middle East

Africa, Asia, and Europe meet in the Middle East. Since ancient times, great powerful empires have fought to control these lands, their resources, and their trade routes. Today, the oil that many Middle Eastern countries produce is valuable to rich countries. There are also deep-rooted cultural conflicts among the peoples of the region.

Oil pumpjack

AZAKHSTAN

UZBEKISTAN

Amu Darya

TURKMENISTAN

Ashgabat

Mashhad

rān

IRAN

Bīrjand

AFGHAN.

Şfahān

Yazd

Daryācheh-ye Hāmūn

Kermān

Zāhedān

Shīrāz

nehr

Bandar-e 'Abbās

an Gulf

Strait of Hormuz

OMAN

RAIN
ama

QATAR

Dubai

Gulf of Oman

Doha

Şuḩār

Abu Dhabi

Muscat

UNITED ARAB EMIRATES

Tropic of Cancer

Şūr

OMAN

Şalālah

ARABIAN SEA

Al-Ghaydah

Socotra (Yem.)

INDIAN OCEAN

© Rand McNally
Made in U.S.A.
M-101119-3

0 10 20 30 40 50 Miles
0 20 40 60 80 Kilometers

MEDITERRANEAN

SEA

Beirut

Sidon LEBANON

Nahr al-Līṭānī

Tyre

SYRIA

'Akko

Golan Heights

Sea of Galilee

Haifa

Tiberias

(A)

Nazareth

(A) **Golan Heights.** Occupied and unilaterally annexed by Israel.

Hadera

Irbid

Janīn

Netanya

Ṭūlkarm

Jordan

Nābulus

(B) **West Bank.** Controlled by Israel, parts administered by the Palestinian Authority. Permanent status to be determined.

Tel Aviv-Yafo

West Bank

As-Salṭ

(B)

'Ammān

(C) **Gaza Strip.** Administered by the Palestinian Authority following unilateral withdrawal by Israel in 2005. Permanent status to be determined.

Rehovot

Jericho

Ashdod

Ashqelon

Jerusalem

Bethlehem

Gaza

Hebron

Dead Sea

Gaza Strip (C)

Khan Yūnis

Beersheba

Al-Karak

Port Said

Khalig el-Tina

El-Arish

Dimona

Suez Canal

El-Qantara el-Sharqīya

ISRAEL

Aṭ-Ṭafīlah

Ismailia

JORDAN

Negev (desert)

Great Bitter Lake

Ma'ān

EGYPT

Suez

Sinai Peninsula

Elat

Al-'Aqabah

Gulf of Suez

Gulf of Aqaba

N-CLA61400-P1- -1-1-1

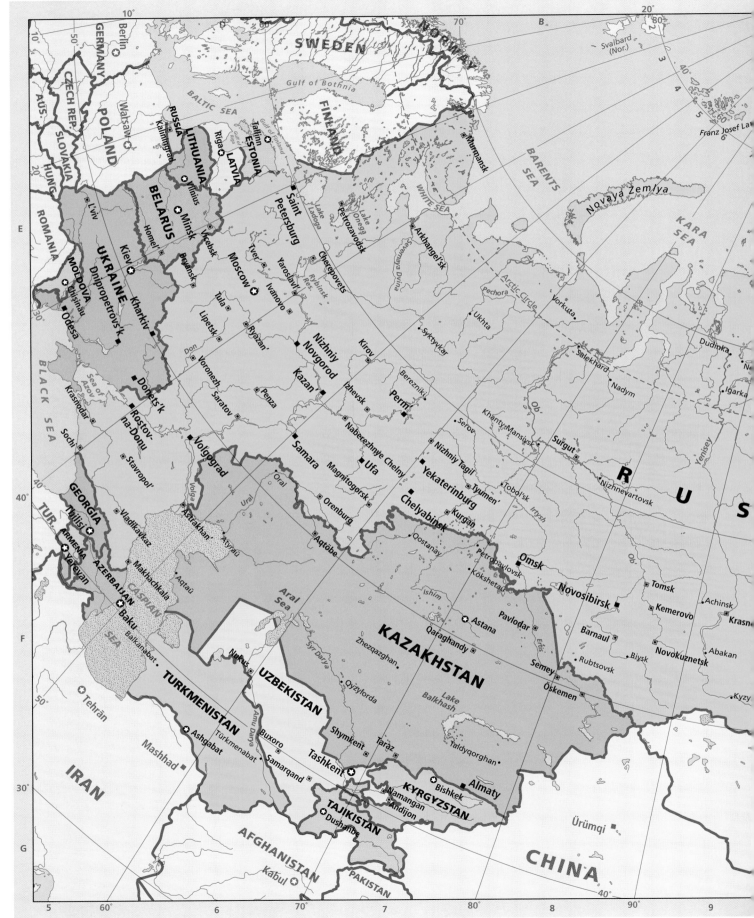

GERMANY
Berlin

CZECH REP.
SLOVAKIA
AUS.
HUNG.
ROMANIA
POLAND
Warsaw

SWEDEN
NORWAY
Svalbard
(Nor.)

Gulf of Bothnia

FINLAND

BALTIC SEA

Gulf of Finland

Tallinn
ESTONIA
Riga
LATVIA
LITHUANIA
Vilnius
Kaliningrad

RUSSIA

Franz Josef La

BARENTS
SEA

Novaya Zemlya

KARA
SEA

WHITE SEA

Murmansk

Arkhangel'sk

MOLDOVA
Chişinău
UKRAINE
Kiev
Lviv
BELARUS
Minsk
Homel'
Vitebsk
Pukansk

Saint
Petersburg
Lake
Ladoga
Petrozavodsk
Lake
Onega
Severnaya Dvina

Arctic Circle

Vorkuta

Pechora

Salekhard

Dudinka

Igarka

Odesa
Dnipropetrovs'k
Kharkiv
Donets'k

Tver'
Moscow
Ivanovo
Yaroslavl'
Rybinsk
Res.
Cherepovets
Kirov

Ukhta

Syktyvkar

Nadym

BLACK
SEA
Krasnodar
Sea of
Azov
Rostov-
na-Donu
Stavropol'

Don
Voronezh
Lipetsk
Tula
Ryazan'
Penza
Saratov

Nizhniy
Novgorod
Kazan'
Izhevsk
Berezniki
Perm'

Khanty-Mansiysk
Serov
Ob'
Surgut

Nizhnevartovsk

R   U   S

Yenisey

Volgograd
Astrakhan'
Vladikavkaz
Makhachkala

Volga
Ural
Oral

Naberezhnye Chelny
Samara
Magnitogorsk
Ufa
Orenburg

Nizhniy Tagil
Yekaterinburg
Tyumen'
Tobol'sk

Omsk
Novosibirsk
Tomsk
Kemerovo
Achinsk
Krasn

GEORGIA
Tbilisi
TUR.
ARMENIA
Yerevan
AZERBAIJAN
Baku

CASPIAN
SEA
Aqtau
Balkanabat

Aral
Sea

Aqtöbe

Qostanay
Kökshetau
Petropavlovsk
Kurgan
Chelyabinsk
Ishim
Irtysh

Barnaul
Rubtsovsk
Biysk
Novokuznetsk
Abakan

Kyzy

IRAN
Mashhad
Tehrān

TURKMENISTAN
Ashgabat
Türkmenabat

Nukus
Balkanabat
Atyrau

Syr Darya
Amu Darya
Buxoro
Samarqand

UZBEKISTAN
Tashkent
Shymkent
Taraz

Zhezqazghan
Qyzylorda

KAZAKHSTAN
Astana
Qaraghandy
Pavlodar
Semey
Öskemen

Lake
Balkhash
Taldyqorghan
Almaty

AFGHANISTAN
Kabul
PAKISTAN

TAJIKISTAN
Dushanbe
KYRGYZSTAN
Bishkek
Namangan
Andijon

Ürümqi

CHINA

10°   20°   70°   80°
30°   40°   50°   60°   90°
5   6   7   8   9

ARCTIC OCEAN

UNITED STATES

Bering Strait

CHUKCHI SEA

BERING SEA

Saint Lawrence Island

Wrangel Island

EAST SIBERIAN SEA

Pevek

Anadyr

LAPTEV SEA

New Siberian Islands

Ostrov Novaya Sibir

Ostrov Kotel'nyy

Arctic Circle

Tiksi

Indigirka

Kolyma

Komandorski Islands

Ust'-Kamchatsk

Ust'-Nera

Susuman

Kamchatka Peninsula

Petropavlovsk-Kamchatskiy

Magadan

Lena

Vilyuysk

Yakutsk

Aldan

SEA OF OKHOTSK

Mirnyy

I A

Aldan

Okha

Nizhnyaya Tunguska

Lena

Sakhalin

Kuril Islands

Angara

Ust'-Ilimsk

Nikolayevsk-na-Amure

Amur

Zheleznogorsk

Bratsk

Zeya

Komsomol'sk-na-Amure

Tatar Strait

Yuzhno-Sakhalinsk

Cheremkhovo

Lake Baikal

Amur

Svobodnyy

Chita

Blagoveshchensk

Khabarovsk

La Perouse Strait

PACIFIC OCEAN

Angarsk

Irkutsk

Ulan-Ude

Birobidzhan

Hokkaidō

Sapporo

JAPAN

Ulaanbaatar

Harbin

MONGOLIA

CHINA

Vladivostok

Nakhodka

SEA OF JAPAN (EAST SEA)

Shenyang

NORTH KOREA

P'yŏngyang

© Rand McNally
Made in U.S.A.
N-100133-2

Northern Eurasia Political Map

National capitals	Towns	Population
✪	■	Over 1,000,000
✪	▣	250,000 – 1,000,000
✪	•	Under 250,000
		── International boundary

0	100	200	300	400	500 Miles
0	200	400	600	800 Kilometers

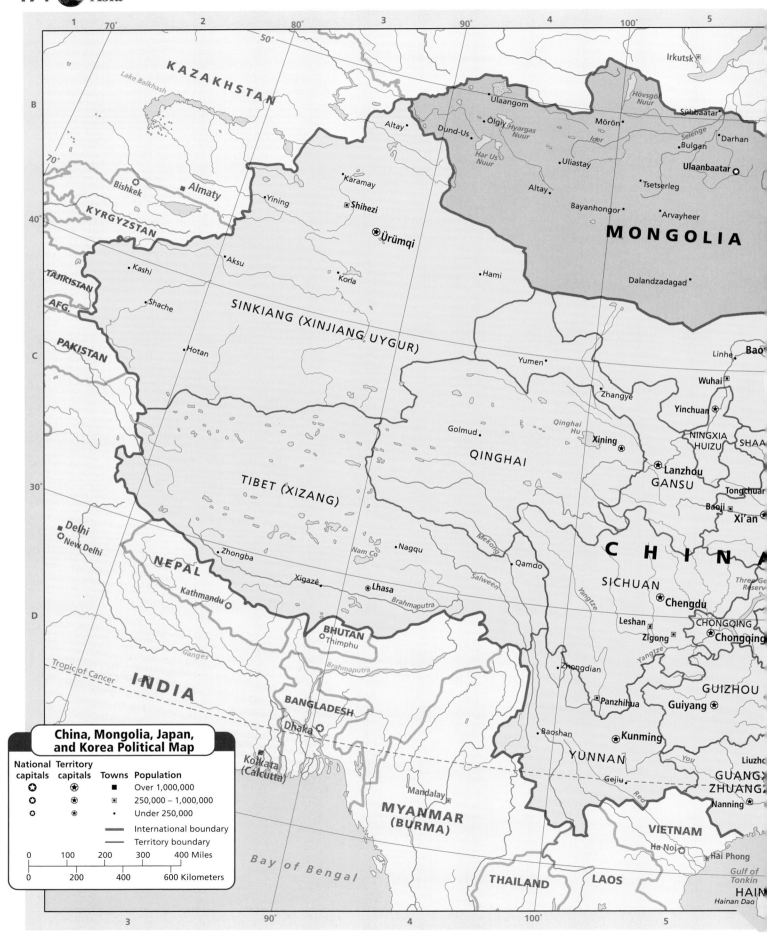

B

70°

50°

KAZAKHSTAN

Lake Balkhash

Irkutsk

Ulaangom

Hövsgöl Nuur

Sühbaatar

Altay

Ölgiy *Hyargas Nuur*

Dund-Us

Mörön

Darhan

Ider

Selenge

Bulgan

Har Us Nuur

Uliastay

Ulaanbaatar ✪

70°

Bishkek ✪

Almaty ■

Yining

Karamay

Altay

Tsetserleg

KYRGYZSTAN

Shihezi ▣

40°

✪**Ürümqi**

Bayanhongor

Arvayheer

MONGOLIA

TAJIKISTAN

Kashi

Aksu

Korla

Hami

Dalandzadagad

AFG.

PAKISTAN

Shache

SINKIANG (XINJIANG UYGUR)

Yumen

Linhe

Bao

C

Hotan

Wuhai ▣

Zhangye

Yinchuan ✪

NINGXIA HUIZU

SHAA

Golmud

Qinghai Hu

Xining ✪

QINGHAI

Lanzhou ✪

GANSU

Tongchuar

30°

Delhi ■

New Delhi ✪

TIBET (XIZANG)

Baoji ▣

Xi'an ▣

NEPAL

Zhongba

Nam Co

Nagqu

Mekong

Qamdo

C H I N A

Kathmandu ✪

Xigazê

Lhasa ✪

Salween

Brahmaputra

SICHUAN

Chengdu ✪

Three Ge Reserv

Yangtze

Ganges

BHUTAN

Thimphu ✪

Brahmaputra

Leshan ▣

CHONGQING

Zigong ▣

Chongqing ✪

D

Tropic of Cancer

INDIA

BANGLADESH

Dhaka ✪

Zhongdian

Yangtze

GUIZHOU

Panzhihua ▣

Guiyang ✪

Kolkata (Calcutta) ■

You

Baoshan

YUNNAN

Liuzho

Gejiu

GUANGX ZHUANG

Kunming ✪

Nanning ✪

Mandalay ▣

MYANMAR (BURMA)

Red

VIETNAM

Ha Noi ✪

Hai Phong

Bay of Bengal

THAILAND

LAOS

Gulf of Tonkin

HAI

Hainan Dao

China, Mongolia, Japan, and Korea Political Map

National capitals	Territory capitals	Towns	Population
✪	✪	■	Over 1,000,000
✪	✪	▣	250,000 – 1,000,000
✪	✪	•	Under 250,000

International boundary

Territory boundary

0   100   200   300   400 Miles

0   200   400   600 Kilometers

RUSSIA

• Ergun Zuoqi
• Hailar
• Yakeshi
Choybalsan •
• Baruun-Urt
• Heihe
• Bei'an
HEILONGJIANG
• Hegang
• Shuangyashan
• Qiqihar
• Daqing
• Suihua
Songhua
• Jixi
Ulaan-Uul •
☆ Harbin
• Mudanjiang
JILIN
Baicheng •
• Jilin
• Changchun ☆
• Liaoyuan

NEI MONGGOL
Hulun Nur
Kerulen
Ergun
Nonni
Amur

• Ch'ŏngjin
• Kimch'aek

NORTH KOREA

SEA OF
JAPAN
(EAST SEA)

Sakhalin

SEA
OF
OKHOTSK

La Perouse Strait
Kuril Islands

• Asahikawa
■ Sapporo
Hokkaidō
• Hakodate
• Aomori
• Morioka
• Akita
Honshū
• Sendai
Niigata
■ Iwaki
JAPAN

• Chifeng
Fuxin •
• Fushun
Shenyang ☆
• Benxi
• Anshan
LIAONING
Jinzhou •
Dandong •
• Sinŭiju
• Wŏnsan
☆ P'yŏngyang
• Hohhot
• Zhangjiakou
☆ Beijing
• Tangshan
• Dalian
Namp'o •
Datong •
☆ Tianjin
Korea
Bay
• Seoul
SOUTH
KOREA
Baoding •
Bo Hai
Shijiazhuang •
HEBEI
• Yantai
YELLOW
SEA
Ch'ŏngju •
• Taegu
yuan •
Yangquan •
Huang (Yellow)
• Zibo
• Jinan
Taejŏn •
Chŏnju •
• Ulsan
HANXI
• Handan
• Anyang
• Qingdao
SHANDONG
Kwangju •
• Masan
• Pusan
Hiroshima
Toyama •
Kanazawa •
Oki-shotō
Kyōto ■
Kōbe ■
Nagoya
• Shizuoka
Hamamatsu •
☆ Tōkyō
Yokohama
• Nagano
Utsunomiya •
• Xinxiang
• Kaifeng
• Zhengzhou
• Xuzhou
JIANGSU
• Yancheng
ang •
Korea Strait
Cheju-do
(S. Korea)
Matsuyama •
Shikoku
dingshan •
HENAN
• Huainan
ANHUI
Kitakyūshū •
Fukuoka •
• Ōita
• Kumamoto
Nagasaki •
• Miyazaki
Kyūshū
• Xiangfan
☆ Hefei
Nanjing ☆
• Nantong
• Wuxi
Suzhou ☆
☆ Shanghai
• Wuhu
Kagoshima •
EAST
Yaku-shima
Tanega-shima •
EI
Yichang •
☆ Wuhan
Yangtze
☆ Hangzhou
CHINA
• Huangshi
• Ningbo
Dongting
Hu
• Jingdezhen
ZHEJIANG
SEA
Amami-Ō-shima
ngsha ☆
☆ Nanchang
Poyang
Hu
• Wenzhou
Tokuno-shima
PACIFIC OCEAN
JNAN
• Pingxiang
JIANGXI
Ryukyu Islands (Japan)
Okinawa-jima
• Hengyang
FUJIAN
☆ Fuzhou
• Naha
• Chilung
☆ T'aipei
Iriomote-jima
• Miyako-jima
Ishigaki-shima
Tropic of Cancer
• T'aichung
• Shaoguan
• Xiamen
• Chiai
PHILIPPINE
SEA
GUANGDONG
T'ainan •
• Kaohsiung
TAIWAN
• Shantou
uangzhou ☆
☆ Hong Kong
• Macau
jiang
SOUTH CHINA SEA
• Pratas Island
(Occupied by Taiwan, claimed by China)
Luzon Strait
PHILIPPINES

Taiwan Strait

Vladivostok

© Rand McNally
Made in U.S.A.
M-101118-4

N
W E
S

ASIA
MONGOLIA
CHINA
NORTH KOREA
JAPAN
SOUTH KOREA
TAIWAN

Climate

Climate Map

Tropical
- Rain all year
- Seasonal rain

Dry
- Desert
- Some rain

Moderate
- Dry summer
- Humid summer
- Rainy summer

Continental
- Long summer
- Short summer
- Very short, cool summer

Polar
- Tundra
- Ice cap

Highlands
- Varies

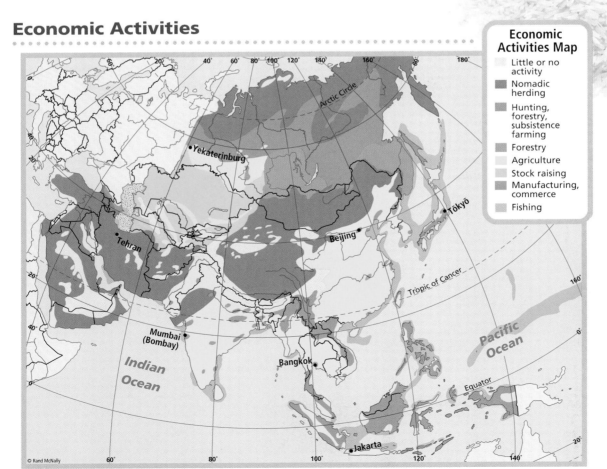

Rain forests thrive in the hot, rainy climate of Southeast Asia.

Eastern China has a moderate climate with humid summers. This is like the climate of the eastern United States.

Economic Activities

Economic Activities Map

- Little or no activity
- Nomadic herding
- Hunting, forestry, subsistence farming
- Forestry
- Agriculture
- Stock raising
- Manufacturing, commerce
- Fishing

Rice is the most important food crop in Southeast Asia.

Japan sends many of its exports to the United States, but it trades with other countries, as well. Trading with many countries helps a country continue to earn money if one trading partner has economic problems.

Populations

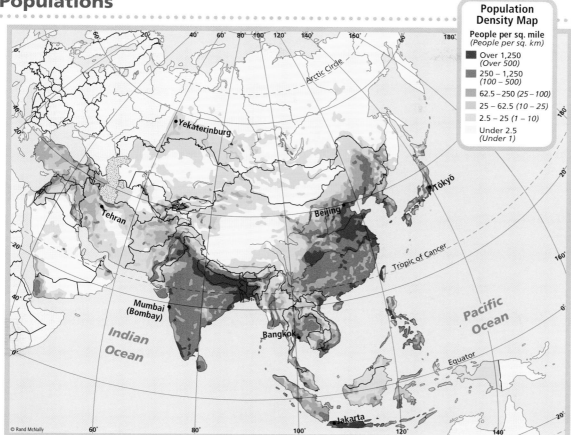

Population Density Map

People per sq. mile
(People per sq. km)

- Over 1,250 (Over 500)
- 250 – 1,250 (100 – 500)
- 62.5 – 250 (25 – 100)
- 25 – 62.5 (10 – 25)
- 2.5 – 25 (1 – 10)
- Under 2.5 (Under 1)

Seoul, South Korea, is home to more than 9.7 million people.

Bangladesh is one of the most densely populated countries in the world.

Much of Mongolia is sparsely populated.

India and China

China and India are the world's population giants. Both have populations of more than one billion people. India's population, however, is growing faster. By 2040 it will be larger than China's. Since about 1980, China has brought down its rate of population growth by strictly limiting how many children a family may have.

India and China Population Growth

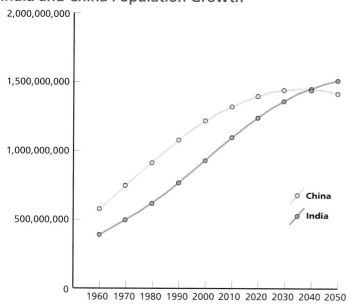

○ China
○ India

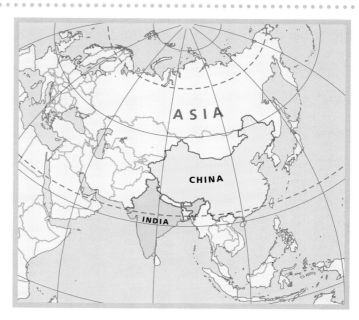

WHAT IF?

What do you think life in India will be like if the population continues to grow rapidly?

Transportation

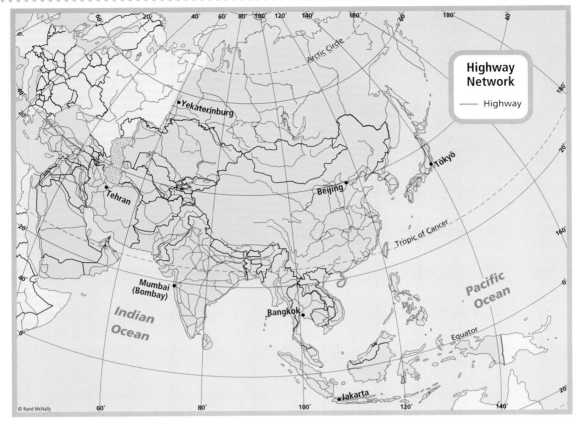

Highway Network

— Highway

Yekaterinburg

Tōkyō

Tehran

Beijing

Arctic Circle

Tropic of Cancer

Mumbai
(Bombay)

Bangkok

Indian
Ocean

Pacific
Ocean

Equator

Jakarta

© Rand McNally

Japan's bullet trains can travel at speeds of up to 155 miles per hour (249 kilometers per hour).

Mountainous terrain makes road-building difficult in many parts of Asia.

The country of Nepal lies along the southern edge of the Himalayas. Thick woodlands cover some of the lower elevations.

Environments

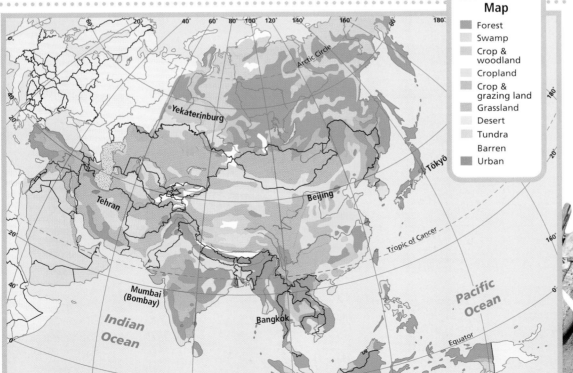

Environments Map

- Forest
- Swamp
- Crop & woodland
- Cropland
- Crop & grazing land
- Grassland
- Desert
- Tundra
- Barren
- Urban

Yekaterinburg

Tōkyō

Tehran

Beijing

Arctic Circle

Tropic of Cancer

Mumbai
(Bombay)

Bangkok

Indian
Ocean

Pacific
Ocean

Equator

Jakarta

© Rand McNally

Grasslands called steppes cover much of Central Asia.

Camel

Natural Hazards

Natural Hazards Map

- • Earthquakes*
- △ Volcanoes*
- \ Tsunamis
- ↗ Tropical storm tracks (over 5 per year)

*Since 1900

Tsunamis

Tsunamis are huge ocean waves caused by underwater earthquakes or volcanoes. They usually travel at speeds of about 300 miles per hour (500 km/hr).

Tsunamis that reach the shore can cause terrible damage to coastal areas. On December 26, 2004, a strong earthquake off the coast of Sumatra in Indonesia caused a tsunami that destroyed huge coastal areas in Indonesia, Thailand, India, and Sri Lanka and also hit Madagascar and continental Africa. More than 200,000 people were killed. Most other tsunamis have occurred in the Pacific Ocean.

© Rand McNally
M-102186-1

Energy

On the Mineral Fuel Deposits map, note the cluster of symbols indicating petroleum deposits around the Persian Gulf, which is near the left edge of the map. This area is part of the Middle East, which produces one-third of the world's oil.

Mineral Fuel Deposits Map

- Coal
- ▲ Petroleum
- △ Natural gas

© Rand McNally
M-102187-2

Oil exporting has brought great wealth to the countries in the Persian Gulf region of the Middle East. This photo shows an oil refinery in the United Arab Emirates.

A pipeline delivers oil to an oil tanker in Saudi Arabia.

China produces more than 45% of the world's coal.

AUSTRALIA AND OCEANIA

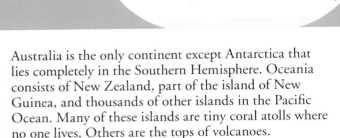

Uluru, also known as Ayers Rock, in central Australia

Sydney, Australia

A dairy farm on New Zealand's South Island

Australia is the only continent except Antarctica that lies completely in the Southern Hemisphere. Oceania consists of New Zealand, part of the island of New Guinea, and thousands of other islands in the Pacific Ocean. Many of these islands are tiny coral atolls where no one lives. Others are the tops of volcanoes.

Australia is the smallest continent. It is about the size of the conterminous 48 U.S. states. It has a drier climate than every other continent except Antarctica. Because Australia is in the Southern Hemisphere, it is warmer in the north than in the south.

Australia's vast, dry interior is called the Outback. Few people live there. Much of the land is used for grazing cattle and sheep on huge ranches called "stations." For many years, children on stations have "gone to school" by two-way radio connection with their teachers and other students called the School of the Air. Today, computers also provide connections for such children.

Australia's first people are the Aborigines. They came to Australia from Asia thousands of years before the first Europeans came. People from Asia also settled other islands of Oceania. New Zealand was the last place they reached. English people started coming to Australia and New Zealand in the late 1700s. People from the British Isles still make up most of the population, but Asians and people from the Pacific Islands have joined them. In both Australia and New Zealand, most people live along the coasts in modern cities.

Kangaroos

A Historical Look At Australia

Circa 40,000 B.C.E.–30,000 B.C.E.
Aborigines arrive in Australia from Asia.

1788
The British establish the first Australian penal colony in Sydney.

1800s
Chinese settlers arrive in Northern Territory

1851
Gold is discovered in New South Wales and Victoria.

Australia's Extremes

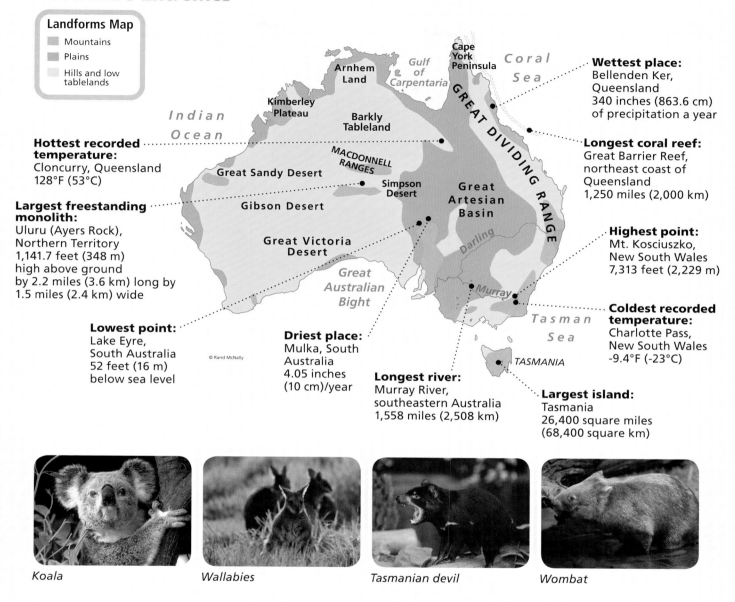

Landforms Map
- Mountains
- Plains
- Hills and low tablelands

Indian Ocean

Gulf of Carpentaria

Cape York Peninsula

Coral Sea

Arnhem Land

Kimberley Plateau

Barkly Tableland

MACDONNELL RANGES

GREAT DIVIDING RANGE

Great Sandy Desert

Simpson Desert

Gibson Desert

Great Victoria Desert

Great Artesian Basin

Darling

Murray

Great Australian Bight

Tasman Sea

TASMANIA

© Rand McNally

Hottest recorded temperature:
Cloncurry, Queensland
128°F (53°C)

Largest freestanding monolith:
Uluru (Ayers Rock), Northern Territory
1,141.7 feet (348 m) high above ground
by 2.2 miles (3.6 km) long by
1.5 miles (2.4 km) wide

Lowest point:
Lake Eyre, South Australia
52 feet (16 m) below sea level

Driest place:
Mulka, South Australia
4.05 inches (10 cm)/year

Longest river:
Murray River, southeastern Australia
1,558 miles (2,508 km)

Wettest place:
Bellenden Ker, Queensland
340 inches (863.6 cm) of precipitation a year

Longest coral reef:
Great Barrier Reef, northeast coast of Queensland
1,250 miles (2,000 km)

Highest point:
Mt. Kosciuszko, New South Wales
7,313 feet (2,229 m)

Coldest recorded temperature:
Charlotte Pass, New South Wales
-9.4°F (-23°C)

Largest island:
Tasmania
26,400 square miles (68,400 square km)

Koala

Wallabies

Tasmanian devil

Wombat

1893
New Zealand is the first country to give women the right to vote.

1901
Australia becomes a self-governing dominion within the British Empire.

1976
The First Aboriginal Land Rights Act is passed.

2000
Sydney hosts the summer Olympic Games.

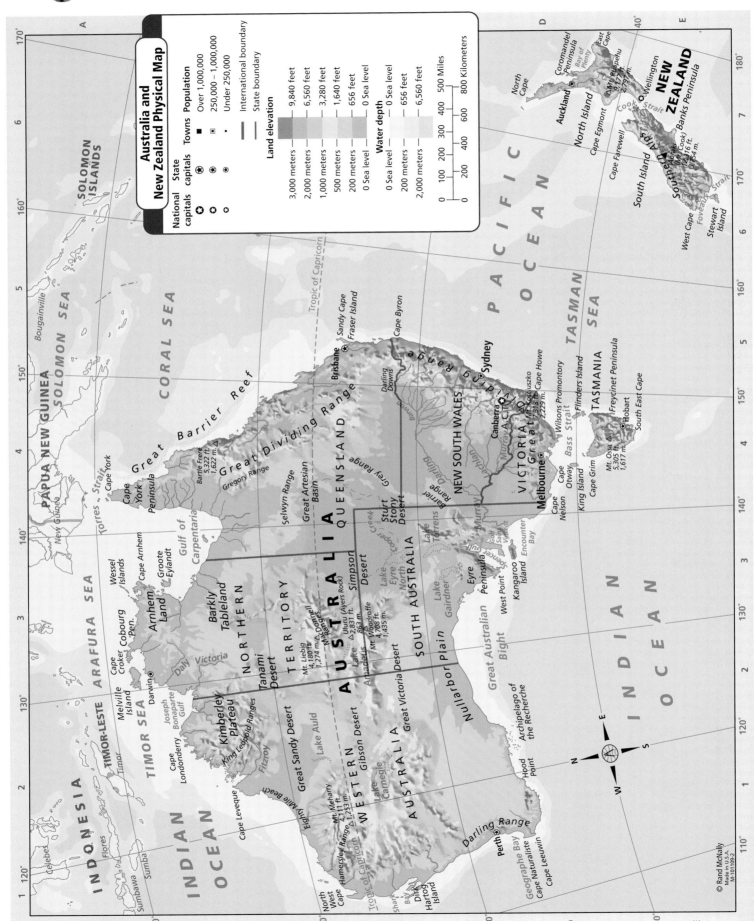

**Australia and
New Zealand Physical Map**

National
capitals

State
capitals

Towns Population

Over 1,000,000

250,000 – 1,000,000

Under 250,000

International boundary

State boundary

Land elevation

9,840 feet   3,000 meters

6,560 feet   2,000 meters

3,280 feet   1,000 meters

1,640 feet   500 meters

656 feet   200 meters

0 Sea level   0 Sea level

Water depth

0 Sea level   0 Sea level

656 feet   200 meters

6,560 feet   2,000 meters

0   100   200   300   400   500 Miles

0   200   400   600   800 Kilometers

© Rand McNally
Made in U.S.A.
M-101109-2

**Australia and
New Zealand Political Map**

	National capitals	State capitals	Towns	Population
	⊛	⊛	■	Over 1,000,000
	◉	◎	▣	250,000 – 1,000,000
	⊙	⊚	•	Under 250,000

International boundary
State boundary

0 100 200 300 400 500 Miles
0 200 400 600 800 Kilometers

INDIAN OCEAN

INDONESIA

Celebes

Sumbawa Sumba Flores

TIMOR-LESTE

Timor

TIMOR SEA

ARAFURA SEA

PAPUA NEW GUINEA

New Guinea

Port Moresby

SOLOMON SEA

Bougainville

SOLOMON ISLANDS

Honiara

VANUATU

Port Vila

CORAL SEA

Joseph Bonaparte Gulf

Darwin

Katherine

Day

Groote Eylandt

Gulf of Carpentaria

Weipa

Cape York Peninsula

Torres Strait

Normanton

Mount Isa

Cairns

Halifax Bay

Townsville

Mackay

Rockhampton

Bundaberg

Fraser Island

Brisbane
Southport

Emerald

Longreach

Charleville

Toowoomba

Coffs Harbour

Taree

Newcastle

Sydney

Wollongong

Dubbo

Bourke

Broken Hill

Penrith

Canberra
A.C.T.

Wagga Wagga

Albury

Bendigo

Ballarat

Geelong

Melbourne

VICTORIA

Mount Gambier

Mildura

Murray

Lachlan

Darling

NEW SOUTH WALES

QUEENSLAND

Tropic of Capricorn

NORTHERN TERRITORY

Tennant Creek

Alice Springs

Lake Amadeus

WESTERN AUSTRALIA

AUSTRALIA

SOUTH AUSTRALIA

Cooper Creek

Lake Eyre North

Lake Gairdner

Lake Torrens

Port Augusta

Whyalla

Adelaide

Spencer Gulf

Kangaroo Island

Encounter Bay

Newman

Lake Carnegie

Meekatharra

Kalgoorlie-Boulder

Esperance

Great Australian Bight

Archipelago of the Recherche

Albany

Bunbury

Geographe Bay

Perth

Broome

Port Hedland

Karratha

Carnarvon

Shark Bay

Dirk Hartog Island

Geraldton

Exmouth

Derby

Fitzroy

Tropic of Capricorn

Bass Strait

Flinders Island

King Island

Launceston

TASMANIA

Hobart

TASMAN SEA

PACIFIC OCEAN

Norfolk Island (Austl.)

NEW ZEALAND

North Island

Whangarei

Auckland

Hamilton

Bay of Plenty

Tauranga

Rotorua

Napier

New Plymouth

Palmerston North

Wellington

Cook Strait

Nelson

Christchurch

Timaru

South Island

Dunedin

Invercargill

Foveaux Strait

Stewart Island

N E S W

© Rand McNally
Made in U.S.A.
M-100309-2

Climate

Climate Map

Tropical
- Rain all year
- Seasonal rain

Dry
- Desert
- Some rain

Moderate
- Dry summer
- Humid summer
- Rainy summer

Continental
- Long summer
- Short summer
- Very short, cool summer

Polar
- Tundra
- Ice cap

Highlands
- Varies

Transportation

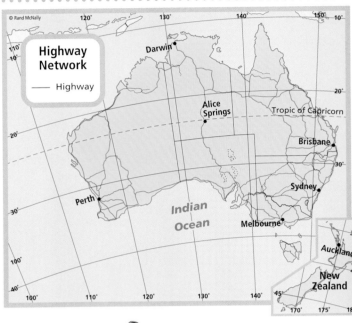

Highway Network
— Highway

DID YOU KNOW?

About 35% of Australia can be classified as desert. In fact, Australia is the driest continent in the world after Antarctica.

Australia's highways provide important links between widely separated towns and cities, especially in the Outback.

Environments

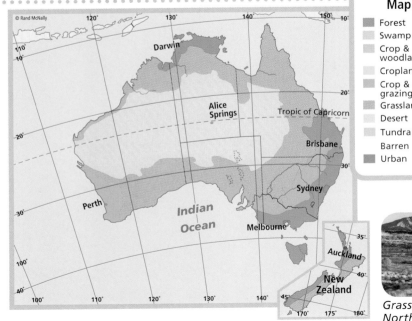

Environments Map
- Forest
- Swamp
- Crop & woodland
- Cropland
- Crop & grazing land
- Grassland
- Desert
- Tundra
- Barren
- Urban

Pinnacles Desert in Nambung National Park, Western Australia, Australia

Grassland in Northern Territory, Australia

Rain forest in Queensland, Australia

Grazing sheep, South Island, New Zealand

Economic Activities

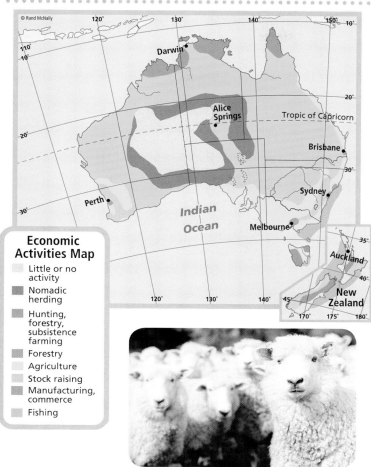

Economic Activities Map

- Little or no activity
- Nomadic herding
- Hunting, forestry, subsistence farming
- Forestry
- Agriculture
- Stock raising
- Manufacturing, commerce
- Fishing

In Australia, sheep outnumber humans four to one. In New Zealand, the ratio is seven to one. Together, the two countries produce nearly 30% of the world's wool.

The Great Barrier Reef

The Great Barrier Reef stretches for roughly 1,429 miles (2,300 km) along the northeast coast of Queensland, Australia. It is made up of more than 3,000 separate coral reefs. Together, they cover 132,974 square miles (344,400 square kilometers). The Great Barrier Reef is the largest group of coral reefs and islands in the world.

Scientists believe that the reef began forming millions of years ago. More than 600 types of soft and hard corals, in a great variety of colors, form the reef. In addition, about 1,500 species of fish live in the warm waters around the reef. Scientists warn that some human activities are causing serious damage to the reef.

Population

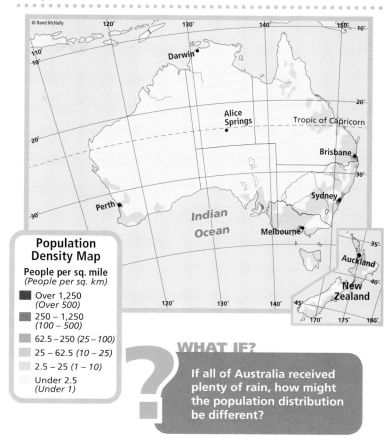

Population Density Map

People per sq. mile
(People per sq. km)

- Over 1,250 (Over 500)
- 250 – 1,250 (100 – 500)
- 62.5 – 250 (25 – 100)
- 25 – 62.5 (10 – 25)
- 2.5 – 25 (1 – 10)
- Under 2.5 (Under 1)

WHAT IF?

? If all of Australia received plenty of rain, how might the population distribution be different?

More than 600 islands are found along the Great Barrier Reef. Some of them have been developed as tourist resorts, but many are uninhabited.

Green turtle

A whale shark

Acropora plate coral

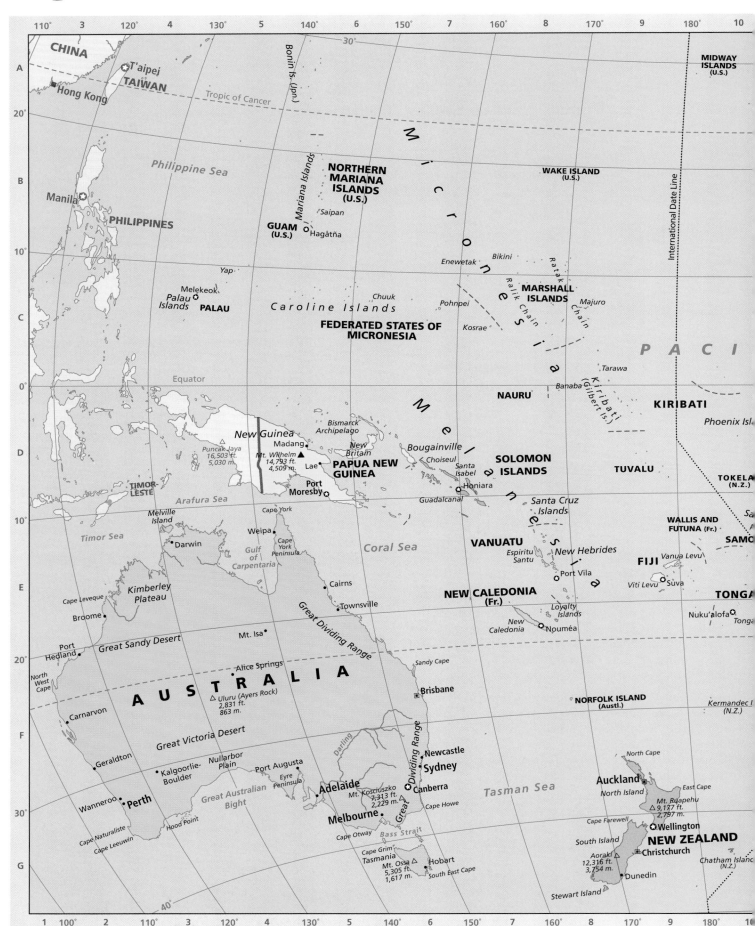

110°   3   120°   4   130°   5   140°   6   150°   7   160°   8   170°   9   180°   10

CHINA

T'aipej
TAIWAN

Hong Kong

Tropic of Cancer

Bonin Is. (Jpn.)

30°

MIDWAY
ISLANDS
(U.S.)

A

20°

Philippine Sea

Mariana Islands

**NORTHERN
MARIANA
ISLANDS
(U.S.)**

Micronesia

WAKE ISLAND
(U.S.)

International Date Line

B

Manila

PHILIPPINES

Saipan

**GUAM
(U.S.)**

Hagåtña

Enewetak

Bikini

Ratak Chain

Ralik Chain

**MARSHALL
ISLANDS**

Majuro

10°

Yap

Melekeok
**Palau
Islands**   **PALAU**

Caroline Islands

Chuuk

Pohnpei

**FEDERATED STATES OF
MICRONESIA**

Kosrae

P A C I

C

Tarawa

Equator

Melanesia

Banaba

NAURU

*Kiribati
(Gilbert Is.)*

KIRIBATI

Phoenix Isl

0°

New Guinea

△ Puncak Jaya
16,503 ft.
5,030 m.

Madang

Mt. Wilhelm ▲
14,793 ft.
4,509 m.

Bismarck
Archipelago

New
Britain

**PAPUA NEW
GUINEA**

Lae

Port
Moresby

Bougainville

Choiseul

Santa
Isabel

Honiara

**SOLOMON
ISLANDS**

Guadalcanal

TUVALU

TOKELA
(N.Z.)

D

**TIMOR-
LESTE**

Arafura Sea

Santa Cruz
Islands

**WALLIS AND
FUTUNA (Fr.)**

SAMO

10°

*Melville
Island*

Darwin

Timor Sea

Cape York

Weipa

Cape
York
Peninsula

*Gulf
of
Carpentaria*

Coral Sea

VANUATU

Espiritu
Santu

New Hebrides

Port Vila

Vanua Levu

FIJI

Viti Levu   Suva

TONGA

E

*Kimberley
Plateau*

Cape Leveque

Broome

Cairns

Townsville

Mt. Isa

**NEW CALEDONIA
(Fr.)**

*Loyalty
Islands*

New
Caledonia   Nouméa

Nuku'alofa

Tonga

Port
Hedland

Great Sandy Desert

North
West
Cape

Alice Springs

Sandy Cape

**NORFOLK ISLAND
(Austl.)**

Kermadec I
(N.Z.)

20°

Carnarvon

A U S T R A L I A

△ Uluru (Ayers Rock)
2,831 ft.
863 m.

Great Dividing Range

Brisbane

F

Great Victoria Desert

Geraldton

Kalgoorlie-
Boulder

*Nullarbor
Plain*

Port Augusta

*Eyre
Peninsula*

Darling

Great Dividing Range

Newcastle

Sydney

North Cape

North Island

Auckland

East Cape

Mt. Ruapehu
△ 9,177 ft.
2,797 m.

30°

Wanneroo

Perth

*Great Australian
Bight*

Adelaide

Mt. Kosciuszko
7,313 ft.
2,229 m.   **Canberra**

Tasman Sea

Cape Howe

Great

South Island

Cape Farewell

Wellington

Cape Naturaliste
Cape Leeuwin

Hood Point

Melbourne

Bass Strait

NEW ZEALAND

Aoraki △
12,316 ft.
3,754 m.   **Christchurch**

Chatham Island
(N.Z.)

G

Cape Grim
Tasmania
Mt. Ossa △
5,305 ft.
1,617 m.

Cape Otway

Hobart

South East Cape

Dunedin

Stewart Island

40°

1   100°   2   110°   3   120°   4   130°   5   140°   6   150°   7   160°   8   170°   9   180°   10

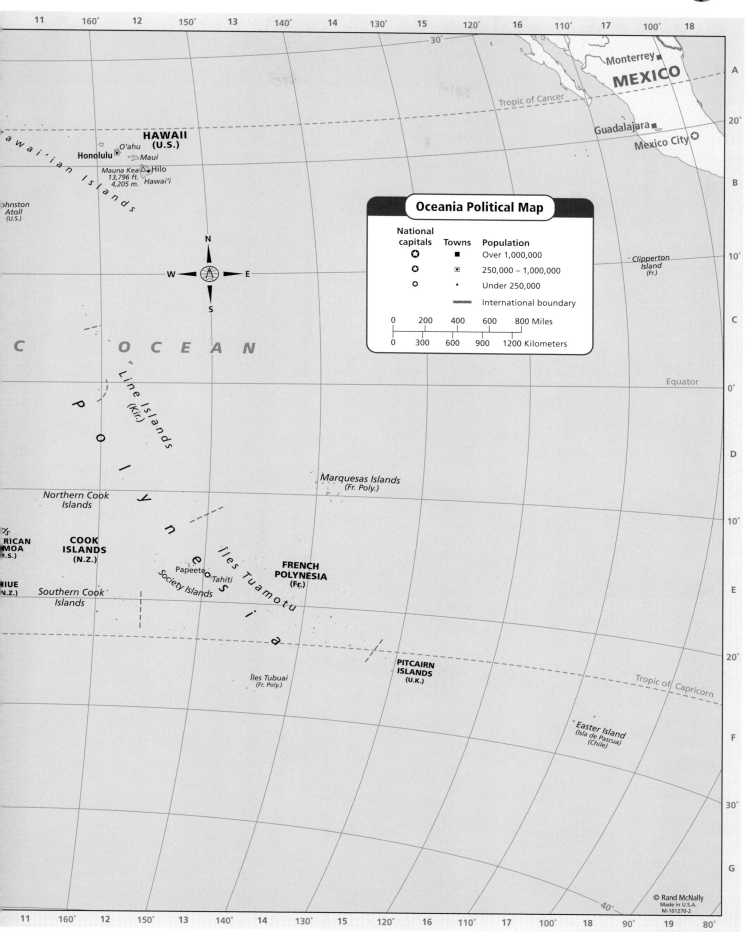

Oceania Political Map

National capitals
- ⊛ ⊛ ⊛

Towns
- ■
- ▣
- ·

Population
- Over 1,000,000
- 250,000 – 1,000,000
- Under 250,000
- ▬▬▬ International boundary

```
0    200   400   600   800 Miles
0   300   600   900  1200 Kilometers
```

MEXICO
Monterrey ■
Tropic of Cancer
Guadalajara ■
Mexico City ⊛

HAWAII (U.S.)
Honolulu ▣
O'ahu
Maui
Mauna Kea △ Hilo
13,796 ft.
4,205 m.
Hawai'i

Hawaiian Islands

Johnston Atoll (U.S.)

Clipperton Island (Fr.)

C OCEAN

Line Islands (Kir.)

Equator

P O L Y N E S I A

Marquesas Islands (Fr. Poly.)

Northern Cook Islands

RICAN MOA .S.)

COOK ISLANDS (N.Z.)

NIUE N.Z.)

Southern Cook Islands

Society Islands

Papeete ⊛ Tahiti

Îles Tuamotu

FRENCH POLYNESIA (Fr.)

PITCAIRN ISLANDS (U.K.)

Îles Tubuai (Fr. Poly.)

Tropic of Capricorn

Easter Island (Isla de Pascua) (Chile)

© Rand McNally
Made in U.S.A.
M-101270-2

ANTARCTICA

Kayaking along the Antarctic coast

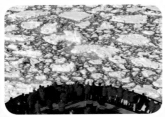
Passengers crowd the deck of an icebreaker ship as it plows through pack ice.

Explorer in a wind tunnel

Antarctica is the world's fifth-largest continent. Most of it lies within the Antarctic Circle. It is the world's most isolated landmass. The nearest land is the southern tip of South America, about 769 miles (more than 1,238 km) from the Antarctic Peninsula.

All the land within the Antarctic Circle has days in winter when the sun never rises and days in summer when the sun never sets. At the South Pole, between March 20 and September 21 the sun never rises, and between September 21 and March 20 it never sets.

Antarctica is the coldest place on earth. Average summer temperatures may reach only about 0° F (-18° C). Such a cold, frozen landmass produces cold winds that collide with warmer air around the coast and form a belt of storms. Antarctica receives very little precipitation. What precipitation does fall produces ice, which accumulates into thick ice sheets that gradually push toward the coast and form ice shelves over the edge of the land.

People discovered Antarctica only about 200 years ago. Exploration on land started a little more than 100 years ago. No people live on Antarctica permanently. More than a dozen countries have established scientific stations where scientists study such things as global climate change, the atmosphere's thinning ozone layer, and plant and animal life. A growing number of tourists visit the continent each year.

Scientists know that the continent has such resources as coal, but an international agreement prohibits exploiting these resources. Perhaps the most important resource is the abundant life in the cold waters off the coast.

Snow petrel

A Historical Look At Antarctica

1918–1821
Fabian von Bellingshausen, a Russian, is the first European to see Antarctica.

1895
A Norwegian expedition is the first to land on Victoria Land.

1911
Roald Amundsen is the first person to reach the South Pole.

1929
Richard Byrd flies over the South Pole.

Scientific Stations in Antarctica

Frozen and isolated as it is, Antarctica offers some important advantages for researchers. Its darkness makes it a good place to study the stars. Its clean air allows studies of air quality. Scientists can see the effects of human activity. Antarctica has no borders—although seven countries have made territorial claims—so scientists from different countries can share the information they find.

A scientific station operated by Argentina

Telecommunications equipment at a scientific station

Palmer Station
The only U.S. station north of the Antarctic Circle

Argentina
Brazil
Chile
China
Korea
Poland
Russia
Uruguay

United States · Chile
Ukraine · Argentina
United Kingdom · Argentina
Argentina

McMurdo Station
Home to Antarctica's largest community and capable of supporting up to 1,200 people

United States
New Zealand

Halley Station
The site of important ozone research

Argentina · United Kingdom

Germany

South Africa

India

Russia

United States
South Pole · **Amundsen-Scott South Pole Station**
Located about 1,150 feet (350 m) from the geographic South Pole

ANTARCTICA

SANAE IV
Built on poles, since 60-80 inches (150 to 200 cm) of snow piles up in winter

Russia

France

Dumont d'Urville Station
Built in 1956 to replace a station that burned down

Vostok Station
The coldest recorded temperature on Earth, -128° F. (-89.2° C), was measured here on July 21, 1983.

China
Russia

Japan

Russia

Mawson Station
The oldest continuously inhabited station south of the Antarctic Circle

Australia

Australia

Australia

Australia

Russia

Davis Station
The southernmost Australian station

Mirny Station
Opened in 1956

Animals in Antarctica

Orcas, also known as killer whales

Wandering albatross

Emperor penguins

Leopard seal

1957-1958
The International Geophysical Year (IGY) focuses on the scientific study of Antarctica.

1959
The Antarctic Treaty is signed. It provides for peaceful scientific cooperation in Antarctica.

1991
The Protocol on Environmental Protection to the Antarctic Treaty bans commercial mining operations in Antarctica.

2000
An iceberg 170 miles long and 25 miles wide breaks off the Ross Ice Shelf.

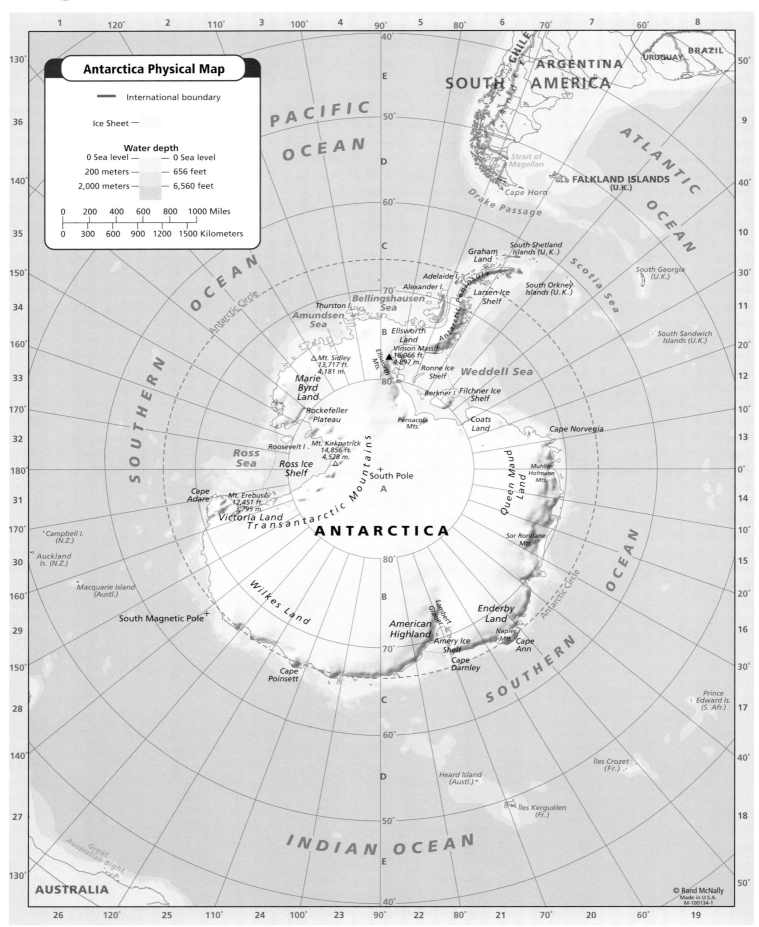

Antarctica Physical Map

International boundary

Ice Sheet —

Water depth

0 Sea level	— 0 Sea level
200 meters —	— 656 feet
2,000 meters —	— 6,560 feet

0   200   400   600   800   1000 Miles

0   300   600   900   1200   1500 Kilometers

PACIFIC OCEAN

CHILE

ARGENTINA

URUGUAY

BRAZIL

SOUTH AMERICA

ATLANTIC OCEAN

Strait of Magellan

FALKLAND ISLANDS (U.K.)

Cape Horn

Drake Passage

South Georgia (U.K.)

SOUTHERN OCEAN

Antarctic Circle

South Shetland Islands (U.K.)

Graham Land

Adelaide I.

Alexander I.

Thurston I.

Bellingshausen Sea

Amundsen Sea

Larsen Ice Shelf

South Orkney Islands (U.K.)

Scotia Sea

South Sandwich Islands (U.K.)

Ellsworth Land

△ Mt. Sidley 13,717 ft. 4,181 m.

Marie Byrd Land

Vinson Massif 16,066 ft. 4,897 m.

Ronne Ice Shelf

Weddell Sea

Rockefeller Plateau

Berkner I.

Filchner Ice Shelf

Roosevelt I.

Mt. Kirkpatrick 14,856 ft. 4,528 m. △

Pensacola Mts.

Coats Land

Cape Norvegia

Ross Sea

Ross Ice Shelf

Transantarctic Mountains

South Pole +

ANTARCTICA

Queen Maud Land

Muhlig-Hofmann Mts.

Cape Adare

Mt. Erebus △ 12,451 ft. 3,795 m.

Victoria Land

Sor Rondane Mts.

Campbell I. (N.Z.)

Auckland Is. (N.Z.)

Wilkes Land

Enderby Land

Napier Mts.

Cape Ann

Macquarie Island (Austl.)

South Magnetic Pole +

American Highland

Lambert Glacier

Amery Ice Shelf

Cape Darnley

SOUTHERN OCEAN

Antarctic Circle

Prince Edward Is. (S. Afr.)

Cape Poinsett

Îles Crozet (Fr.)

Heard Island (Austl.)

Îles Kerguélen (Fr.)

Great Australian Bight

INDIAN OCEAN

AUSTRALIA

© Rand McNally
Made in U.S.A.
M-100134-1

Thematic Content Index

This index makes it easy to compare different continents and regions of the world in terms of climate, economies, and other major themes covered in the atlas.

State	Population	Rank in Population	Area in Square Miles	Rank in Area	Year Admitted to the Union	Order Admitted to the Union	State Capital	Largest City
Alabama	4,779,736	23	50,645	28	1819	22	Montgomery	Birmingham
Alaska	710,231	47	570,641	1	1959	49	Juneau	Anchorage
Arizona	6,392,017	16	113,594	6	1912	48	Phoenix	Phoenix
Arkansas	2,915,918	32	52,035	27	1836	25	Little Rock	Little Rock
California	37,253,956	1	155,799	3	1850	31	Sacramento	Los Angeles
Colorado	5,029,196	22	103,642	8	1876	38	Denver	Denver
Connecticut	3,574,097	29	4,842	48	1788	5	Hartford	Bridgeport
Delaware	897,934	45	1,949	49	1787	1	Dover	Wilmington
Florida	18,801,310	4	53,625	26	1845	27	Tallahassee	Jacksonville
Georgia	9,687,653	9	57,513	21	1788	4	Atlanta	Atlanta
Hawaii	1,360,301	40	6,423	47	1959	50	Honolulu	Honolulu
Idaho	1,567,582	39	82,643	11	1890	43	Boise	Boise
Illinois	12,830,632	5	55,519	24	1818	21	Springfield	Chicago
Indiana	6,483,802	15	35,826	38	1816	19	Indianapolis	Indianapolis
Iowa	3,046,355	30	55,857	23	1846	29	Des Moines	Des Moines
Kansas	2,853,118	33	81,759	13	1861	34	Topeka	Wichita
Kentucky	4,339,367	26	39,486	37	1792	15	Frankfort	Lexington
Louisiana	4,533,372	25	43,204	33	1812	18	Baton Rouge	New Orleans
Maine	1,328,361	41	30,843	39	1820	23	Augusta	Portland
Maryland	5,773,552	19	9,707	42	1788	7	Annapolis	Baltimore
Massachusetts	6,547,629	14	7,800	45	1788	6	Boston	Boston
Michigan	9,833,640	8	56,539	22	1837	26	Lansing	Detroit
Minnesota	5,303,925	21	79,627	14	1858	32	St. Paul	Minneapolis
Mississippi	2,967,297	31	46,923	31	1817	20	Jackson	Jackson
Missouri	5,988,927	18	68,741	18	1821	24	Jefferson City	Kansas City
Montana	989,415	44	145,546	4	1889	41	Helena	Billings
Nebraska	1,826,341	38	76,824	15	1867	37	Lincoln	Omaha
Nevada	2,700,551	35	109,781	7	1864	36	Carson City	Las Vegas
New Hampshire	1,316,470	42	8,953	44	1788	9	Concord	Manchester
New Jersey	8,791,894	11	7,354	46	1787	3	Trenton	Newark
New Mexico	2,059,179	36	121,298	5	1912	47	Santa Fe	Albuquerque
New York	19,378,102	3	47,126	30	1788	11	Albany	New York
North Carolina	9,535,483	10	48,618	29	1789	12	Raleigh	Charlotte
North Dakota	672,591	48	69,000	17	1889	39	Bismarck	Fargo
Ohio	11,536,504	7	40,861	35	1803	17	Columbus	Columbus
Oklahoma	3,751,351	28	68,595	19	1907	46	Oklahoma City	Oklahoma City
Oregon	3,831,074	27	95,988	10	1859	33	Salem	Portland
Pennsylvania	12,702,379	6	44,743	32	1787	2	Harrisburg	Philadelphia
Rhode Island	1,502,567	43	1,034	50	1790	13	Providence	Providence
South Carolina	4,625,364	24	30,061	40	1788	8	Columbia	Columbia
South Dakota	814,180	46	75,811	16	1889	40	Pierre	Sioux Falls
Tennessee	6,346,105	17	41,235	34	1796	16	Nashville	Memphis
Texas	25,145,561	2	261,231	2	1845	28	Austin	Houston
Utah	2,763,885	34	82,169	12	1896	45	Salt Lake City	Salt Lake City
Vermont	625,741	49	9,217	43	1791	14	Montpelier	Burlington
Virginia	8,001,024	12	39,490	36	1788	10	Richmond	Virginia Beach
Washington	6,724,540	13	66,455	20	1889	42	Olympia	Seattle
West Virginia	1,852,994	37	24,038	41	1863	35	Charleston	Charleston
Wisconsin	5,686,986	20	54,158	25	1848	30	Madison	Milwaukee
Wyoming	563,626	50	97,093	9	1890	44	Cheyenne	Cheyenne